Soviet and Post-Soviet Politics and Society (SPPS) Vol. 88
ISSN 1614-3515

General Editor: Andreas Umland, *Catholic University of Eichstaett-Ingolstadt,* umland@stanfordalumni.org

Editorial Assistant: Olena Sivuda, *Dragomanov Pedagogical University of Kyiv,* sivuda@ukrcognita.com.ua

EDITORIAL COMMITTEE*

DOMESTIC & COMPARATIVE POLITICS
Prof. **Ellen Bos**, *Andrássy University of Budapest*
Dr. **Ingmar Bredies**, *Kyiv-Mohyla Academy*
Dr. **Andrey Kazantsev**, *MGIMO (U) MID RF, Moscow*
Prof. **Heiko Pleines**, *University of Bremen*
Prof. **Richard Sakwa**, *University of Kent at Canterbury*
Dr. **Sarah Whitmore**, *Oxford Brookes University*
Dr. **Harald Wydra**, *University of Cambridge*
SOCIETY, CLASS & ETHNICITY
Col. **David Glantz**, *"Journal of Slavic Military Studies"*
Dr. **Rashid Kaplanov**, *Russian Academy of Sciences*
Dr. **Marlène Laruelle**, *EHESS, Paris*
Dr. **Stephen Shulman**, *Southern Illinois University*
Prof. **Stefan Troebst**, *University of Leipzig*
POLITICAL ECONOMY & PUBLIC POLICY
Prof. em. **Marshall Goldman**, *Wellesley College, Mass.*
Dr. **Andreas Goldthau**, *Stiftung Wissenschaft und Politik*
Dr. **Robert Kravchuk**, *University of North Carolina*
Dr. **David Lane**, *University of Cambridge*
Dr. **Carol Leonard**, *University of Oxford*

Dr. **Maria Popova**, *McGill University, Montreal*
FOREIGN POLICY & INTERNATIONAL AFFAIRS
Dr. **Peter Duncan**, *University College London*
Dr. **Taras Kuzio**, *George Washington University, DC*
Prof. **Gerhard Mangott**, *University of Innsbruck*
Dr. **Diana Schmidt**, *University of Bremen*
Dr. **Lisbeth Tarlow**, *Harvard University, Cambridge*
Dr. **Christian Wipperfürth**, *N-Ost Network, Berlin*
Dr. **William Zimmerman**, *University of Michigan*
HISTORY, CULTURE & THOUGHT
Dr. **Catherine Andreyev**, *University of Oxford*
Prof. **Mark Bassin**, *University of Birmingham*
Dr. **Alexander Etkind**, *University of Cambridge*
Dr. **Gasan Gusejnov**, *University of Bremen*
Prof. em. **Walter Laqueur**, *Georgetown University*
Prof. **Leonid Luks**, *Catholic University of Eichstaett*
Dr. **Olga Malinova**, *Russian Academy of Sciences*
Dr. **Andrei Rogatchevski**, *University of Glasgow*
Dr. **Mark Tauger**, *West Virginia University*
Dr. **Stefan Wiederkehr**, *DHI, Warsaw*

ADVISORY BOARD*

Prof. **Dominique Arel**, *University of Ottawa*
Prof. **Jörg Baberowski**, *Humboldt University of Berlin*
Prof. **Margarita Balmaceda**, *Seton Hall University*
Dr. **John Barber**, *University of Cambridge*
Prof. **Timm Beichelt**, *European University Viadrina*
Prof. em. **Archie Brown**, *University of Oxford*
Dr. **Vyacheslav Bryukhovetsky**, *Kyiv-Mohyla Academy*
Prof. **Timothy Colton**, *Harvard University, Cambridge*
Prof. **Paul D'Anieri**, *University of Kansas, Lawrence*
Dr. **Heike Dörrenbächer**, *DGO, Berlin*
Dr. **John Dunlop**, *Hoover Institution, Stanford, California*
Dr. **Sabine Fischer**, *EU Institute for Security Studies*
Dr. **Geir Flikke**, *NUPI, Oslo*
Dr. **David Galbreath**, *University of Aberdeen*
Prof. **Alexander Galkin**, *Russian Academy of Sciences*
Prof. **Frank Golczewski**, *University of Hamburg*
Dr. **Nikolas Gvosdev**, *Naval War College, Newport, RI*
Prof. **Mark von Hagen**, *Arizona State University*
Dr. **Guido Hausmann**, *Trinity College Dublin*
Prof. **Dale Herspring**, *Kansas State University*
Dr. **Stefani Hoffman**, *Hebrew University of Jerusalem*
Prof. **Mikhail Ilyin**, *MGIMO (U) MID RF, Moscow*
Prof. **Vladimir Kantor**, *Higher School of Economics*
Dr. **Ivan Katchanovski**, *University of Toronto*
Prof. em. **Andrzej Korbonski**, *University of California*
Dr. **Iris Kempe**, *Heinrich Boell Foundation Tiblissi*
Prof. **Herbert Küpper**, *Institut für Ostrecht München*
Dr. **Rainer Lindner**, *Stiftung Wissenschaft und Politik*
Dr. **Vladimir Malakhov**, *Russian Academy of Sciences*
Dr. **Luke March**, *University of Edinburgh*

Prof. **Michael McFaul**, *Stanford University, California*
Prof. **Birgit Menzel**, *University of Mainz-Germersheim*
Prof. **Valery Mikhailenko**, *The Urals State University*
Prof. **Emil Pain**, *Higher School of Economics, Moscow*
Dr. **Oleg Podvintsev**, *Russian Academy of Sciences*
Prof. **Olga Popova**, *St. Petersburg State University*
Dr. **Alex Pravda**, *University of Oxford*
Dr. **Erik van Ree**, *University of Amsterdam*
Dr. **Joachim Rogall**, *Robert Bosch Foundation, Stuttgart*
Prof. **Peter Rutland**, *Wesleyan University, Middletown*
Dr. **Sergei Ryabov**, *Kyiv-Mohyla Academy*
Prof. **Marat Salikov**, *The Urals State Law Academy*
Dr. **Gwendolyn Sasse**, *University of Oxford*
Prof. **Jutta Scherrer**, *EHESS, Paris*
Prof. **Robert Service**, *University of Oxford*
Mr. **James Sherr**, *Defence Academy of the UK, Swindon*
Dr. **Oxana Shevel**, *Tufts University, Medford*
Prof. **Eberhard Schneider**, *University of Siegen*
Prof. **Olexander Shnyrkov**, *Shevchenko University, Kyiv*
Prof. **Hans-Henning Schröder**, *University of Bremen*
Prof. **Yuri Shapoval**, *Ukrainian Academy of Sciences*
Prof. **Viktor Shnirelman**, *Russian Academy of Sciences*
Dr. **Lisa Sundstrom**, *University of British Columbia*
Dr. **Philip Walters**, *"Religion, State and Society," Oxford*
Dr. **Zenon Wasyliw**, *Ithaca College, New York State*
Dr. **Lucan Way**, *University of Toronto*
Dr. **Markus Wehner**, *"Frankfurter Allgemeine Zeitung"*
Dr. **Andrew Wilson**, *University College London*
Prof. **Jan Zielonka**, *University of Oxford*
Prof. **Andrei Zorin**, *University of Oxford*

* While the Editorial Committee and Advisory Board support the Genera[l] for publication, responsibility for remaining errors and misinterpretation[s]

Soviet and Post-Soviet Politics and Society (SPPS)
ISSN 1614-3515

Founded in 2004 and refereed since 2007, SPPS makes available affordable English-, German- and Russian-language studies on the history of the countries of the former Soviet bloc from the late Tsarist period to today. It publishes approximately 20 volumes per year, and focuses on issues in transitions to and from democracy such as economic crisis, identity formation, civil society development, and constitutional reform in CEE and the NIS. SPPS also aims to highlight so far understudied themes in East European studies such as right-wing radicalism, religious life, higher education, or human rights protection. The authors and titles of previously published and forthcoming manuscripts are listed at the end of this book. For a full description of the series and reviews of its books, see www.ibidem-verlag.de/red/spps.

Note for authors (as of 2007): After successful review, fully formatted and carefully edited electronic master copies of up to 250 pages will be published as b/w A5 paperbacks and marketed in Germany (e.g. vlb.de, buchkatalog.de, amazon.de) and internationally (e.g. amazon. com). For longer books, formatting/editorial assistance, different binding, oversize maps, coloured illustrations and other special arrangements, authors' fees between €100 and €1500 apply. Publication of German doctoral dissertations follows a separate procedure. Authors are asked to provide a high-quality electronic picture on the object of their study for the book's front-cover. Younger authors may add a foreword from an established scholar. Monograph authors and collected volume editors receive two free as well as further copies for a reduced authors' price, and will be asked to contribute to marketing their book as well as finding reviewers and review journals for them. These conditions are subject to yearly review, and to be modified, in the future. Further details at www.ibidem-verlag.de/red/spps-authors.

Editorial correspondence & manuscripts should, until 2011, be sent to: Dr. Andreas Umland, ZIMOS, Ostenstr. 27, 85072 Eichstätt, Germany; e-mail: umland@stanfordalumni.org

Business correspondence & review copy requests should be sent to: *ibidem*-Verlag, Julius-Leber-Weg 11, D-30457 Hannover, Germany; tel.: +49(0)511-2622200; fax: +49(0)511-2622201; spps@ibidem-verlag.de.

Book orders & payments should be made via the publisher's electronic book shop at: www.ibidem-verlag.de/red/SPPS_EN/

Authors, reviewers, referees, and editors for (as well as all other persons sympathetic to) SPPS are invited to join its networks at www.facebook.com/group.php?gid=52638198614 and www.linkedin.com/groups?about=&gid=103012

Recent Volumes

79 Bernd Rechel
The Long Way Back to Europe
Minority Protection in Bulgaria
With a foreword by Richard Crampton
ISBN 978-3-89821-863-4

80 Peter W. Rodgers
Nation, Region and History in Post-Communist Transitions
Identity Politics in Ukraine, 1991-2006
With a foreword by Vera Tolz
ISBN 978-3-89821-903-7

81 Stephanie Solywoda
The Life and Work of Semën L. Frank
A Study of Russian Religious Philosophy
With a foreword by Philip Walters
ISBN 978-3-89821-457-5

82 Vera Sokolova
Cultural Politics of Ethnicity
Discourses on Roma in Communist Czechoslovakia
ISBN 978-3-89821-864-1

83 Natalya Shevchik Ketenci
Kazakhstani Enterprises in Transition
The Role of Historical Regional Development in Kazakhstan's Post-Soviet Economic Transformation
ISBN 978-3-89821-831-3

84 Martin Malek, Anna Schor-Tschudnowskaja (Hrsg.)
Europa im Tschetschenienkrieg
Zwischen politischer Ohnmacht und Gleichgültigkeit
Mit einem Vorwort von Lipchan Basajewa
ISBN 978-3-89821-676-0

85 Stefan Meister
Das postsowjetische Universitätswesen zwischen nationalem und internationalem Wandel
Die Entwicklung der regionalen Hochschule in Russland als Gradmesser der Systemtransformation
Mit einem Vorwort von Joan DeBardeleben
ISBN 978-3-89821-891-7

86 Konstantin Sheiko in collaboration with Stephen Brown
Nationalist Imaginings of the Russian Past
Anatolii Fomenko and the Rise of Alternative History in Post-Communist Russia
With a foreword by Donald Ostrowski
ISBN 978-3-89821-915-0

87 Sabine Jenni
Wie stark ist das „Einige Russland"?
Zur Parteibindung der Eliten und zum Wahlerfolg der Machtpartei im Dezember 2007
Mit einem Vorwort von Klaus Armingeon
ISBN 978-3-89821-961-7

Thomas Borén

MEETING-PLACES OF TRANSFORMATION

Urban Identity, Spatial Representations and Local Politics in Post-Soviet St Petersburg

ibidem-Verlag
Stuttgart

Bibliografische Information der Deutschen Nationalbibliothek
Die Deutsche Nationalbibliothek verzeichnet diese Publikation in der
Deutschen Nationalbibliografie; detaillierte bibliografische Daten sind im
Internet über http://dnb.d-nb.de abrufbar.

Bibliographic information published by the Deutsche Nationalbibliothek
Die Deutsche Nationalbibliothek lists this publication in the Deutsche Nationalbibliografie;
detailed bibliographic data are available in the Internet at http://dnb.d-nb.de.

Frontcover Picture: Russia and Sankt-Petersburg, spaces of transformation. Digital Collage of Maps
© Thomas Borén 2005.

∞

Gedruckt auf alterungsbeständigem, säurefreien Papier
Printed on acid-free paper

ISSN: 1614-3515

ISBN-10: 3-89821-739-6
ISBN-13: 978-3-89821-739-2

© *ibidem*-Verlag
Stuttgart 2009

Alle Rechte vorbehalten

Das Werk einschließlich aller seiner Teile ist urheberrechtlich geschützt. Jede Verwertung
außerhalb der engen Grenzen des Urheberrechtsgesetzes ist ohne Zustimmung des Verlages
unzulässig und strafbar. Dies gilt insbesondere für Vervielfältigungen,
Übersetzungen, Mikroverfilmungen und elektronische Speicherformen sowie die
Einspeicherung und Verarbeitung in elektronischen Systemen.

All rights reserved. No part of this publication may be reproduced, stored in or introduced into a retrieval
system, or transmitted, in any form, or by any means (electronic, mechanical, photocopying, recording or
otherwise) without the prior written permission of the publisher. Any person who does any unauthorized act
in relation to this publication may be liable to criminal prosecution and civil claims for damages.

Printed in Germany

To my parents Karin and late Linnar Borén

Contents

List of Figures 11
List of Abbreviations 13
Note on Transliteration and Russian words 15
Preface and Acknowledgements 17

1 Modelling time-space – urban meeting-places 19
   1.1 Point of departure – landscapes of courses 23
   1.2 Introducing a model for spatial change 26
   1.3 Total action-space 30
   1.4 Real and actual action-spaces: system and lifeworld 32
   1.5 Disposition of the thesis 38

2 The cultural geography of Russia 43
   2.1 The cultural turn 44
   2.2 Lifeworlds and semiotics 47
   2.3 The cultural turn – revisited 51
   2.4 On post-modernism and the subject as "wide-awake" 55
   2.5 On the concept of practice 56
   2.6 Soviet and post-Soviet geography – a cultural turn? 60
   2.7 Symbolic landscapes of the Moscow-Tartu School 64
   2.8 Conclusions 70

3	Taming the hermeneutic animal – field method	73
	3.1 The (empirical) bodily imperative	76
	3.2 Inside – outside	80
	3.3 Critique and the taming of the hermeneutic animal	82
	3.4 The city as field	83
	3.5 Theoretical interpretation	85
	3.6 Logical inference and generalisability	86
	3.7 Ethics	90
	3.8 The position of the researcher as a foreigner	94
	3.9 Funnels, serendipity and abduction	103
	3.10 Conclusions	106
4	A Soviet type high-rise housing district	109
	4.1 Ligovo – a background	109
	4.2 (War) history inscribed in public space	114
	4.3 Thinking big – planning big	117
	4.4 The *pustyr'*, and the houses	123
	4.5 The greenery, the benches and other spatial details	126
	4.6 A *spal'nyi* raion?	131
	4.7 Conclusions	134
5	Symbolic landscapes and Ligovo's genius loci	137
	5.1 Rozhkov's history of Ligovo	140
	5.2 The artificial spatial language of Sankt-Peterburg as text	146
	5.3 Location and status	147
	5.4 Cultural heritage context (persons) – the Heroes	149
	5.5 Stories of modernisation – Ligovo's main functions	153

	5.6	Time-spatial strategies of continuity – the creation of continuity	155
	5.7	Juxtaposition in space over time	155
	5.8	Juxtaposition of Ligovo with Sankt-Peterburg	158
	5.9	Triangulating the results	162
	5.10	Anti-codes	166
	5.11	Conclusions	167
6		Secret space, mental maps and stiff landscapes	173
	6.1	The semiotics of maps	174
	6.2	Soviet maps	176
	6.3	Historical maps	179
	6.4	City maps	180
	6.5	Maps of Ligovo	185
	6.6	End note on Soviet maps	188
	6.7	The Soviet fear of accurate information	194
	6.8	Maps, people and the stiff landscape	195
	6.9	Conclusions	197
7		Political structure and communication	199
	7.1	The new local democracy – introduction	201
	7.2	Soviet and post-Soviet political structures	204
	7.3	Munitsipal'nyi okrug No 40 "Uritsk"	210
	7.4	The Municipal Council and its influence	217
	7.5	Direct impact on the place	218
	7.6	Financial and organisational help	219
	7.7	Control and safety measures	220
	7.8	Finances, plans and problems	220
	7.9	Local media	222

	7.10	The media situation in Ligovo	223
	7.11	The local TV-channel	224
	7.12	Local TV as a political tool at the local level	229
	7.13	Conclusions	232
8	Ligovo essays of Sankt-Peterburg – Conclusions		235
	8.1	The double hermeneutic circle	236
	8.2	Theoretical assessment – the first hermeneutic circle	237
	8.3	Empirical assessment – the second hermeneutic circle	239
	8.4	Generalising spatial change – looking forward	244
	8.5	Lines, instead of fields	246

Appendix A: Issues of local self-government — 251

Appendix B: The Municipal Council — 253

    Age, sex, profession and education among the deputies — 253

    Local connection and earlier political experience of the deputies — 256

Bibliography — 259
Maps and atlases — 283
Films — 284
Homepages — 284

List of Figures

1.1	Model of scale-sensitive space construction	27
1.2	Time-spatial connections between system and lifeworld	36
1.3	Cars on a lawn in Ligovo	37
4.1	Map of Ligovo and Krasnosel'skii raion in Sankt-Peterburg	111
4.2	Historical Ligovo, wooden houses at Nikolaevskaia Street	112
4.3	A war monument to Alexander V. German, who has give his name to one of the main streets of Ligovo	114
4.4	A war monument to mark the front	115
4.5	Berezovaia Alleia Slavy in Ligovo	116
4.6.	Map of Ligovo	119
4.7.	Polezhaevskii Park	120
4.8.	The "Rubezh" cinema	122
4.9.	The building of the administration of Krasnosel'skii raion	122
4.10.	View of Ligovo from a 14-storey house, the Gulf of Finland in the background	124
4.11.	Façade with "freezers", glassed-in balconies, flower-boxes, antennas and satellite dishes	125
4.12.	The greenery as a mix of planned and spontaneous plantation, and a football ground	127
4.13.	An extreme example of the "wild" character of the greenery in the yards	128
4.14.	View over a yard, to the left is a school located in-between the houses	129
4.15.	A post-Soviet shopping centre, a Soviet shopping centre in the back	132

4.16.	The market at Ligovo train station	132
4.17.	Small scale traders outside Dom Tkanei	133
6.1.	Social composition of population of city of Kazan in the 1970s	184
6.2.	Ligovo map from 1981	187
6.3.	Ligovo map from 2002	190
6.4	An inaccurate cartographic representation of Ligovo in a map from 1996	191
6.5.	Aerial photo of Ligovo from late autumn 2000	192
6.6	Aerial photo of Ligovo. Farm buildings at the sovkhoz are pictured in the foreground	192
7.1.	Election posters in Munitsipal'nyi okrug No. 40 "Uritsk"	215
8.1.	The double hermeneutic circle	237
8.2.	Fields of different types of spatial change	245
8.3.	Lines of different types of spatial change	247
8.4.	Types of change following each other	248

List of Abbreviations

ASSR	Avtonomnaia Sovetskaia Sotsialisticheskaia Respublika (*Autonomous Soviet Socialist Republic*)
GAI	Gosudarstvennaia avtomobil'naia inspektsiia (*State Automobile Inspectorate*)
Glavlit	Glavnoe upravlenie po okhrane gosudarstvennykh tain v pechati (*Main Administration for Safeguarding State Secrets in the Press*) originally: Glavnoe upravlenie po delam literatury i izdatel'stv (*Main Administration for Literary and Publishing Affairs*)
GUGK	Glavnoe upravlenie geodezii i kartografii (*Central Board of Geodesy and Cartography*)
KGB	Komitet gosudarstvennoi bezopasnosti (*The Committee of State Security*)
FSB	Federal'naia sluzhba bezopasnosti (*The Federal Security Service*)
NKVD	Narodnyi komissariat vnutrennykh del (*Peoples Commissariat for Internal Affairs*).
RUVD	Raionnoe upravlenie vnutrennykh del (*District Board of Internal Affairs*)
KPSS	Kommunisticheskaia Partiia Sovetskogo Soiuza (*Communist Party of the Soviet Union, CPSU*)
USSR	Union of Soviet Socialist Republics (Soiuz Sovetskikh Sotsialisticheskikh Respublik, SSSR)

Note on Transliteration and Russian words

Concerning transliteration I have followed the system used by Princeton University Library throughout the text. There are, however, a few exceptions: the letters Ё, Й, Ц, Э, Ю and Я are transliterated E, I, Ts, E, Iu and Ia without "diacritic marks". Personal names that have established English translations are not transliterated, for example Yeltsin (and not El'tsin). The last exception to the Princeton system concerns the references in which I have strictly kept to the transcription of the names, titles etc. used by the authors.

Since a couple of years the transliteration of place names is standard cartographic procedure on international maps and therefore Sankt-Peterburg, and not Saint-Petersburg, St. Petersburg or St Petersburg, Petergof and not Peterhof, and so on in this text. Toponyms, apart from names of the countries or seas (Soviet Union, and not Sovetskii Soiuz; Russia, and not Rossiia; Gulf of Finland, and not Finskii zalif), are thus transliterated throughout the text, even if an English name exists. Exceptions, however, do exist. For ease of reading, certain details in names are translated when deamed relevant, such as highway instead of *shosse*, street instead of *ulitsa*.

"Soviet", with a capital "S" is used when the word is an adjective relating to the proper noun of the country (e.g. Soviet authorities), but when the same word is used with a lower case "s", it denotes the political units (councils) that governed the different territorial levels throughout the Soviet Union. Raion is another case in point. The word is in many texts treated as an English word, and is so also here. In general, however, Russian words are otherwise transliterated into the form (singular, plural, the accusative, the dative, etc.) they have in the Russian context.

Preface and Acknowledgements

The main part of this work was presented in December 2003 as a seminar manuscript. It was then called *Urban Life and Landscape in Russia in the Aftermath of Modernity: Ligovo Essays of St Petersburg*, which has been the working title of the present text. In April 2005 I defended the manuscript as a doctoral thesis at the Department of Human Geography, Stockholm University, and it was made available in print in one of the department series (Meddelanden No. 133, 2005) under its present title. The text at hand now is the same as in the theses – only marginal changes and language corrections has been made.

Acknowledgements: First of all, many thanks to my supervisors – Bo Lenntorp, who guided me through the final stages, and Karl-Olov Arnstberg, who got me started and followed my work for a long time. Many thanks also to Thomas Lundén as assisting supervisor. All of you have been very important to me and to this work.

This book started in the context of the research project "Life-forms in the Suburbs of Large Cities in the Baltic Sea Region" carried out by the Swans research group and financed by The Foundation for Baltic and East European Studies (Östersjöstiftelsen). The project was based at Södertörn University College and led by Karl-Olov Arnstberg. Thanks also to my Swan-companions: Ulla Berglund, Siv Ehn, Bettina Lissner, Eleonora Narvselius, Erik Olsson and Juan Velasquez.

In Russia I was associated with the Faculty of Political Science and Sociology, European University at St Petersburg. I would like to thank this faculty and especially Vadim V. Volkov for academic affiliation and supervision during fieldwork. Thanks also to the other staff and graduate students at the faculty.

When the Swans-project ended I returned to Stockholm University and the Department of Human Geography, where I received additional funding for finishing my work from the Faculty of Social Sciences. The two major financiers are hereby greatly acknowledged, as are Lillemor och Hans W:son Ahlmanns fond för geografisk forskning, Stiftelsen Carl Mannerfelts Fond, and Axel Lagrelius fond för geografisk forskning for complementary financing. The grants from the Swedish Institute which helped to finance the fieldwork are also greatly acknowledged.

Thanks also to late Galina Lindquist for reading an earlier version of this text, as well as to an anonymous reviewer. Special thanks to Andrew Byerley for proof-reading the English and for valuable comments on the text, and to Elena Tchebanova, Elina Demenkova, Irina Timofeeva, Yuliya Konovalova, Oleg Pachenkov and Ina and Dmitrii Frank-Kamenetskii for all kinds of help and support. Many thanks to Lia Iangoulova for her excellent interview transcriptions. And to Sodobe Hamedani and Jonas Winnerlöv for providing help in the early stages of fieldwork when it was really needed. Special thanks to an old lady in the northern part of the city, to Anatolii Mikhailovich Rozhkov, to the people of Ligovo, and especially to the family where I stayed.

Apart from the scientific support from supervisors and colleagues at both Stockholm University and Södertörn University College, apart from the material support from the financiers, apart from the help and moral support from family and friends in Sweden and Russia, last but not least I wish to acknowledge the spiritual support from God. Thanks.

Thomas Borén

1 Modelling time-space – urban meeting-places

Dunk, dunk, dunk, dunk. The sound of the pounding knife is rhythmic, steady and secure. Cabbage is chopped to salad. Elena Alekseevna sits on a small stool in the middle of the kitchen floor with a sack on one side and a number of cabbage heads on the other. On the floor in front of her is a cracked wooden bowl and she works with a mezzaluna, the blade of which fits the curvature of the bowl. Outside the window newly fallen snow has adorned Ligovo, one of Sankt-Peterburg's worn outer high-rise districts, in a beautiful winter apparel. Elena has taken in the cabbages from the small glassed-in balcony on the west side of the apartment block which is more usually used as the prolonged pantry of the flat. The cold outside seems to have come as a surprise despite it already being mid-November, and the balcony is now too cold and some of the cabbages have frozen. Elena Alekseevna peels off the outer leaves that have been spoiled by the cold and then inspects the colour and consistency of the remaining part. If it is green and soft the cabbage is cut in two and the stem removed. The two halves are chopped up, whereas the stem and the damaged outer leaves are put aside to be composted at the dacha. The cabbage heads that are white and hard are put back into the sack for later use. She talks uninterruptedly while working.

I watch astonished. A couple of days have passed since I moved in with Elena Alekseevna and her family, and the sense of un-substantiality has started to pass. I sit on a stool at the kitchen table with my back turned to the wall. The task of chopping the cabbages into fine shreds looks like hard work. I ask if I may help but the offer is rejected. These everyday kitchen practicalities in Ligovo seemed a world removed from those played out in my own Stockholm kitchenette. Someone who grew up under similar circumstances in the same country or region would probably already have a relatively accurate picture of what was taking place behind the closed doors of people otherwise strange to him or her. They would largely share the same lifeworld and, with some reflection, would be reasonably aware of what was going on in other people's everyday lives. Although the specific life forms may vary, people would be aware of the general structures of the lifeworld. The place, in this case Ligovo, or Uritsk which is the Soviet name, is one part of the general lifeworld structure of the people living here. They all encounter the same physical environment, and all would have some kind of relation to the high-rise buildings and the large-scale urban landscape that radiates out from the historical centre of Sankt-Peterburg. They would know how the city works, would follow its rhythms and all be included in the world of thoughts that encompasses it. There is a practical understanding of the city, and on a daily basis the urbanites handle the claims and opportunities of their lifeworld, both in relation to that very lifeworld, and also in relation to the systems that act in a given city space. However, the situation is almost the opposite for an outside researcher. A premise for this kind of research is that life in other places is different, and it was with great interest that I sat down at the kitchen table when I heard the pounding and saw that Elena was busy doing something that I did not immediately understand.

It was clear that Elena Alekseevna had sorted and chopped cabbage many times before. Careful use of the resources at hand in order to have food on the table was self-evident to her, as self-evident as the return of all that was not edible to the soil, nothing should be wasted. What was not self-evident to Elena Alekseevna, however, was that there would always actually be something to eat. Indeed, hunger was no abstract condition, as a teenager she had herself experienced the famine in Leningrad during the blockade in the early 1940s. During the winter of 1941–42, it was January, her younger brother had starved and frozen to death and his body had lain for one month in a room of the flat waiting for removal and burial. Hunger also existed in the stories she related about her two sisters whom she had never met; sisters who had died in infancy during the hard years following the revolution.

For someone who has at one time experienced starvation, food is rarely if ever taken for granted, even to the extent that one might neglect one's family. Elena Alekseevna relates a story about something edible that she had to, but did not want to share, and her pain, the remembrance of hunger – the panicked and drained desperation – etched into her face like *The Cry* of Munch, silent and deafening at the same time. During the war, moreover, people's lives were not only threatened by hunger, cold and the detonating shells of the attacking forces, but also by a total collapse of Soviet society. The disintegration of the system had been so immanent that the memories of what had taken place still exist – and are cared for – as a formative element in the lifeworlds today, over 60 years later.

In a discussion of lifeworlds it would be easy to stop at one or a couple of aspects of the concept, and in the following the focus is first and foremost on the spatial system of relevances of the lifeworld. At the same time, however, it is important to remember that the concept aims to understand a type of a whole. It is the whole that consist of the collected experience that all persons have, and it is also directed forwards in time as expectations, plans and goals for action. The sum total of the lived experiences in this very now makes up the lifeworld of an individual. This sum total thus includes the memories, knowledges and practices that one carries along in life, as well as ideas about the future, both concrete personal goals, as well as the overarching views that exist in society at large pertaining to the prospects and vistas to come.

The things that are found in the surroundings of one's existence also constitute a part of the social world, and partake in the forming of lifeworlds. One ages not only together with other people with whom one shares the lived experience, but also with the material world that encompasses the self. And just as communication between people may vary from the smallest of gestures and briefest of utterances from strangers, to deep exchanges with family, friends, neighbours and colleagues with whom one shares space for larger parts of the day and for long periods of time, the contact with the things one shares space with, and which are within the reach of one's consciousness, may vary. Certain things are more present than others and may be found within the physical distance needed to have a direct, tactile contact with them. A large part of the social system within which the things are arranged, is constructed to regulate this very direct and tactile contact. To mention but one example, there was a very obvious lack of tactile contact with food during the famine in Leningrad.

The social system that regulates access and contact to things functions in a different way than the practice-oriented and moral and emotionally based regime that orders experiences in the lifeworld. At the most general of levels, the system is all about power and money that are formed around norms. Morals and emotions constitute the base of the system, but in contrast to the feelings and values of the lifeworld, these have evolved in direct relation to the power over, and the organisation of, a space that widely transgresses in size, and in technical and social complexity the space that people via their lifeworlds are in direct contact with and which they form and are formed by. The space of the lifeworld and the space of the system are not different or discrete spaces in the physical environment. Rather, the space where both lifeworld and system take place is created as a composite arising from the intermingling and over-layering of the system and the lifeworld into each other. Space, viewed in this way, is essentially a meeting-place of lifeworld and systemic forces.

These meeting-places are, in the final analysis, about survival, as the example of food provisioning in the city has shown. In most cases, however, space is taken for granted and is not reflected upon on a daily basis by the general public. We practice our everyday spatialities on a routine basis, and, for as long as everything functions as usual, the place where we live and it's functioning does not occupy the front regions of the mind. Consequently, if it is of more or less decisive importance for the general welfare of people that these places work, a geographically interesting task is to problemize them, and I think of them exactly as meeting-places defined in time and space by a series of cultural, social and physical necessities and opportunities. In this chapter I outline a scale-sensitive model for how this may be understood. In the following chapters I apply the model in empirical descriptions and analyses of some specific aspects on these meeting-places.

The aim of this study is to understand how meeting-places are constructed and, in the light of this construction, to understand the transformation from the Soviet times to today. The purpose of the study is hence twofold: firstly to develop a model for understanding spatial change and the construction of space as a meeting-place, and secondly, to employ this model to show an otherwise little-known picture of urban Russia and the outer high-rise districts in Sankt-Peterburg and their transformation from Soviet times to the present day.

In connection with these theoretical and empirical objectives, I pursue a methodologically aimed thesis of logic, namely that the model is a tool that makes the worldview of time-geography and the epistemology of the landscape of courses applicable to concrete research. The model, I argue, is situated in-between geographic theory and the chosen object of research, and from it research questions which are hence both theoretically and empirically grounded may be constructed. These research questions may include heuristic and explorative searches, as well as concretely formulated questions. By no means is this the only way to bring theory and empirical material close to each other, but it is one way to make the idea of the landscape of courses researchable without losing track of this idea's ontological foundations and principles.

Empirically this is carried out by focusing on meeting-places, in the context of this study on Ligovo, an outer city district in Sankt-Peterburg, to illustrate the train of thoughts presented. To a large extent the study builds on spatial narratives, and the period of analysis approximately spans the years between 1970 and 2000. Fieldwork in the form of participant observation was carried over a 16 month period during 1998 to 2000, 14 months of which were spent in Ligovo. I have worked abductively and hence tried to interweave and synthesise theory and empirical material in the model discussed below. In terms of both the objective and the research approach I have embraced a desire to be "empirical" for the reason that the existing knowledge concerning formerly Soviet and current Russian everyday places is limited. I thus hope to fill in a few of the blanks on the Western map of the Russia that developed during the Soviet era. I proceed from a view on places and landscapes that derives from the time-geographical perspective and complement this with a spatialised discussion on Jürgen Habermas' lifeworld and system.

1.1 Point of departure – landscapes of courses

Meeting-places. Life and landscape. Concepts intertwined in each other. My own view of landscape originates in the general worldview of time-geography, and more specifically in the idea of *förloppslandskap*, the landscapes of courses (Hägerstrand 1993).[1] This perspective views the world as being in constant motion and flux and focuses on the dynamic interface between time, space, humans and things (nature, material artefacts). It further views the world as loaded with human intentions expressed in the form of projects, and with energy from the sun, as well as with the dynamic aspects of a general ecology. It is constructed to understand the totality and multi-dimensionality of the geographical object of study – the earth as the home of mankind.

The landscape of courses hereby concurs with the core of the geographic tradition in which the principle of nearness – rather than the principle of likeness – is applied, and it thus proceeds from ideas of co-existences of differences, and how these are packed and jostle with each other in time-space. In this view time-space is essentially a meeting-place, and the study of this may be called a *gefügekunde*, or the logic of how things are put together. This logic would try to explain and understand how all that is present in a given scenery keeps together, and how the processes of time-space proceed in collaboration, competition, or independently of each other, or how they may be pushed aside (Hägerstrand 1985a). In such a scenery it is not only the material existents – corpuscles – that take place, but also ideas, intentions, plans, perceptions, wishes, knowledges, narratives, relations and other socially and immaterially conditioned occurrences are seen as part of the totality, and from which the physical landscape is subsequently materialised or demolished. All that is present is of interest in creating the sought for contextual synthesis, and the

> only totality that fulfils the condition of the presence of all components, but still is confined, is a piece of a populated landscape. With landscape is meant not only that which is visible in the surroundings, but *all that is present within the defined border, inclu-*

---

[1] Landscapes of flows would be an alternative translation. However, Hägerstrand often found and used words with a special flavour, although more ordinary words well could have about the same meaning. Therefore I have translated *förlopp* to courses and not to flows. Moreover, the word flow would in most instances be translated to Swedish as *flöde* and not *förlopp*. For reviews and discussions of time-geography, see Hägerstrand 1985b, 1991, Asplund 1983, Carlestam & Sollbe 1991, Åquist 1992, Gren 1994, Lenntorp 1998, Borén 1999.

sive of that which moves in and out of the border during the chosen time-period. (Hägerstrand 1993:26, *original emphasis, my translation*)

It is about "blocks of reality without gaps", and it is only in the next stage that it becomes interesting to specify and organise the material on the basis of the research questions one is interested in. With regard to this, Bo Lenntorp (1998) writes that geography may be seen as a "logic of excerption" (*excerperingslära*) in which the epistemologically important idea is not to sew together the ideas of different schools of thought, but to excerpt or "pick out" the relevant parts of such a block for detailed examination, without misrepresenting the geographic perspective of the totality of reality. To understand how the world is put together in the first place, it is thus the finetuned excerpts that are important. The point of departure is not to add detail to detail from "below", but rather to divide the totality from "above", to understand how

> [t]he configurations of nature and society compete about place in a defined budget of space, time and energy. Hereby cause and effect is not only a question of before-and-after as in a laboratory, but also of the practicabilities of the budget, due to the surroundings' resistance or willingness to be traversable. Without a notion of the landscape of courses as a budget frame, it is not possible to decide what is pushed aside as an effect of something new penetrating, or what is expanding because something formerly unresisting withdraws. *The study of the landscape of courses becomes a question of how to observe and interpret the physical "wielding of power" of different phenomena in relation to each other.* (Hägerstrand 1993:27, *original emphasis, my translation*)

One of the keys to understanding spatial change is thus to be found in the nature and qualities of the surroundings, and they should therefore feature prominently in any theory or model that tries to understand this change.

1.2 Introducing a model for spatial change

As I have pointed out above, one of the keys to understanding time-spatial change resides in the character of the surroundings. To the extent that everything in a landscape of courses is constantly in motion, these surroundings function as media that are themselves also in motion and continuous transformation. One of these agile media, or surroundings, that I want to focus on is the "social", in a broad meaning of the term. While this causes me to depart slightly from the corporeally addressed corpus callosum of time-geography, I do retain a focus on its intention to consider the time-spatial configurations of co-existences. Rather I look at this from another direction, from the immaterial world to the material.[2]

The social functions as a medium for ideas, practices and knowledge, and is thereby also a medium – to a greater or lesser extent – for order. I divide the social as medium into four parts; *language, power, money* (Habermas 1984, 1987a) and what I conceptualise as *serious enthusiasm*. However, before I account for the details in this constructed order (and the concepts we as researchers use to understand this are sometimes part of the construction of that very same order), it should be made clear that time-geography needs to be complemented with both a methodology and a method that are adjusted to the study of this medium. Sometimes that which has been divided from above, must be seen from with-in.

To do this, I proceed from a time-spatial model of power-forces in and between what I call *total* action-space, *real* action-space and the *actual* action-space. These action-spaces, which are concerned with different levels of scale, are formed in relation to space, time, lifeworld and system, and the general ideas that are prevalent in society at a certain time, as well as

---

2 Time-geography is open to these kinds of theoretical experiments, as shown in the studies that combine it with other theories, see Kersti Nordell (2002) discussing time-geography and Schütz, Jennie Bäckman (2001) discussing Tönnies, my own attempts with regards to the lifeworlds and system (1999), Åquist discussing Giddens (1992). Anthony Giddens has used it in his works and structuration theory was influenced by it. Also, Nigel Thrift (1996) refers to it and places some of Hägerstrand's ideas in line with the thinking of Heidegger, Wittgenstein, Merleau-Ponty, Bourdieu, de Certeau and Shotter. The "list" of works could probably be made longer; what the referred examples indicate is that time-geography is open to use in a broader context, may be aligned with mainstream social theory, and is adaptable to research problems of various kinds.

by the *course-relations* which mainly originate in the fact that people are active creatures engaged in projects (Figure 1.1). Apart from these elements, the model features an important additional aspect, i.e. the pertinence of (today's perception of) the history of science for the understanding of the world. (See also Borén 1999.)

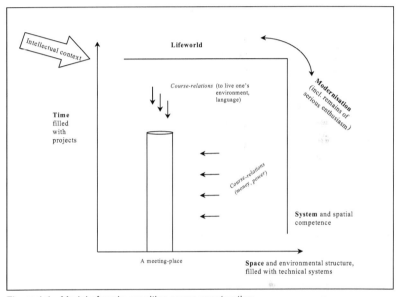

Figure 1.1   Model of scale-sensitive space construction

The model is general and almost anything may be positioned at its centre, i.e. be placed in relation to the components of the model to understand the object of study in a geographic time-spatial context. In this case, and according to the purpose of the study, a part of the city of Sankt-Peterburg is positioned at the centre. *The purpose of the model then becomes to show, in a scale-sensitive way (i.e. from the nearness in everyday life to time-space-enclosing factors) the components of and the dynamics in the construction of space* – or expressed in a more time-geographic way *to show how a block of the landscape of courses appears in a methodologically applicable form.* This is the overarching thesis of this work.

It should be noted that in this thesis I mainly treat the *societal* budgeting of time-space and, further, that the ecological time-spatial budgeting that takes place between man, plants and animals is, if treated at all, simply regarded as a definite limit to what the societal budgeting is capable of. The main difference between the different types of budgeting is that ecological budgeting is not coloured by ideological standpoints. As soon as it is, it becomes by definition part of the societal budgeting.

Concerning the components of the model, space is one of them. In the model, space is regarded as "absolute" until lifeworld and system are included. When lifeworld and system are included space becomes relational, but still retains many of its absolute traits.[3] These traits of space as absolute constitute the environmental structure, which in its turn consists of nature and technical support systems, i.e. technology and infrastructure of various kinds. These figure as fundaments to the different action-spaces I will describe. If we turn to relational space, I will call this "action-space" since it is filled with projects and practices of the lived environment, spatial competencies and course-relations, all of which evolve over time. But "action-space" as an analytical concept can hardly be said to suffice for the purpose of this research. To be scale-sensitive to a world that ranges from the everyday projects of people, to space-overarching historical developments, time-space must be divided further, and I find the division of action-space into the three above mentioned levels useful for this purpose.

Time and projects are further components of the model. Time is regarded as absolute, or definite, and filled up with projects.[4] Projects are here treated in the time-geographical meaning where they are regarded as future oriented "goals for action". No specific differentiation is made between unreflected routine behaviours, spontaneous or impulsive actions, planned actions, or whether the project contains one or several people. Neither are projects differentiated according to their relation to common

---

3   This move from an absolute conception of space to a relational conception also means that time-geography becomes sensible to epistemological critique, a trait it would not have otherwise (at least not explicitly, as its intention is to move beyond the political and provide a politically neutral frame of mind, or worldview).

4   This does not rule out that the *perception* of time may vary among people, or due to circumstances (see Lundén 2002:26). In this model such aspects are considered as a part of lifeworlds.

norms and values, or to other interests. Two ideas require specific mention here. Firstly, that projects are often enfolded in other projects, and secondly that an action aimed at a certain goal often gives rise to unexpected side-effects. Projects could be concisely summarised as "cultural" process and is a general concept for human action. I leave it at this for the time being but in the following chapters I discuss at length both "culture" and "action" in terms of the acting subject as competent and wide-awake and examine this in terms of signifying systems and (everyday) practices.

In the model, the concept of course-relation fulfils an important role. In the landscape of courses, the determination of the *where* and *when* of that which exists is dependent on its surroundings, i.e. a course, existent or project is dependent on all the other things and projects that exist in its time-spatial surroundings, and therefore it must of necessity have some kind of force balancing mutual relation to them. This relation I call course-relation, and it is the relation between courses, and between courses and existents and projects that are intended. In interplay with each other, the course-relations determine the position of a particular course, existent or project. If these relations did not exist, a particular course, existent or project would diffuse forwards in time to cover all in time-space. Apart from the pressure that the surroundings exert on a course, existent or project, it may have internal, centripetal forces that keep it together, concentrating it from within. In the model the course-relations are illustrated with arrows, and as is shown these stem from the two lines illustrating lifeworld and system. The course-relations, it must be clear, exert a transforming force on that which they are directed towards.

An additional factor in the model is the thick arrow in the upper left corner. The arrow symbolises the intellectual context, i.e. the historical context of thought in which we as researchers understand the problems and material at hand. This course-relation relates to a context that does not necessarily affect, at least not directly, the spaces under study, although it surely affects the manner in which these are understood. It is included in the model to show that our understandings (as expressed in this model, and further discussed in Chapters 2 and 3, and as "shown" empirically in Chapters 4–7) are not detached from the intellectual and social context in which they develop. A note on this is that the intellectual context is dynamic and in the dynamics of the reproduction of the intellectual web of significances, new ideas are constantly added and some of the old ones become redundant.

Let us now turn to where spatial change really takes place, to the action-spaces and their respective course-relations.

1.3 Total action-space

The total action-space of a certain society "overarches" it and is made up of a limited number of "meta-projects". The bent arrow in the upper right corner in Figure 1.1 symbolises the course-relations of the meta-projects that exists in time-space. Meta-projects are those projects that have extended existence in both time and space. They may have centres and peripheries but they primarily strive toward spatial coverage and penetration over and into almost all that exists. They are messianic and colour both the lifeworlds of people and the institutions of the system at all scale levels, often or maybe always by establishing a specific language (*langue*) for the structuration and transaction of meaning. To a meta-project, and based on the specific language, certain master narratives are so closely connected that it is difficult to separate the three. Meta-texts, which contain instructions on how to decipher the language of the master narratives, are also attached to meta-projects. The master narratives include general directions on how to describe and interpret the world, to make the meta-projects realisable. Formulated simply, the meta-project relates to the "doing", the language to how the world is codified, the master narrative to how the message of the meta-project is organised, and meta-texts are pedagogical tools that help to install the language throughout the social body.

Meta-projects are extended over long durations in time and the ideas on which they are built take on a dynamic of their own, since within them there are many actors and institutions that act to carry out these meta-projects. Meta-projects are large-scale goals for action. In an earlier study I related this to sustainable development (Borén 1999), but here I think of the project of "modernity" as such a meta-project, including aspects such as electrification, industrialisation, urbanisation, etc. The master narrative connected to

Soviet modernity can be summed up in four words: the building of communism. However physical the *expressions* of the meta-project are when they are materialised in the form of power plants, industries, cities, etc., meta-projects' main ground for change is in the minds of people. Meta-projects become a kind of culturo-structuring social paradigm. A further trait is that they do not seem to respect political borders, but spread irrespective of them. They are not primarily place specific, although they may receive a local character when implemented in real action-space.

The course-relations connected to meta-projects are forceful in terms of their power to convince, but can not in and by themselves bring about the changes that they espouse and envisage. They (meta-projects and their course-relations) are initially founded on the energy of *enthusiasm*, which forms a social medium of its own in that people sacrifice money, power and language-ordered lifeworld-based relations to engage in them, and it (the medium) mainly lives in texts and in the world of formulation. Moreover, these texts and the world of formulation are taken as important and *serious* by its actors. In sum, *serious enthusiasm* characterises the core of a meta-project, and its actors endeavour to translate this medium into textual form, since it is mainly an unformulated mind-body sensation, or gut-feeling that underlies the medium.[5] However, to be realized, a meta-project must be broken down into part-projects that are realisable. The space that relates to this may be called *real* action-space. Here the part-projects of the meta-project come to be allocated to specific actors and institutions, and to people in general, all of which start to carry them out. Accordingly, these actors also confront the restraining effects of the real world.

---

5   Before a meta-project becomes established and gets *followers*, the *establishing group* would by many other people be characterised as fanatics with unrealistic dreams, especially if they envision rapid change. In the case of Russia, I think especially of people like Kropotkin, Plekhanov, Lenin, Trotskii and the other core revolutionaries.

1.4 Real and actual action-spaces: system and lifeworld

To understand the real action-space and the actual action-space we have to look at the core of the model. This is made up of course-relations and the four axes. In Figure 1.2 these factors are lifted out of the main model and shown in simplified form. In addressing their role in the model it is necessary to briefly discuss the work of Jürgen Habermas and the concepts of lifeworld and system.

Habermas has written prodigiously on language, morals, society and other key areas of social theory.[6] While his work constitutes a rich source from which geographers and others have drawn, his work has not had any major impact on the cultural geography discussed in Chapter 2. In one of his most central works – *The theory of communicative action* published in two volumes from 1981[7] – he discusses the interaction between system and lifeworld and argues that social evolution (modernisation) involves the colonisation of the lifeworld by the system. In his argument, Habermas proceeds from the lifeworld-concept of Alfred Schütz, and a concept of the system that is based on the ideas of Talcott Parsons.

Central to Habermas' theory on communicative action are communicative and instrumental reason. With communicative reason, Habermas refers to the reason embedded in the speech act. These acts in large aim for mutual understanding, and it is also through this aim and understanding that the actions of the lifeworld are co-ordinated. By speech acts, which use language as the medium, a (spirit of) community is founded, and the mutual understanding that arises in terms of what should be done and how, is acted upon. Instrumental reason, on the other hand, is communicated through the media of power and money, and these in turn co-ordinate the actions of the state and the market, which together constitute the system.

---

6 For discussions of Habermas' works, see Månson 1998, Giddens 1985.
7 The original German title of the two volumes are *Theorie des Kommunikativen Handels, Band 1: Handlungsrationalität und gesellsschaftliche Rationaliserung.* (Suhrkamp Verlag, Frankfurt am Main. 1981.) and *Theorie des Kommunikativen Handels, Band 2: Zur Kritik der funktionalistischen Vernunft.* (Suhrkamp Verlag, Frankfurt am Main. 1981.) In this work I refer to Habermas 1984 regarding the first volume and to Habermas 1987a for the second, both of which are English translations made by Thomas McCarthy.

Habermas underlines the importance of seeing society concurrently as system and lifeworld, and in a comment on Habermas' work, Karl-Olov Arnstberg (1997, cf. 1996) argues that such a perspective may be taken very far, but also states that the perspective should not be understood as one in which the lifeworld is one-sidedly "wiped out" by the system. Lifeworlds are perpetually created, and with illustrations drawn from the world of work, Arnstberg exemplifies how a manager may take employees into his or her confidence, or how the office may be decorated with things of the lifeworld, such as photographs of one's family.

The problem, as Habermas argues, is rather that communicative reason, which he means has prevailed in the lifeworld, has come to be increasingly replaced with the instrumental reason that governs actions in the system. The rationalisation of the lifeworld that comes with modernisation is not the main problem – Habermas believes in the modern project – but rather one of its consequences: the rationalisation strikes against the language-based, lifeworld-conditioned mutual understanding by affecting the way we interlocutarly reach this mutual understanding, without however, that we are explicitly conscious of this. He writes:

> The effects of the system on the lifeworld, which change the structure of contexts of action in socially integrated groups, have to remain hidden. The reproductive constraints that instrumentalize a lifeworld without weakening the illusion of its self-sufficiency have to hide, so to speak, in the pores of communicative action. This gives rise to a *structural violence* that, without becoming manifest as such, takes hold of the forms of intersubjectivity of possible understanding. (Habermas 1987a:187, *original emphasis*)

It is thus a form of deception. In the Soviet Union however, it is justified to ask whether or not the opposite process also happened, namely that the lifeworld occupied the system. Maybe this would be due to the fact that attempts by the state to instrumentalize the lifeworlds were over-explicit and based in rhetoric that ordinary people were quick to unravel. In short, people were sensible of the system and of what it tried to do. Another likely contributing factor is that the system did not work as intended. An example of this is, as shown by Alena Ledeneva (1998) in her discussion of the informal economy in the Soviet Union, that the state bureaucracy was "personified". The civil servants in the bureaucratic system came to perform their duties mainly in relation to the *personal* contact that the citizen had with the civil servant as a "friend", and not as a representative of established regulations in the decided order. Without such a personal contact the system worked slowly, poorly and sometimes not at all.

This example shows, if nothing else, that while the general structures of the lifeworld may have been colonised, social solidarity was not extinguished. Indeed, on the contrary, it was realized in a new way, and in relation to the system, a strategic way. One is loyal to one's friends and people assist one another in order to solve problems. In the context of the Soviet era this was not occasional practice but formed into widely spread lifeworld-based networks of personal relations that were necessary to live a "normal" life. These networks also had a mediating function between the private and the public (Borén 2003a), and hereby created an actual action-space with wider boundaries for most people than the action-space determined by the system. The rationalisation of the lifeworld that Habermas means has been pressed upon it from the ordering principles of the system (power and money from the state and market sub-systems respectively) had in this case not replaced the *communicative reason* that direct the actions in the lifeworld. In much else however, and maybe foremost in the lifeworld-based spatial system of relevances, the Soviet system and its variant of the modern project, came to "fragmentize" the cultural consciousness of the everyday, and hereby exert a much stronger influence on the actual action-spaces. This fragmentation, according to Habermas (1987a:355), would then be an obstacle to "enlightenment" of the effects of the subsystems.

Be that as it may, from the account so far it is clear that the system and the lifeworld are two qualitatively different aspects of society. But in terms of their respective spatialities, the system and lifeworld nevertheless share space with each other, and where one is present, the other is too. The relations and communication between them, as well as their relative degrees of presence in a given place, may vary according to the circumstances. How these very aspects relate to each individual place will be determining for how space there is formed. How matters stand spatially between the system and the lifeworld is summarised in Figure 1.2.

As is evident in the figure, the system and lifeworld are drawn as two partly overlapping circles which are placed in relation to a spatial axis and to an arrow that indicates time. The overlap illustrates the spatial points of contact between the lifeworld and the system, and the time arrow is meant to show that the points of contact develop together over time. To understand the picture, the course-relations that stem from the system, its institutions and regulations are vital. These set the limits for the real action-space by the technology available and utilised, the rules that specify what is legitimate institutional behaviour, the violence that may be summoned for the conformation to rules, the material resources allocated to a place, and the desired ethics and morals, as well as the knowledge at hand.

A strictly spatial aspect of this knowledge is the spatial competence (Hägerstrand 1993:47) that the system commands. The concept of spatial competence signifies the actors that draw plans and set guidelines for how space should be used. With the realisation of these plans by the institutions of the system, the system asserts itself in the time-space of individual people, i.e. the place they live in. Presupposing that the time-space of people is characterised by nearness and lifeworld based communication, i.e. something other than the system, the system and the lifeworld will consequently meet, which is shown by the overlap of the two circles. Spatially, however, it is not only the system that makes an impact on the place, but people continue to live and use the environment at hand. They do this according to the premises of the lifeworld, and they thereby take part in forming the terrain according to the pragmatic demands valid right then, right there. Not considering all of the regulations of the real action-space, people will use their lived experiences, their perceptions, practices and feelings to live their environments, and from this originates what I call the actual action-space. Over time, the course-relations that stem from this will impinge upon space and how it is formed.

To sum up, the course-relations that stem from the system and the lifeworld respectively make up the forces that in interplay with and against each other form space. Space hereby becomes a meeting-place in which the different action-spaces, so to say, are superimposed on each other. Based on the demands of the system and its means at hand, the actors of the system act to fulfil its plans, and in so doing the real action-space ensues, and with it the course-relations of the system. What I have called the actual action-space on the other hand, and the course-relations related to it, is the result of actions that are founded in and rest upon what is imposed by the lifeworld.

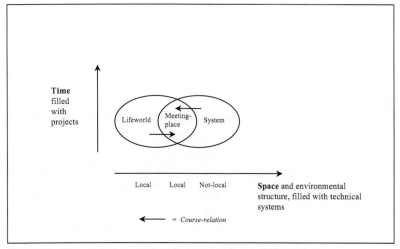

Figure 1.2   Time-spatial connections between system and lifeworld

A concrete and simple example is that in Ligovo the system had not planned enough parking places for private cars, at least not where the car owners wished to park. Instead they park the cars on the small roads and on the lawns just outside the entrances to the houses (Figure 1.3). A direct consequence of this is that the grass, which by the spatial competence was planned to be used in a different way, is worn and the ground turns to mud when it rains. The actors in the real action-space did not have the force to stop this practice and the course-relations of the system are in this case weaker than the course-relations that are mobilised by the lifeworld of the car-owners. This meeting of course-relations resulted in a damaged lawn – the damaged lawn is a spatial expression of the meeting of the course-relations. *In this meeting, space was created and a relational meeting-place constructed*. One may expect that with time the system will react and eventually build more parking places, or perhaps endeavour to increase adherence to the regulations through recourse to increased violence (e.g. by putting up road blocks), or, alternatively, the car-owners may become aware of the lawn's significance through language based communicative action with the neighbours.

Figure 1.3   Cars on a lawn in Ligovo (1999). (Photo: Thomas Borén)

The example is taken from Elena Alekseevna's world. The cars and the fact that their owners, besides parking on the lawn, do not pay any fees to park them inside the district irritate her. On occasions she discusses this at home, and she has raised the matter at a political meeting in the district. However, during my stay in Ligovo little happened to placate Elena's irritation, rather the opposite would be true. Concurrently with the improving economic situation in the country after the economic crisis of 1998, increasing numbers of people can afford to purchase cars. The photograph shows how the parking place is sometimes also used to carry out repair work on the cars.

1.5 Disposition of the thesis

The first three chapters of this work are theoretically directed. In the first of these I account for the model (Chapter 1) which is at the heart of the thesis and which grounds the following inquiries. This introduction is then followed by an epistemologically oriented overview of literature, which focuses on cultural geography (Chapter 2). This approach to geography is mainly based on qualitative methods, including cultural semiotics, and these are thoroughly discussed in relation to fieldwork (Chapter 3). Taken together, the two latter chapters represent an attempt to problemize the production of knowledge, a pertinent part of which concerns the controlled interpretation used to read the empirical material. The reading builds (by necessity) on epistemological and theoretical ideas included in earlier studies, and these are therefore an important component to understand the understanding (i.e. the meta-understanding) of the construction of meeting-places, which is at the core of the model described in this chapter. However, the meta-understanding of geography is dynamic and changes as new ideas are incorporated – and older ones diminish in importance – in geographical research. Accordingly, in these chapters I also discuss alternative tools for interpretation that might add to the understanding of the object of research, and to the meta-understanding. Moreover, in Chapter 2, in addition to a discussion of general epistemological prerequisites, I also introduce to geography the theoretical thinking of Yuri Lotman and the "cultural semiotics" of the Moscow-Tartu school. To my knowledge, and somewhat surprisingly, this has not been discussed in geography before.

Fieldwork, which is the focus of Chapter 3, has long been a more or less taken-for-granted matter in geography, and what we actually do in the field has only recently become a subject for theoretical discussion. In opening up the black box of geographical fieldwork I use my own experiences (based on about 16 months of participant observation) of the Sankt-Peterburg field to add to the discussion concerning methodology and the construction of knowledge. In short, I argue for field research to be theoretically informed, in the process of which, among other things, the role of the fieldworker as person is highlighted. It is the field researcher as person that is engaged in learning the practices and semiotic systems of a place and, it is argued, he or she should make use of and reflect upon the "perceived position" he or she possesses in the field. Rather than the fieldworker's gender, colour or class position in his or her home society, information from respondents is first and foremost given to him or her in relation to the categorical and situated knowledge of the subjects. In my case the respondents initially placed me in the category "foreigner", and the chapter discusses this in terms of "perceived positions".

In Chapter 4, the aim of which is to acquaint the reader with Ligovo as the site of research, the thinking presented in Chapters 1–3 is applied only in a cursory manner, as the chapter concentrates on describing some of the features of this high-rise suburb. The chapter accounts for the appearance of Ligovo today and the focus is on the material aspects of the district, although its history and some of the everyday practices of people are also described and analysed. Although the chapter is mainly descriptive, in some "obvious" cases concerning for example the greenery in the yards and the façades of the houses, I could not resist discussing how such space has been created as a result of local and extra-local factors and as clear-cut examples of Ligovo as a meeting-place. With regards to the greenery, and thus to how a substantial part of urban space is formed, the research results presented in the chapter are empirically new, and should have general value to the broader body of knowledge on Soviet cities. To some extent this is also the case for the findings regarding the vacant plots (*pustyria*) found in the district, and for some of the other spatial details that are described.

In Chapters 5–7 the approach is more heuristic and inquiring than descriptive. With Ligovo as the base for this work, I have excerpted or "picked out" certain aspects of time-space and to these I apply the model and the theoretical ideas described in the first three chapters. These analyses, which are empirically grounded on studies of texts, maps, interviews, informal talks and observations, shows the action-spaces and the course-relations related to the transformations Sankt-Peterburg and Russia from Soviet to post-Soviet times. In short, these are concerned with identity and the spatial codes with which Sankt-Peterburg is understood (Chapter 5), maps and the Soviet politics on spatial representations (Chapter 6), and local self-government and the newly established municipalities (Chapter 7).

In the first of these chapters (Chapter 5) I explicate, among other things, three codes that govern the perception of the identity of Sankt-Peterburg, and thereby also what it means to be a post-Soviet Sankt-Peterburgian. In this chapter I also show how Ligovo is textually juxtaposed in time and space to create a sense of continuity. The juxtapositions also create a perceptual unity of time and space that makes it easier for the inhabitants to connect to the histories of Sankt-Peterburg, and hence also to the new historicist master narrative of the total action-space of what the city is becoming as it transforms from its Soviet past. The chapter is, aside from literature and field experiences, empirically based on a text that deals with the history of Ligovo. The text on Ligovo is, I argue, a performative map that formulates the genius loci of the district and, accordingly, also intervenes in place-making processes. As with the case of any map, it is used for orientation in the landscape of the-not-so-taken-for-granted, a very necessary aid after the fall of communism and the entry of a new era.

In the next chapter (Chapter 6), the focus is on cartographic maps. These, no doubt, also represent an attempt to intervene in the world of lived experiences and affect how the surroundings are (or should be) perceived. The chapter includes a map study of Ligovo, and a review of Soviet cartography and map policy, as well as references to my own experiences of the field. Among other things, the chapter discusses and identifies some of the falsification practices that were used by the Soviet authorities, and which I show have at least to some extent also been used in post-Soviet maps. The main results, however, are presented in the discussion where I develop the theoretical proposition of a "stiff landscape", which together with a proposition on the special characteristics of Soviet mental maps, may explain the extensive knowledge of the city exhibited by its inhabitants. To develop these propositions I also explain the Soviet fear of accurate spatial information and connect this to the socio-spatial sphere of practice and lived experience, as well as to the peculiarities of the Soviet urban economic landscape. In the final analysis it is concluded that the Soviet politics of the sign did not work as the system had intended.

In Chapter 7, I turn to post-Soviet politics regarding control over space and analyse the newly implemented "third" level of political power in Russia. This political level is spatially based in municipalities, which should be locally self-governing. The idea of self-governing municipalities represents a major change, and eventually a break, in the Russian tradition of political governance. More concretely however, the impact of the self-governing municipality in Ligovo has been rather limited and the chapter concludes that it has not fulfilled its potential as an important actor in forming the action-spaces of Ligovo. It is also concluded that the municipal reform has in some respects impacted in favour of the lifeworld, as local decision-making regarding certain issues is now closer to the population than before. The chapter account for the concept of local self-government, the Soviet and post-Soviet history of local government, how the Ligovo municipality works, and what it has actually accomplished, as well as the local political communication and media situation. The chapter is based on observations, talks, interviews, and texts published by the Municipality, and the chapter adds empirical results that support earlier research findings on local self-government. In both Chapter 5 and 6, the research not only supports earlier findings but also adds new general(ised) knowledge, that I take to be of value for the cultural geography of Russia.

In the last chapter (Chapter 8), the results of the empirical studies in chapters 5–7 are summarised and evaluated in relation to the general thesis and purposes of this work, i.e. the model that has informed the research is evaluated. This evaluation, or assessment, of the model is made with regards to the model's validity, and to its capacity to help generate new theory. The evaluation, moreover, is done both with regards to the model's theoretical foundations, and to the empirical results of the studies, in what I term the "double hermeneutic circle". At the end of the chapter, attempts are made to develop, or rather to abstract the model further. In this discussion time-spatial change is generalised into five types and this abstraction covers in a highly generelised way all change that any area of any size may go through.

2 The cultural geography of Russia

> How places are made is at the core of human geography. Overwhelmingly the discipline has emphasized the economic and material forces at work. Neglected is the explicit recognition of the crucial role of language, even though without speech humans cannot even begin to formulate ideas, discuss them, and translate them into action that culminates in a built place. (Tuan 1991:684)

In 1979 R.A. French and Ian Hamilton wrote that the socialist city was the most neglected research field in urban studies in the west. Since then the literature on the subject has grown considerably although several empirical gaps still exist. Tiit Tammaru (2001) notes that not much has been written on the suburbanisation of Soviet cities that started in the 1950s. An even less studied urban phenomenon is how people who live in the outer districts relate in everyday life to their city, their place and lived environment. During Soviet times, western field-based studies with an inside perspective hardly existed at all, and Soviet research neglected to examine many important areas of social life. When it comes to socially oriented research, the years of transformation have in many respects been an empirical and theoretical *terra incognita* (Piirainen 1997). This is especially so concerning high-rise districts on the outskirts of cities. The bulk of the literature on Sankt-Peterburg is about buildings in the centre, and not on the lived environments in the outskirts.

One may have expected such gaps to have been filled following the dissolution of the Soviet Union and the opening up of the country to field research by foreign researchers. Furthermore, one may have expected that Russia and the other former communist countries would have become inundated with geographers eager to study the transformation in general, or the impact of communism on the landscape, or to test theses and questions with their own primary material from a range of perspectives. This is not least the case since it was known that the epistemological bases for research differed in the Soviet Union and researchers therefore could be pretty sure that from certain perspectives this vast country would be largely unstudied. These studies could have been done out of normal scientific curiosity, or for more serious reasons; Russia is after all still the largest country on earth and its importance to not only its neighbours but also at the global scale would, one would think, demand detailed geographical knowledge on this part of the world. This, however, did not happen and the research that has been conducted is impressive neither in terms of quantity nor in variation of perspectives.

In this chapter I discuss cultural geography and my reason for doing so is that geographical understandings of the questions under study can be considered neither scientifically nor socially independent of the scientific historical context in which they are conducted. The approaches discussed in this chapter are thus important to understand the geographical understanding of how meeting-places are constructed. Apart from the general development and epistemological bases for cultural geography, I examine western studies of the cultural geography of Russia,[8] as well as introduce to geography the cultural semiotics of Jurii Lotman and the Moscow-Tartu school. The chapter also includes a discussion on practices and on the subject as a social actor in geographical studies, which lately have complemented the cultural turn.

2.1 The cultural turn

Sometime in the 1970s, the dominance of the spatial science school was broken and the "quantitative revolution" in geography ended. Two major schools of thought, radical or Marxist geography and humanistic geography established themselves firmly in the discipline and statistical and mathematical approaches were to be complemented by a plethora of qualitative methods. These were not new to the subject in the sense that similar ap-

---

[8] For those interested in the history of the discipline in pre-Revolutionary Russia and the Soviet Union, see Anuchin 1977, Gerasimov 1981, Hooson 1984, De Souza 1989, Mazurkiewicz 1992.

proaches had not existed earlier. The first are to be found in late-19th century French geography and in early-20th century British geography (Rugumayo 1997:39–40, Philo 2000:31–32). What was new however, was the volume of work within qualitatively oriented discourses.

The directions of research also changed. The overarching theme in geography from the 1980s to the beginning of the 1990s was the relationship between society and space (Gren 1994:19). Not only did social aspects gain more space in geography, but also spatial concerns grew in social theory. The spatial dimension must up till this point be regarded as having been neglected in social analyses (Gregory & Urry 1985, Harvey 1985a & b).[9] In an often-quoted passage, David Harvey states that

> Marx, Marshall, Weber, and Durkheim all have this in common: they prioritise time and history over space and geography and, where they treat the latter at all, tend to view them *unproblematically* as the *stable* context or site for historical action. (Harvey 1985b:141, *my emphasis*)

Uniting spatial and social theory may be seen as a part of a larger change within social science at large. The transgressions of disciplinary boundaries have increased and disciplines "borrow" models, methods and theories from each other (Marcus & Fischer 1986), a trend that is similarly relevant for Swedish geography (Lenntorp 1995).[10] One pertinent example is the "New Cultural Geography" that developed as a specific geographic contribution to the broad and interdisciplinary field known as "Cultural Studies", which in its turn may be said to have taken a geographical turn as it directed interest to places and other spatial phenomena. Of general interest in these studies is the role of language as a constituent element in the social construction of society, and the subsequent interest in reading the physical and social sides of the surface of the earth as a text. This interest in language is not specific to geography, indeed similar developments have

---

9   Also in the subject of history, space as a category in its own right has not been subject to research (Harrison 1998/2003).
10 Lenntorp also shows that the discipline was internationalised during the period, i.e. more of the works concerned other countries, and a larger share of the PhD students working in Sweden originally came from other countries. However, as I have shown elsewhere (Borén 2002) rather few Swedish geographers studied the Soviet Union/Russia or other parts of Eastern Europe during the period 1980–2001.

been noticed in many of the social and human sciences (Barnes & Duncan 1992:2).

Within geography, this development has implied preponderance towards qualitative methods and a focus on the construction of meaning. The epithet for the new geography is "the cultural turn", and the core of this turn is seen by its hard-line proponents as something very different from the "old" cultural geography with its roots in the 1920s and the tradition founded by Carl Sauer and the Berkeley school. As the "new" cultural geography, with leading names such as James Duncan, Peter Jackson and Daniel Cosgrove, settled with its Sauerian history in the 1980s by framing it as oriented towards material culture (Price & Lewis 1993), the "material" was pushed into the background and "the immaterial", i.e. webs of meaning and systems of signification, came to completely dominate the intra-disciplinary discussions. Mark Bassin sums up this development:

> For if "classical" cultural geography taught us to examine a material landscape shaped by the social, economic and cultural forces of the inhabiting groups, and if "humanistic" cultural geography went on to explore how such material landscapes were perceived and interpreted at a subjective cognitive level, then the "new" cultural geography has opened our eyes critically to landscape as an act of representation. (Bassin 2000:249)

By and large what "culture" is taken to mean in the new cultural geography is (the construction, and reconstruction of) "meaning". More or less explicitly, these directions are based on a conception of the sign, and proceeding from this, the directions also concern the semantics and semiotics of social life. Fundamental to the approach is the notion that anything can be "read as texts". For geographers, this "anything" has, for the most part, concerned the inherently spatial, e.g. various cultural aspects of places, cities or landscapes, but in principle anything (history, events, people, practices, etc.) can be taken to represent a text. The "reading" of the texts is the interpretation(s) that can be made (by the researcher).

However, as (these) interpretations are based on the researcher's own preconceptions and apperceptions, the researcher would first have to learn and then make conscious the preconceptions and apperceptions of the people under study, at least if the researcher wishes to portray the issue under study from "within", in order to make "thick" descriptions (Geertz 1973). To do this, the researcher would have to learn the organising principles in the local lifeworlds.

2.2 Lifeworlds and semiotics

In the lifeworld the lived experiences of each individual are in focus. These are, however, not private in the sense that they belong to only one person. Rather, lifeworlds are social and used to manage the sharing of space and living together with other people, and the experiences of sharing space and living together is organised in accordance with a certain complex of ideas. To put it simply, the meaning of lived experiences are organised into webs of significances, or sign systems, which people use to understand and communicate things about the world, often with the goal of reaching a level of mutual understanding of different situations to solve real life problems. The sign systems are thus closely connected to language as the medium underlying speech and practices that make up the course-relations stemming from the lifeworld.

Accordingly, to understand lifeworlds the researcher has to understand how the sign system is organised, and how it is applied in practice in specific situations in the actual action-space. The approach is based on the idea that there is a difference between something as a symbol and that something itself. Following the Swiss linguist Ferdinand de Saussure, the internal relationship of the sign can be drawn thus:

s (the signified)
S (the Signifier)

Empirically it is only "S" that can be perceived (through sight, sound or other senses) whereas "s" is the interpretation that we ourselves make of the perceived. Following from this, what we see with our eyes (or perceive with other senses) is intelligible only when it is interpreted. The interpretation is not arbitrary, but follows a certain cultural pattern – a certain complex of ideas on how the world is arranged. These learned complexes of ideas can perhaps best be described as follows: to every single symbol is linked a number of connotations that together constitute a network of meanings in which every single symbol can be understood only in relation to other symbols. That is, in relation to what it is not. The symbols' relations to each other form a semantic whole – webs of meaning, structures of signification, typifying constructions – which constitutes our conception of the world, and which has a bearing on how we act in the world. Finding out what this conception looks like for the Other is an important geographical quest which, if anything, can teach us something about the lifeworlds of people and why they do what they do in various places in the world. Accordingly, this is also one of the keys to understanding the spatial variations ("areal differentiation") on the surface of the earth.

That differences exist in the webs of meaning between people, groups and, if you like, cultures, is rather obvious, but if we turn to the sign itself, can there really be differences in the (social) meaning of the sign? Yes, it *is* possible to argue that the sign has a special position in Russia vis-à-vis the western world. With its basis in the orthodox belief and tradition, a special relation has, according to Per-Arne Bodin, developed between the original image and the copy. Writing of the icon as a Signifier he argues that "a special view on the sign [is created] which becomes absolutely central for the understanding of the *entire Russian culture in all its parts*: the sign is not conventional but owes something of the power of the signifier" (1995:21, *my translation and emphasis*). To put it somewhat differently, the relation between the Signifier and the signified is "closer", the Signifier carries, or comprises more of its "signified" in the Russian cultural context than in the Western – the difference, or the distance between the copy and the original has diminished (see also Bodin 1987). The Russian relation to the sign, which is founded in the semiotics of icons, is "one of the most important ideational invariants in the Russian cultural history" (Bodin 1993:82, *my translation*).[11]

---

11   See also Lotman & Uspenskii (1977/1985). There might be other ways to explain the special relationship which I will not treat at length here. For instance Joseph Brodsky makes no references to icons or religion when asked about these matters, although he clearly recognises the special position of the word in Russian, compared to English. Joseph Brodsky has, in an interview with Bengt Jangfeldt, expressed this in terms of "acoustic mass". "For a Russian ear or a Russian eye,

Further support for Bodin's claims can be found in Gunnar Olsson's discussion on the sign in *Western* culture. According to Olsson, there is no doubt that the Western sign is clearly divided by the Saussurian bar. He argues that in the Saussurian sign we see the dual western cultural and historical heritage, i.e. the difference between the Jewish and the Greek, between the visible and invisible, between matter and meaning (1998a&b, cf. Olsson 1992). Put in less minimalist terms, he means that the whole cultural history of the Western world is expressed in the division of the sign in two parts.

If this is so, i.e. that the sign is related to (social) history and not (only) to an idealistic-objectivistic scientific way of conceptualising the human capacity to think, communicate and understand, then it is not difficult to imagine that the relation between the parts within the sign differs in Russia since neither Antiquity nor the Renaissance had any greater impact in Russian cultural history, not to mention the special characteristics of the Russian Enlightenment story.

Further support for the thesis of the specificity of the sign in the Russian context is to be found in the work of Boris Gosporov (1985). He discusses the role of literature in Russian society and its modelling effects on everyday life, as well as the special academic discipline that the study of these texts gave rise to. He calls this the discipline of *the semiotic aspects of social behaviour*, and argues that because disciplines that in the west studied social behaviour (e.g. social anthropology) were not allowed in the Soviet Union, the study of literary texts became a way to circumvent these political restrictions. The discipline of semiotics should not, however, be seen as directly analogous with its western counterparts, but rather as providing, among other things, the "missing link" that makes possible the study

---

the word has", he argues "a much larger specific weight, simply a larger acoustic mass, than the same word in for example English." He relates this to Russian being a more polysyllabic language than English is. He also states that the word is "physically more real for a Russian than for anybody else" since the word in Russian history always has been persecuted. (All quotes are from Jangfeldt 1987:447, *my translations*). Moreover, I do not problemize the relationship between the word and the image. Both may be seen as signs in a semiotic way, even though there are differences between them, e.g. when simultaneity is concerned (see Hägerstrand 1985a).

of "culture as lived by individuals within the traditional typological and historical study of complex literate civilizations" (Gosporov 1985:29).

The main argument is that literature becomes a guide, or model for life as one lives it. Concisely put, cultural semiotics

> examines social life as the realization of cultural codes developed by society. Cultural codes are systems of more or less conventional signs that a member of a given society must internalize in order to participate competently in that society's life. The possessor of such a cultural code is able to distinguish within the flow of raw experience those elements significant from the point of view of his culture, identify their value, and react to them. Like any native language, the codes of social behavior are not consciously created or learned, they are acquired during the ordinary practice of social relations. Any system with a heightened and de-liberate internal organisation will tend to play an important role in this process of internalization. (Gosporov 1985:16–17)

So, if the thesis of the special relation of the sign holds, which I believe it does, and this makes people more inclined to act according to the models expressed by different sign systems or languages, this has implications for how society at large functions. Just one example is that signs relating to politics become sensitive and the use of them thus has to be restricted (censorship). A further example is that the actors in the total and real action-spaces may be expected to be more inclined to use the sign systems so that people's understanding of reality are in congruence with their goals and worldview (propaganda). This is done with a range of tools of political technology of which schooling and the control of mass media, including maps, stand out as the most pertinent. In short, the control over texts becomes crucial to control space.

One and the same text may, however, be read differently at different times and by various actors – the meaning of a text can be contested (Duncan 1990). This insinuates contestations over what codes should be used when deciphering a text in order to reveal its meaning. Studies of such contestations over the preferential right to the interpretation of a text might reveal the power-forces at work at a certain place, as well as to help illuminate the social structures and stratifications of social life. So, what then of the role of language in western cultural geography-studies of place?

2.3   The cultural turn – revisited

The study of linguistic place construction can take different forms and Yi-Fu Tuan (1991:85–86) divides the approaches of this cultural geographic discourse into three categories. The first is also the most linguistic and focuses on the metaphorical power of words, i.e. how they invoke emotions and give the place a certain character. The place, hereby, also receives "visibility". The second line of reasoning emphasises socio-linguistics and can be subdivided into four general ideas:

- Language as a practical activity (i.e. as a force and medium for co-ordinating the physical construction of places)
- Language at the level of epistemology (what and how a geographer knows what she or he knows)
- Hermeneutic interpretations of landscapes (the landscape as text)
- Language in relation to power over places (techniques of surveillance and control)

The third approach, which Tuan himself adopts and names, is the "narrative-descriptive". Tuan means that this approach absorbs and draws upon the insights of the first two, without however, going into analytical detail or theoretical overview. He has a very critical attitude to theory and argues that theory

> tends to drive rival and complementary interpretations and explanatory sketches out of mind, with the result that the object of study – a human experience, which is almost always ambiguous and complex – turns into something schematic and etiolated. Indeed, in social science, a theory can be so highly structured that it seems to exist in its own right, to be almost "solid," and thus able to cast (paradoxically) a shadow over the phenomena it is intended to illuminate. By contrast, in the narrative-descriptive approach, theories hover supportively in the background while the

complex phenomena themselves occupy the front stage. (Tuan 1991:686)

As I argue in the following chapter, theories are used as interpretative tools and should therefore not only "hover in the background" but be made explicit, and inform the descriptions.

The general aspects of the approaches outlined by Tuan were not only confined to the subdiscipline of cultural geography but were later, in the 1990s, to gain recognition and acceptance within the subject at large. New textbooks on the general history of geography included chapters dealing with cultural-geographic issues, its theory, development and place in the subject (e.g. Johnston 1997, Holt-Jensen 1999, Peet 1998), and several readers for students have been published that deal with qualitative methods.

The cultural turn should not, however, be regarded as a unitary or discrete school of thought, but rather as a diverse set of approaches that have one or several traits in common. A difficulty in ordering these, if one would wish to do so, is that the different labels are not definite. Michael Dear (2000) labels more or less all studies that use qualitative methods as postmodern, although I doubt that all of their respective authors would have chosen to place their work under this umbrella-term. Other alternative designations that could be used are: post-structural, linguistic, reflexive, hermeneutic, feminist and interpretative. This confusion of labels is itself a part of the cultural turn. Most of its proponents would, I believe, wish to interpret the diversity in the subject as a reflection of the multifaceted character of society and of differences in epistemological approaches and ontologies. In the cultural turn all are sceptical of having one "grand theory" that endeavours to account for all aspects of social and cultural life in the great diversity that exists in space, e.g.; different ethnic groups, social groups, genders, professional categories, ages, abilities, sizes, etc. Differences in research approaches to the differences in space would instead be regarded as an asset, and no one would be interested in conforming research as that would be a first step towards totalising the subject.

Another trait which the different directions of the cultural turn have in common with each other is a relativistic view of knowledge. Knowledge is regarded as relative to the social and historical context in which it is produced and thus the focus on the construction of meaning (in different place and time specific contexts) is more than just a research interest, it is also an ontological prerequisite. In focusing on meaning, the studies often centre on some aspect of language. However, since the late 1990s, not only are language and representational issues of interest but so too are practices of everyday life. In geography this is sometimes referred to as "non-representational" theory.

So, the theoretical development of the subject continued and already by the latter half of the 1990s the freshness of the "representation" approach had diminished. In 1996 Pamela Shurmer-Smith argued that the time of "excitement at ideas has passed and the layering up of examples begins" (quoted in Matless 1997:393). The layering up of examples seems to have been carried out to the extent that the cultural turn at the end of the millennium had become not only "*too* successful", but also "*too* hegemonic" (Philo 2000:28, *original emphasis*). The danger is that too much geography is written as if the material world no longer existed, as if the physicality or corporeality of things and human bodies were no longer of importance or consequence, and as if real experiences and everyday life disappears in-between various representations and other more or less blurred reflections in a world conceived of as a hall of mirrors full of texts, texts and texts.

A reaction was bound to come, and the two major currents that interest me will be treated in short accounts that will also mark the end of this story. The first concerns the materiality of geography, and the second the social actor. The former is discussed in terms of "rematerialising" cultural geography. It is argued that this approach should not concern itself with "the object fetishism" that characterised the "old" cultural geography, but should instead be sensitive to "when and where the materiality of material culture makes a difference" (Jackson 2000:13). The examples raised by Jackson are drawn from his own research and principally examine how commodities, magazines and consumer places are used and treated discursively. He focuses on material culture and the relation between people and things. Chris Philo (2000) makes a broader claim as he discusses the need to take not only the material world but also the social life of people more seriously (see also Gregson 2003). The "material" here should be understood not in terms of material culture but as a geography where matter matters. These calls must be understood in the light of cultural geography as a subdiscipline in the larger family of geographical traditions, and as Loretta Lees (2002) argues in response to Philo, this is what urban geographers have been doing all along. In subdisciplines other than cultural geography, the cultural turn has not replaced other perspectives – it has added to them.

The second current, that of the social actor, has included calls to include the individual and his or her world of lived experiences, as well as things, thus stressing action, practices and performance, in what Nigel Thrift has called "non-representational" theory (1996).[12] As something of a comparison, a somewhat analogous development seems to have evolved within social anthropology after the first years of symbolic, or interpretative anthropology in the 1970s (Umiker-Sebeok 1977, Ortner 1984). In social theory more generally, the writings of Pierre Bourdieu (1977, 1990) stand out as important in this respect. He represents an approach which thinks of people as people and not primarily as part of a structure, culture or system. He thought, among other things, in terms of practical kinship and practical economy as these take form for the individual given certain restrictions with regard to spatial, temporal and power aspects of social life. His writing has, according to Joe Painter (2000), not engaged geographers in any depth although it is frequently referred to. In the following I will critically discuss his concept of practice against the background of a critique of the post-structuralists/post-modernists and the idea of the subject as competent and "wide-awake". This discussion is organised in to two shorter sections, or excursuses. The first lays out my general view on the place of the subject in geographical research and the second proceeds from this towards a concept of practice that focuses on the "social going about" – going about living.

---

12 Thrift includes time-geography in this. To suggest to call it time-demography, as he does, is however a mistake. Not only people but also things (nature, material artefacts) are at the centre of the corporeal worldview and time-geographical analyses (see Ellegård & Lenntorp 1980:77–78, and also Hägerstrand 1993, Lenntorp 1993, Anderberg 1996, Borén 1999). Moreover, time-geographical coupling restrictions and space-time budgeting certainly emphasise the role of things other than humans.

2.4 On post-modernism and the subject as "wide-awake"

Concerning divisions within cultural geography, James Duncan and David Ley (1993) distinguish between the radical and the less radical and term the former the post-modernists and the latter the hermeneutics. In its most radical forms the cultural turn hung on to the general critique of reason as formulated by the post-structuralists. These thinkers took the arguments of text analyses to the extreme and used them to question western reason as such, and rejected any kind of foundations for what should be regarded as true knowledge. However, according to Richard Peet (1998), they were not able to produce an alternative philosophy, although their critique contains important insights – e.g. concerning the spatial variations of desire (and its control). Peet holds that the theory generated by the post-modernists endeavours to hide the flaws of its arguments in "terminological vagueness and outrageous theoretical excess" (1998:246).

With regards to representation, Duncan and Ley (1993) have argued that post-modernism *cannot* leave the foundations of representation if they still want their work to have "descriptive force". Presentations along the lines of a "cogito interruptus", to borrow a term and argument from Umberto Eco (1967/1987, cf. 1977/1987), is to cheat the readers as it forces the reader to implicitly enforce reason and rationality into the text, if for no other reason than that the receiving part in the act of communication, according to Habermas and Schütz, wants to make sense of the message as a unified entity. The author of a text could therefore be said to need to structure the text to make the receiver a "model" reader who respects the text and does not overinterpret it (Eco 1992a&b) (this of course may include leaving the text open to various interpretations). Duncan and Ley further argue that neither can post-modern writing ever leave behind the privileged role of the author in textual experiments of destabilising representational conventions. Introducing polyphony or polyvocality – letting the voices of the Other be heard – to engage in a dialogue in the text *with* the other, is still done with the author as supreme director. Only that now that fact is more hidden.

The post-structural critique also had implications that concerned the idea of people as rational subjects. People become "de-centred" and their intentions and (inter)subjectivity lost meaning in how society is constituted.

Habermas points out "that in the various approaches to the critique of reason, no systematic place is envisaged for everyday practice" (1987b:339), although Nigel Thrift modifies this statement by dividing the post-structuralists in two schools regarding the position of the subject (1996:27–30). Nevertheless, neither of the schools would treat the human subject as an actor that acts in the world from a competent position, a position that Alfred Schutz describes as "wide-awake" (Schutz 1945/1962).

> By the term "wide-awakeness" we want to denote a plane of consciousness of highest tension originating in an attitude of full attention to life and its requirements. Only the performing and especially the working self is fully interested in life and, hence, wide-awake. It lives within its acts and its attention is exclusively directed to carrying its project into effect, to executing its plan. This attention is an active, not a passive one. (Schutz 1945/1962:213)

To be sure, the de-centring of the subject is the opposite to thinking of people as living their lives competently. What is evident in the quote is a focus on people as active, and hence it is important to clarify what people actually do, how they carry out projects. If we are to understand how people engage in, and affect their surroundings this kind of thinking must be complemented with a more explicit concept of practice. In the following I discuss the practice concept of Pierre Bourdieu, and show that it is *not* congruent with the view of the acting subject as wide-awake. If we are to understand what people do from the point of view of their intentions and interests at hand, the projects they actually realize, and how they actively set about living the world, it is better to proceed from a concept of practice that presuppose that humans are conscious and strategic beings. Such a concept would also have to be contextual with regards to different situations.

2.5 On the concept of practice

In the following discussion I challenge two concepts of practice by playing them off against each other. The objective is to show, and to begin to formulate, a concept of practice that is "modest", and to my mind better suited for studies of human action in complex societies than the two discussed here. The first is Pierre Bourdieu's concept of practice, and a critical excursion on this will explicate the second, Michel de Certeau's. First Bourdieu:

> In fact, a given agent's practical relation to the future, which governs his present practice, is defined in the relationship between, on the one hand, his *habitus* with its temporal structures and dispositions towards the future, constituted in the course of a particular relationship to a particular universe of probabilities, and on the other hand a certain state of the chances objectively offered to him by the social world. (Bourdieu 1990:64, *original emphasis*)

According to Bourdieu the habitus contains (historically based) dispositions that govern practices, not mechanically but within its inherent constraints (1990:55) and in relation to conditions that make these dispositions compatible (ibid:54). In sum, the habitus can be described as the inner (internalised, especially from childhood, and embodied dispositions) and the outer (the sharing in a social group of the same dispositions) (ibid:59) *milieu*. These dispositions and milieu are reproduced by practices that are compatible with its inner and outer components, which, as I have already mentioned, govern practices.

Much closer in defining practices than this Bourdieu does not come, in fact he never tries to do so and instead speaks of the "logic of practice", a nice contradiction in terms since practices, according to Bourdieu, cannot be grasped either through discourse (the spoken or written word) or by the models of the sciences and the arts. This is so mainly due to the time aspect, practices are "entirely immersed in the current of time" (1990:81) and, using the example of a ball player, are played out "in conditions which exclude distance, perspective, detachment and reflexion" (ibid:82). These conditions are antithetical to the conditions of science, which he uses to paint a contradictory picture for the sake of explanation. Further on, practices are situational in a way science is not. They are acted out according to the unformulated here and now and, according to Bourdieu, if we (researchers) ask informants about their practices "it gives some chance of discovering the truth of practice as a blindness to its own truth" (ibid:91) meaning that the respondent cannot, by other means than the most simple, account for the *raison d´être* of the practice as carried out in different situations.

This might be so in the pre-modern society of the Kabyles, which Bourdieu studied. In a complex modern society the social actor is, maybe not totally but to a much larger extent, aware of why, what, how, when and where he or she involves in practices (even if the reflections and awareness might be a subject of misrecognition and thus a kind of misconception of the nature of the practices). To explain this, using Bourdieu's own terms, this is so since there is no all-embracing and omnipotent *doxa* in complex societies. Doxa, according to Bourdieu (1977) is an experience or "belief" which originates when social and mental structures, objective and personal categories coincide. When Bourdieu writes of objective categories he means that which is shared by the group, i.e. doxa are conceptions of the world that can not be questioned as the people in that very world share these. Besides, they would not have an alternative to compare their conceptions with. Thus, the doxic belief represents the natural and social world as self-evident.

It is questionable if this is true for "pre-modern" societies, and it certainly is not true in complex societies. In complex societies there is knowledge of alternatives (i.e. there is no total correspondence between social and mental structures, or between objective and personal categories), which leads people to active decision making between choices and thus to reflection; on time, the situation and how to formulate or explain to oneself and others what one is doing. Bourdieu thinks that as soon as one starts to reflect on one's practice it is diverted from the action itself, and thus "meshes with the juridical, ethical or grammatical legalism to which the observer is inclined by his own situation" (1990:91) and therefore it looses its truth as practice. I, on the other hand, think that in complex societies one is constantly, but to various degrees, interacting with people with *different* dispositions, which, in my understanding, perspectivises one's own behaviour and lays the fundament for a more or less reflective stance towards time, the situation and the discourse. Of course people in complex societies might misunderstand each other on "juridical, ethical and grammatical" grounds, but this is not always the case. In fact it doesn't happen as often as Bourdieu would lead one to believe – just think of all the inter-*habitus*ial contacts, not only between respondent and researcher but also locally and globally, that govern various kinds of capital and exchange, and this is possible because people in everyday situations in practice can transcend the logic of practice.[13]

This leads me to argue that practices in complex societies might be understood as "de-practilised" (since an action in modern society is seldom just an action but is reflected and not distanced). But, it is nonetheless practices, however de-practilised they might be, that people do engage in since people relate to a practical sense of what is to be done in a particular situation. Importantly, the particular situation is to some extent foreseen or even purposefully created by the social actor, who thus has time to reflect on the when, where and how the practice is to be carried out. Since I find "de-practilised practice" a clumsy term, in this text I will use the more established word "practice", although my use of it allows for a greater degree of an agent's understanding of her or his own behaviour than is inherent in Bourdieu's conceptualisation. In Bourdieu's understanding of the concept of practice, it can not be said that the practices are carried out by subjects that are "wide-awake". His concept covers something else.

Michel de Certeau – "a *tactic* is a calculated action" (1984:36–37, *original emphasis*), it is an everyday behaviour carried out in relation to the strategies of power as conducted by different institutions. In this a tactic circumvents the strategies and creates "opportunities" out of them. This is especially pertinent when discussing economic practices (see Borén 2003a), but can apply for a range of other situations as well. In the Soviet Union, everyday life developed in the explicit context of subordination to state directives and discourse, and people had to be careful to not challenge the system, at least openly. The adaptive behaviours that developed thus come pretty close to what de Certeau calls "tactics". It should also be noted that these acts of tactical behaviour have open-ended properties, there are no "rules" for how they should be carried out in every imaginable situation. Concisely stated, people in complex societies must use tactics in time, and

---

13 A telling example of the result of "inter-habitusial" contacts is provided by Yuri Lotman (1984). He describes how the Russian nobility in the 18th century (the time when Petrine style modernity started to enter Russia), due to contact with and acquisition of west-European manners, "theatrilized" their everyday behaviour. This become the absolute opposite of "practices" – the everyday was a stage on which you could act, play a role and indulge in highly semiotized gestures.

in relation to the situation and the discourse in which a subject finds him or herself, and not, as he or she would be according to a strict interpretation of Bourdieu, restricted in his or her practices by the pre-modern habitus he describes for the Kabyles.

In concluding this argument, I find myself wanting a concept of practice that does not swing, as de Certeau's does, to the other extreme of awareness of what one is doing in everyday life. To me it seems that there is a need for a concept that covers the "middle range" of acting in the world, one that is neither totally unreflected nor strategic to the extent that it becomes congruent with de Certeau's concept of tactic. It should be a practice concept that includes "the social going about", but where there are "alarm bells" ringing when that "social going about" is stressed and strained by the limits of the doable, irrespective of whether these limits are set by power forces of the system, time-geographical restrictions in Hägerstrand's (1970, 1985b) sense, or changes in one's micro-social environment or lifeworld. When I use the term practice, it will be informed by this statement, however rudimentary the theoretical argument is in its current form.

2.6 Soviet and post-Soviet geography – a cultural turn?

In the western subdiscipline of Soviet geography, and later post-Soviet geography, the general development of cultural geography in the 1980s and 90s was largely ignored. Geographers studying the Soviet Union did not, with the exception of Mark Bassin (1983, 1988, 1991, 1992, 1999), take part in the general development of geographical theory during these formative years of "new" cultural geography.[14] Moreover, western geographers studying the Soviet Union were stuck with an old epistemological base for their research. Michael Bradshaw argued in 1990 that geographers studying Russia should be more theoretically oriented. The following quote is illustrative:

---

14 Anssi Paasi's studies of the Finnish-Russian border might be an exception, if one wants to count his work as cultural geography (see Paasi 2003).

> We do not know whether – and if so, how far – the geography of Soviet socialism can be understood by applying theories of Western capitalism or any of these other models. Unfortunately, geographers of the Soviet Union (in both the West and the Soviet Union) are as guilty as anybody for not trying to think theoretically about the nature of Soviet society. Faced with a lack of theory, the response has been to concentrate on the empirical description of geographical issues. We must work actively to take our research beyond the parade of statistical facts which we so frequently offer as the end-point of our studies, to adopt, adapt, critique and inform theoretical thinking outside our subdiscipline [i.e. the geography of the Soviet Union]. (Bradshaw 1990:318)

Judging from this quotation, research was rather uniform in approach and further support for this argument is found in Nicholas Lynn's notation that British and American geographers have not been active participants in the debates "beyond empirical regional studies" concerning the transition in Russia and the other countries in the former Soviet Union, and the "general result of all this is that very few commentators have taken geography into account when theorizing the process of postsocialist change" (1999:824). Lynn's own theoretical perspective stems from the "New Regional Geography" and he, together with the authors in *Theorising Transition* (1998) edited by John Pickles and Adrian Smith, are among the small number of academics who seem to have responded to Michael Bradshaw's (1990) call for foreign area-specialists to study the (post-)socialist countries from a theoretically informed perspective. It should also be mentioned that the bulk of critical, theoretically informed geographers seldom noticed, or compared the capitalist economical system with its socialist neighbour in the east. Andrew Sayer (1992) touches upon how fruitful such comparisons can be, and from this point criticises David Harvey and others for failing to correctly understand the role of shear complexity in capitalistic societies.

The above studies by Pickles, Smith and others all have a politico-economical perspective, which in a way could be seen as the critical counterpart to the research of the area that dominates the field, i.e. questions of political and economic reform by political scientists and economists. Craig Young and Duncan Light (2001:941–942) write that political scientists have studied the establishment of political parties, democracy-building, elections, constitutions and the building of civil society. The economists in their turn have focused on economic reform including aspects such as privatisation, price liberalisation and currency convertibility. However, in these analyses

> the focus has been disproportionately on the technical processes of post-socialist transformation, with an often unspoken assumption that building a capitalist multi-party democracy involves little more than just a set of technical transformations. (Young & Light 2001:942)

There are at least three general transformations taking place in the former communist countries. Two of them – political and economical transformation – relate to the above mentioned studies, whereas the third form of transformation, the social, and hence questions relating both to social and cultural spheres, are severely neglected by (geographic) research.

So, the "social" seems to have been largely forgotten by the Western researchers who set out to study these countries when this became possible following the fall of the Berlin wall. There can, however, be no doubt that as the political and economical system changed, the social and cultural sides of these societies were affected as well, and the spatial implications of this should be of great interest for geographers. But what have socially and culturally oriented studies in geography achieved?

In 2002 Tim Unwin and Bettina van Hoven called for contributions to a book to be entitled *Lives in transition*.[15] It was argued that although the transition had been analysed at length, the voices and experiences of the people in the region had "rarely, if ever been allowed to speak for themselves" concerning what it was like living in the region during this period. It was also stated that although women as a group in Eastern and Central Europe had been studied, men and children had not (see also van Hoven 2004). Additional support for these statements comes from Alan Dingsdale (1999), one of the few writers who has summarised the English language literature of geographical interest concerning change in post-Soviet Eastern Europe and Russia. The works Dingsdale refers to are few and it should be noted that he tries to cover the whole of Eastern Europe, Russia included.

---

15 Published in 2004 by Bettina van Hoven.

Accordingly, the geographical studies that cover Russia are even fewer. Dingsdale divides this work into four categories:
- Redefining personal and territorial identity, meaning and place perception.
- Transition and transformation, mainly political and economical.
- The New Europe.
- Global processes and the New World Order.

Regarding the first category, Dingsdale states that (cultural) geographers have not taken part in the debate to any significant extent (1999:147). This is also congruous with Andrew Dawson's (1999) account of the perspectives that have not been used in the study of post-socialist cities, most of which could be placed in the broad and loosely defined category of sociocultural geography. The situation is very much the same concerning Swedish geographical periodicals and chronicles. The articles on the cultural geography of Russia and Eastern Europe are few, as are the perspectives that are used (Borén 2002). The situation has somewhat improved with the publication of an anthology concerning the Balkans (Lundén & Book 2003), although the chapters hardly belong to core areas of cultural geography. Concerning larger works within a loosely defined cultural geography up to 2002, the only major studies are Tiina Peil's (1999) dissertation on Estonian islands and islanders, and Tommy Book's (2000) study of political landscapes regarding symbols such as names, monuments and heraldry in Russia/Soviet Union and Eastern Europe.[16]

Another sign that could be taken as symptomatic of the precarious situation for the (study of the) cultural geography of the post-socialistic countries is that the special issue of the journal *Ecumene* in 2000 (Vol. 7, No. 3), devoted to Russian and Soviet art, includes only one article written by a geographer, the other three being written by historians. Moreover, in a recent "handbook" of cultural geography, the cultural geographies of the former Soviet Union and Eastern Europe are more or less totally ignored (Ander-

---

16 With the exception of Gunnar Olsson's work, the perspective has not been prominent in Swedish human geography at all (Gren 1994:164, fn.142). However, at the end of the 1990s the cultural turn became a small but established and growing line of research also in Swedish universities (concerning Stockholm University, see

son et al. 2003), both empirically and hence also theoretically. The situation might, however, be improving. Recently, two cultural geographical studies of Moscow have been published that examine place symbolism (Sidarov 2000, Forest & Johnson 2002).

However, that persons other than geographers join forces with geography in understanding space is symptomatic of a general trend in the social sciences of lending theories, models and methods from each other. Subsequently, when researchers in other subjects turned their attention to space and place, studies of cultural geographic interest have emerged. Compared to the situation within the specific field of the cultural geography of Russia, the wealth of relevant literature that has developed has been considerable, see e.g. Czaplicka & Ruble 2003, Hellberg-Hirn 2003, Boym 1994. This trend started, however, rather late and in 1999 Jeremy Smith introduces the anthology *Beyond the limits: the concept of space in Russian history and culture*, by writing that the "study of space as a category in its own right is in its infancy" (1999:11).

2.7 Symbolic landscapes of the Moscow-Tartu School

But did Soviet geographers engage in cultural geographic studies of cities? With a few exceptions the general answer is no, they did not. Soviet (human) geography focused on economic issues and, as I have discussed above regarding culture and structures of signification, from the 1960s the discipline that was to approach more socially and cultural oriented questions was semiotics, and to some extent this was also applied to spatial issues.

Within this line of thought, the writings of Yuri Lotman and Boris Uspenskij, two semioticians and cultural historians, whose main studies date back to 1960s, 70s and 80s, stand out. They have applied this type of thinking, together or alone, to a range of historical phenomena, and among them are studies of the historical cityscape of Sankt-Peterburg (Lotman & Uspenskij

---

Jansson 2003), and at the beginning of the 3rd millennium, it figures heavily in an introductory reader to human geography (Gren & Hallin 2003).

1984a, Lotman 1990:191–202). To Robin Milner-Gulland these studies have been "instrumental in opening up a whole new area of, or approach to, Russian cultural history, an approach that at least gives due weight to what one might call the 'iconization' of Russia itself" (1994:96). As these scholars have had no impact within geography, it seems appropriate to begin with an introduction to their ideas on the semiotics of culture.

Lotman and Uspenskij belonged to the so-called Moscow-Tartu School, a group of Russian and Estonian semioticians who took as their starting point, and subsequently developed, the ideas first introduced by the Russian formalists in the 1920s. The formalists' original idea was that a piece of art was a semiotic device that could be analysed as a conscious modification of social rules or norms. According to Umberto Eco, the Russian formalists never managed to develop a full structural awareness but remained at the level of formal analyses as they never fully realised the idea that "putting into form" also meant "organisation of content" (1990:viii, see also Gosporov 1985). The formalists had been working on signifying systems but had not understood the role of semiotic systems, which Lotman and the circle around him made central in their own analyses. When the 1920s were coming to its end, and when Stalin rose to power, the formalists were forced off the scene and their ideas moved to Praha (Prague), and from there on to Paris. In the Soviet Union, the intellectual thread of the formalists was picked up by Lotman and the Moscow-Tartu school.

In his book *Universe of the mind* (1990), Lotman also pays tribute to Roman Jakobson, Mikhail Bakhtin, and Vladimir Propp. But first and foremost among his sources of inspiration was Ferdinand de Saussure. Beginning with the 1968 seminars at Tartu University, this group of scholars made "the move from structural analysis in isolation to the study of the interrelationship between a literary work and its real-life context" (Gosporov 1985:15) and Lotman can not be said to be a "pure" structuralist. At the end of the 1970s and especially in 1980s, Lotman under the influence of Bakhtin "softened the edges" of his semiotics and opened up for a more "dialogistic" perspective (Bethea 1997). But even before this, Lotman regarded culture as something dynamic and in constant change, and he viewed finding the codes of cultural grammar – a project so important to Claude Lévi-Strauss – not as an end in itself, but a prerequisite for understanding the dynamics of culture in a more social manner. Especially important in this regard was the creative role of choice in translating between different sign systems, or languages.

For Lotman and the Moscow-Tartu School, the most central feature of their interpretative frame is "the functional correlation of different sign systems" (Lotman et al. 1975:3), or what they term the *semiotics of culture*. Culture is here understood as constructed as a hierarchy of semiotic systems, and a multi-layered extra-cultural sphere that "surrounds" the semiotic systems. The extra-cultural sphere is what culture is not; it is the unknown, the disorganised, chaos – sometimes conceptualised as oppositional to the inherent norms residing in the known, i.e. in culture: Hellenians contra barbarians, us contra them, the church contra sects of sorcerers, etc. They argue that culture, from the view of its practitioners, is often regarded as the model to which non-culture has to conform. However, if culture is viewed from a scientific standpoint, which has at its disposal a metasystem of descriptive concepts, culture and non-culture are mutually conditioned and dependent of each other.[17]

Interesting as the relation to the extra-cultural may be, they nonetheless pertain to the view of culture that

> it is indisputable that it is precisely the inner structure, the composition and correlation of particular semiotic subsystems, which determines the type of culture in the first place. (Lotman et al. 1975:7)

With such a view of culture Lotman and Uspenskii propose that cultural history should be studied as "semiotic physiology". The base for this "physiology" is the total corpus of signs that exist in any society and they conceptualise this corpus as "the semiosphere".

> The semiosphere, if pictured in the momentary film-still of a synchronic cross-section, would include in itself all the totality of semiotic acts, from the signals of animals to the verses of poets and the call-signs of artificial satellites. But the semiosphere, because

---

17 Lotman et al. are of course aware of the fact that science constitutes particular subsystems and that they thus are enclosed in the semiotic system at large, see also below. Moreover, a culture is not, in their view, something fixed and rigid, but open and in a more or less fluid state.

it possesses memory which transforms the history of the system into its actually functioning mechanism, thus includes also the whole mass of texts ever created by mankind as well as programs for generating future texts. /.../ [W]e may regard the semiosphere as a *working mechanism* whose separate elements are in complex dynamic relationships. This mechanism on a vast scale functions to circulate information, preserve it and to produce new messages. (Lotman & Uspenskij 1984a:xii, *original emphasis*)

Obviously, the semiosphere is characterised by considerable diversity and hereby constant meetings or "clashes" will occur within it, and this makes the dynamics within it exuberant. It is the continuous contact and repeated meetings – translations, transcodings, dialogues, etc. – that make up this "exceptional" dynamics.

Let us briefly dwell on what Lotman and Uspenskij mean by the complex dynamic relationships that they mean exist in the semiosphere. The prerequisite is that they regard the semiosphere as consisting of different languages, e.g. the languages of different arts (literature, film, painting, etc.), the language of mythology, the language of etiquette and so on. Language in its turn is defined as a "mechanism which uses a certain set of elementary signs for the communication of content" (1984a:ix), and hereby have some kind of internal coherence to its users.

Language is here seen in its semiotic meaning. Language is the codes, or *langue* in Saussure's terminology, that underlie speech, or any other text (Saussure's *parole*). The relation between them is:

Everything that is relevant in speech (or text) is given in language (or code). Elements occurring in a text without any correspondence in the code cannot be bearers of meaning. (Lotman 1990:11)[18]

The quote is central, and could also be taken to mark a dividing line between linguist-semioticians and those who are more interested in society as a social phenomenon (cf. Umiker-Sebeok 1977:123, 126). Linguists fo-

---

18 This is a definition of text, that comes close to how Clifford Geertz's regards texts (Umiker-Sebeok 1977:122, Geertz 1973), and it is also in line with Claude Lévi-Strauss' argument (1979:5–14) that all meaning has to relate to rules of translation between different languages (i.e. codes).

cused on the language and its codes whereas social scientists concentrated on the meaning, or the message, that is transferred between different actors, with the language as a tool or arena. For the latter it is neither language nor the text themselves that are problemized, but rather the consequences and the position of the message in the social and spatial structure (and not in the linguistic structure). It is the message that is socially and geographically interesting.

But as I will argue in Chapter 5, the understanding of the codes in a specific message in one (1) text is a way to see the spatially general, in that it is valid for a larger area than the area or place covered by the text. Concisely stated, codes are not sensitive to scale in the same way as texts are. When a writer describes that which is spatially specific for a place, he or she uses codes and these codes are talkative about how the space is described – and hence also perceived – in other places. Furthermore, places may be grouped spatially to raise the level of scale. The places I think of in this case are other parts of Sankt-Peterburg than Ligovo, and the higher level of scale that these can be grouped into is the whole city of Sankt-Peterburg. From here it follows that it is possible, on the basis of a text concerning a certain area, to say something of the symbolic landscapes of Sankt-Peterburg. The codes at work in the text of Ligovo, are also at work in Sankt-Peterburg at large. Thus the codes are also socially and geographically interesting.

Lotman's own studies provide here an interesting middle ground between the linguistic-semiotic and the social-semiotic approach. Because Lotman was also an historian, he was not locked into a purely structural approach to culture, but complemented his method such that it was also attentive to the role of codes, or language(s) in the history of culture. As the discussion on the semiosphere shows, there is not one cultural code, but many, existing parallel in time as well as informing each other and changing over time.

As has been noted, the semiosphere is full of intertextual activity and things within it undergo constant change. This change arises from the fact that actors within the semiosphere do not have exactly the same codes, so when they translate – read, interpret – other texts, they also produce a new message. Not only are the codes somewhat different, they are also ordered differently and relate to different linguistic experiences. Ones linguistic memory is different from all others. The creative aspects of culture – the making of new information and new meaning – lie in these translations as the translator has to make choices about how to interpret the texts he or she meets, and choose which metaphors to use. The choices are especially highlighted and made explicit when translations are made between languages that use qualitatively different codes, for example between landscape and history, or between architecture and poetry, or between painting and music (Lotman 1990:123–130).[19]

However, the sender of a message often seeks to control the interpretation (translation, reading) of the text such that the message is received and understood in ways that agree with the intention of the author of the text. To achieve this he or she uses a simplified language. In order to understand the control mechanisms of interpretation, an interesting research task would thus be to identify the simplified, or artificial, language in a text.

A simplified language, or as Lotman put it, an artificial language, models the function of language to transmit messages (1990:13). Simplified language, I take it, corresponds to the core of the intended message and its function is inherent in the overall structure of the language and can be described as stable points of reference as to how we should interpret the rest of the text. I understand this to mean that we can see traces of the artificial language at work in all texts. The simplified language consists of codes that are "bigger", or more important, than other codes since they are shared by many and repeated more often than other codes. Lotman continues:

> When we use artificial languages (or natural and poetic languages as artificial languages, for instance if we transmit a novel by Tolstoy by a brief annotation of the plot), we are isolating meaning from language. Under the complex operations of meaning-generation language is inseparable from the content it expresses. In this last instance we are concerned not merely with a message in a lan-

---

19 I am not here prepared to discuss what Lotman means with languages being "untranslatable", but would like to mention that according to psycho-physics, the human brain is able to translate between different sensory modalities. We understand the message when people say "sweet as sugar" (sense of taste) about someone. The language of interpreting taste is translated into words and applied to things that are not taste. With metaphors we make languages translatable.

guage, but also a message about language, a message in which the interest is shifted on to its language. (Lotman 1990:15)

With this in mind, it is not difficult to argue that language, or codes, are the link between the general and the specific. If we reveal the codes of an artificial language in a specific text, we also have the possibility to say that these codes are at work in other texts as well. This argument is applied in Chapter 5, in which a specific text on Ligovo is analysed. This specific text itself tells us something about the history and geography of Ligovo, but the close reading of the text also reveals some of the codes in the artificial *spatial* language of the wider landscape of Sankt-Peterburg. This is done to reveal traits in the total action-space of Sankt-Peterburg.

2.8   Conclusions

On the basis of this chapter it may be concluded that western researchers have not studied the Soviet Union, or post-Soviet Russia, with cultural geographical questions, methods and techniques to any large extent. As a direct consequence of this it is also possible to conclude that, because places are always becoming, there are several blank spots on the Anglophone map of Russia. Moreover, the chapter has outlined the epistemological basis of cultural geography with a focus on what may be called textual or linguistic approaches, and this has been discussed in relation to the study of Russia. This has been complemented with a discussion of the Moscow-Tartu school of semiotics, and of "non-representational" approaches with a focus on the concept of practice. In this line of thinking the social actor is no longer "de-centred" but stands in focus for analyses of the material and cultural time-spatial context. Furthermore, the approaches outlined above are necessary to realize the intention of the model explicated in the first chapter. The model considers the lifeworld with regards to practices, experiences and signifying systems and how they interact with the pertinent ideas in the total action space and with the system. The understanding of geography (epistemologically speaking) that is to be found in these kinds of studies, when paired together, thus form the intellectual background to understand the construction of meeting-places. *How* such a study is carried out in the light of the purpose of this work, in the light of the discussion above on the landscapes of courses, the general model, and as part of a new (and materialised) cultural urban geography, is discussed in the next chapter.

3 Taming the hermeneutic animal – field method

> "Field-work": a familiar term to geographers. All too familiar, perhaps, for it's striking how rarely we have reflected on the place of field-work in our collective disciplinary imagination. /.../ Where field-work has become the subject of debate amongst historians of geography, it has too often been considered as an unproblematic expression of ruling ideologies or institutional projects. (Driver 2000:267)

As the opening quotation illustrates, fieldwork in geography is only starting to be problemized and its history is not written.[20] It can also be said that the descriptions of what we actually do in the field tend to be mundane and localised (Lorimer & Spedding 2002:227). Furthermore, the teaching of field methodology is not common, if it exists at all (DeLyser & Starrs 2001:vi, Zelinsky 2001:2). Fieldwork in geography seems to be taken for granted to such an extent that what being in the field actually means for the production of knowledge has been neglected. Heidi Nast writes:

> The "field" in fieldwork is treated as a *physical* assignation, a bias stemming from historically centering human and physical geography's contributions around field mapping-related endeavours that were often tied to government-sponsored surveys and resource assessments. /.../ In this sense, human geographers are seen to engage in fieldwork merely by entering a physically designated "field". (Nast 1994:56, *original emphasis*)

To problemize geographical fieldwork will have to begin with a focus on the "work" in fieldwork, to find out what the "field" in fieldwork is really about. To do this, I discuss and reject the critique that has been levelled at qualitative fieldwork in the form of participant observation, and channel the results of this discussion into an argument concerning the role of the fieldworker's person and body, and contextualise these in the current debate on "posi-

---

[20] But see Cloke et al. 2004, Chapter 1 for a short history on practising human geography.

tions", and in my own experiences in Russia. I thus use my experiences of method – about 16 months of more or less explorative fieldwork from 1998 to 2000 – to discuss methodological questions. I find this important for the understanding of field-based construction of knowledge, but it is also important in an empirical sense: the report on me in the field is part of the report on the field.

During my fieldwork time in Russia I spent about 14 months in Ligovo. I lived in a three-room apartment together with a three-generation family of four people: Elena Alekseevna, born in 1927 and mother to Tania, born in 1960, and her two children Elizaveta, born 1981 and Oleg, born 1985. These people were very important in forming my knowledge on Ligovo, but do not feature often in this text. As I will argue, it is primarily the special understanding, or cultural competence, one brings home from the field that is important and not the notes, tapes or other empirical "evidence" (although these are important too, but in a different sense).

A third reason for indulging in a longer discussion on fieldwork in the form of participant observation is that few other geographical studies have discussed these issues in detail.[21] Participant observation as a method has been described, problemized and reflected upon at length, mainly within social anthropology, which has developed the method as a structural element of its disciplinary identity, but it has also been used within ethnology, qualitative sociology and psychology. Geographers as well – although sparingly so – have also used participant observation. In the five-year period between 1994–1998, only 8 (5%) of the 161 articles in *Environment and Planning D: Society and Space*, a journal devoted to qualitative research in human geography, used material based on participant observation. In *Annals of the Association of American Geographers*, during the same time period, the percentage was even lower (Herbert 2000:550). Instead, the large majority of qualitative studies use interview-based methods (Crang 2002:650). However, as Jamie Baxter and John Eyles (1997) discuss, it is uncommon for researchers to report fully on their interview practices and this makes it difficult for the reader to evaluate the rigour of the

---

21   This is so even if two thirds of the 35 granted PhDs in geography at Berkeley from 1986–1991 used participant observation in doing their fieldwork in non-western countries (Price & Lewis 1993:9).

research. As Mike Crang also notes, being asked to write the first "progress report" on qualitative methods indicates that they have finally been accepted within geography as established methods, although they have mainly been associated with social, cultural and feminist geographies (2002:647–648). There is, however, a growing literature on fieldwork in geo-graphy, beside the ones existing in feministic geography and ethnographic studies. Fieldwork as a "black box" is being opened up.[22]

By way of introduction, participant observation is a scientific field method that strives for an understanding of that which takes place in a certain context, and it implies that the researcher has to try to assimilate that cultural context in full. It is about synchronising the personal and academic worldview of the researcher with the material and symbolic world in the place of study, with the ultimate purpose of describing this understanding to a mainly academic audience. To develop the understanding the researcher spends time in the place of study, which makes it possible for him or her to share the conditions of that time-space with the local population.

In relation to the model outlined in chapter one, the strength of the method is that it makes it possible to describe and explicate the close connections that exist between people, their lifeworlds and the places they construct. However, people and places are not bounded or secluded from an imagined outer world, but more or less tightly connected to the world around them, which also exists within them. The local and the extra-local are interwoven in ways not observed in older studies based on participant observations. In 1985 Peter Jackson wrote that participant observation as a method had not developed its full potential to locate the studies in their larger historical and social contexts. To do this, Jackson continues, an appropriate theory would also have been necessary (1985:171–172). However, as Michael Agar (1996) discusses, from the 1980s and onwards, studies based on participant observation became more sensitive to the world outside the strictly local, and issues relating to

---

22 See for example the special issues of *Geographical Review*, vol. 91 (2001), no. 1 & 2 and *Area*, vol. 34 (2002), no. 3, which both are devoted to fieldwork. For an early example, see also *The Professional Geographer*, vol. 46 (1994), no. 1, in which a large section covers fieldwork and feminism. Two recent textbooks on qualitative methods (Limb & Dwyer 2002, Cloke et al. 2004) should also be mentioned here.

the state, the market, the "global" and other more or less place independent factors were up-graded in ethnographic theory. According to Steve Herbert, the method enables the study of the

> moments when [processes of] macro and micro interpenetrate, when constraints and contingencies alternately pattern and perturb daily life. Such research is of undoubted significance to geographers interested in how landscapes are constructed and lived /.../ [and t]he abstract categories of survey data and quantitative analysis simply cannot capture the complex, contextual nature of daily life. (Herbert 2000:555–6)

The method thus makes it possible to study the course-relations from different scale-levels as these relations are expressed in their embodiment in people and emplacement in space. Accordingly, participant observation is one way to empirically support the contextual and scale-sensitive model outlined in the first chapter.

3.1 The (empirical) bodily imperative

Nearly all of the time spent doing participant observation in the field is used to live in and with that environment, and it does not matter if one is consciously and actively researching or not, one's senses are continuously alert, and hence the hermeneutic animal in us works whether we want it to or not. I use the term hermeneutic animal to denote that people interpret their environments on an "unconditional" basis – it is done whether we want to do it or not, and it always includes the knowledge we had prior to the interpreted situation. When conducting a study, however, we control our interpretations and make them open for others to assess. In recent debates the fundamental role of the researcher as a person and his or her "position" has been highlighted. Important as it is to reflect on these issues, the reflections are always preceded by, and filtered and mixed through impressions stemming from the bodily prerequisites of being in the field. Fieldwork involves a presence and nearness, which ultimately implies that one's own interpreting subject is tied to one's body and is thereby also restricted, not only as an existent in the time-space but also in other ways, e.g. ethically and emotionally, linguistically and intellectually. The limited capacity of the body restricts the possible practical and intellectual undertakings in the field.

The nearness of the researcher to the field implied by participant observation is not only about learning ways and means to see and to understand, but also about learning how to do, i.e. "body management", about handling one's own body – acquiring and using embodied practices in a new physical space. Geographic knowledge then, following Felix Driver (2000:267), may be seen as being constituted through a range of embodied practices. Driver mentions practices of travelling, dwelling, seeing, collecting, recording, and narrating, some of which are clearly spatial; movement, performance, passages, and encounters. In all of these, it is the acting, physical body of the fieldworker that, in interaction with other bodies (human and physical entities of other kinds), bases the overall understanding that the fieldworker is striving to attain. And, in order to manage one's body in the field so as to gain locally constructed insights, the fieldworker – the body manager – uses embodied social skills. In the use of these skills, which he or she will have to learn *in situ*, his or her body will also be an agent in the work. Or, as Wilbur Zelinsky writes, apprehending the environment need not be "'work' at all but rather the causal, unstructured sensing of our surroundings or simply an ad hoc, impulsive exercise in getting one's bearings", and in doing this we employ "not only vision but all the many other senses" (2001:6). To coexist in the space of the respondents will be, in the words of J.D. Dewsbury and S. Naylor: "about the surface of the body, the way it contacts the world through movement and sensation; and it is about the viscerality of the body, the gut instincts, the breathless anxieties and the gall that sees us get things done" (2002:257). The body carries empirical imperatives, in the original meaning of the word.

Physically sharing the space of experience is the foundation on which to start building a joint frame of references with the studied persons, a frame based on understanding and practice of, for example, the everyday. It should be noted that the everyday reality is not "original" – rather it is the subjects' interpreted reality which one can take part of by being near the subjects. This is valid not only for the respondents' verbal or written statements where it is evident that they present an interpretation of how they perceive their lives, their place and other aspects of their lifeworld, but *it is also* valid for people's practices.

A practice is an expressed interpretation of its own embodiment. Every repetition of it is new, but since it is a repetition it is an interpretation of all earlier occurrences of the specific practice – practices that since long formed themselves into a script, a scheme, or however one chooses to express the *automation* with which they are performed. Every repetition of a practice also requires a more or less conscious interpretation of the situation in which the practice is to be used, as well as an interpretation of the necessary adjustment of the practice to the situation at hand. That is to say, the practice is, when it is performed, an interpretation of its own embodiment in relation to the interpretation of the situation. Body, doing and situation melt together and forms part of a semiotic context to be mapped.

Furthermore, people are not discursively conscious about taken for granted embodied practices, and practices cannot, according to Pierre Bourdieu (1990:91), be put into words by the respondents. Moreover, people often say one thing but do another. Sharing the space of experience thus makes it possible for the fieldworker to note differences between the statements, e.g. that which is said in an interview, and that which people actually do. It may be pointed out that when studying space, which is filled with everyday matters and unreflected practices as well as matters of complete unawareness, then the nearness that the researcher achieves by being in place is a precondition for contextual studies of the spatial behaviour of the individual. In other words, one cannot ask respondents about everything about the place because they are simply not conscious of everything. Notwithstanding the theoretical, ethical and general aspects pertaining to fieldwork and participant observation, this stands out as the most important. It is about returning to the bodily and material matters and to the place where one is. In Pierre Bourdieu's formulation:

> It is possible to step down from the sovereign viewpoint from which objectivist idealism orders the world, /.../, but without having to abandon to it the 'active aspect' of apprehension of the world by reducing knowledge to a mere recording. To do this, one has to situate oneself *within* 'real activity as such', that is, in the practical relation to the world, the preoccupied, active presence in the world

through which the world imposes its presence, with its urgencies, its things to be done and said, things made to be said, which directly govern words and deeds without ever unfolding as a spectacle. (Bourdieu 1990:52, *original emphasis*)

From this basic perspective participant observation is about what the researcher does in the field. It proceeds from the natural attitude, i.e. from that which is perceived as real by the subjects, which is also the knowledge of the world from which people construct their everyday routines, solve large and small problems and act in the world. By taking part in their lives, under conditions as similar to theirs as possible, the researcher will learn the local structures of signification by way of communication that usually has a practical application (i.e. one *does* things – with one's bodies – together). This implies a process through which the researcher departs from a state of ignorance into a state of being familiar with the internal relations of the structures of signification as she or he learns how these structures function in their practical application. This is a requirement for understanding the background practices that, firstly, might be taken for granted by the subjects, and secondly, not easily lend themselves to linguistic descriptions, if they would be reflected upon. Moreover, the researcher can learn not only how the practice-oriented structures of signification of the place are ordered internally but also, in complex societies, how they relate to each other as parts of a greater whole, such as the state, the global, the market and/or other systems of primarily non-local relations. By participating in the everyday lives of the respondents, the researcher learns the common usage of signifiers in that place, and he or she can then theoretically connect these to the ideational and other courses originating in the total and real action-spaces that flow through and affect the place.

The process is thus about learning to understand. It is through this process that the foundation of knowledge is created, i.e. in the encounter with the unknown to which a bridge must be built. It is the bridging itself that is the essence of the method. This is often metaphorically understood in terms of "insider" and "outsider".

3.2 Inside – outside

Fieldwork is not just about being in a place, looking around, and taking part in what people are doing, nor is it just about taping interviews with them. It is rather about understanding the place and what the people there are doing from their point of view; from the "insider's" point of view. Peter Jackson writes that participant observation is a "method with which an attempt to transcend the epistemological gulf between 'insider' and 'outsider' can be made" (1983:44). In order to do this successfully, Karl-Olov Arnstberg states that it is important for the researcher to place him or herself as "close as possible" (1997:144) to the persons in the study. Metaphorically speaking, participant observation means to "jump from one's 'research raft' to the 'raft of the natives'. Then it is about staying on board long enough to be able to participate in manoeuvring it" (Arnstberg ibid:51, *my translation*).[23]

This manoeuvring can be summed up in James Scott's concept of "mētis", i.e. "practical experience" and "local knowledge".[24] The essence of mētis is "[k]nowing how and when to apply the rules of thumb *in a concrete situation*" (Scott 1998:316, *original emphasis*). Mētis comes from living in, and with a certain environment, and is the opposite of generalised knowledge and scientific theories. It is localised and a form of reasoning most suited to the "complex material and social tasks where the uncertainties are so daunting that we must trust our (experienced) intuition and feel our way" (Scott 1998:327). Based in practical experience, Scott continues, the key test of mētis is its practical efficacy.

To gain access to, and to understand the local mētis would thus tell us a lot about how the world functions from the perspective of the people in a certain place. Thus, mētis is also of central significance for whether a fieldworker is able to manoeuvre in the local waters or not.

But how does one actually bridge the epistemological gulf between the "outsider" and the "insider"? The determining question is whether it is possible

---

23 Although being close to people in a place often is a prerequisite for gaining information on many issues, it should also be noted that sometimes respondents are more willing to speak about sensitive issues with people who are not part of the local community, as Holly Hapke and Devan Ayyankeril (2001:348) point out.
24 The term derives from Greek mythology: Mētis was Zeus' first bride (Scott 1998:424, fn8).

to acquire the necessary communicative skills. Following Alfred Schütz, I believe that this can be made possible by applying the principle of "reciprocity of perspectives" and the thesis of the "natural attitude of daily life". Courtice Rose (1988) writes about the natural attitude that the world, during the course of everyday life, presents itself to the I in self-evident categories. These categories are taken for granted and experienced as real. The world also includes other people and these are assumed to have the same experience of the objects in the world that the I has. The "reciprocity of perspectives" is a principle stating that the everyday world does not change as the I changes his or her biographical position from "here" to "there", i.e. if another person than the I would make a move to the same position, that person would experience the same "there" as the I does. This is not only true regarding the physical objects present "there" but also social constructs can be shared when viewed from the same position. Rose writes:

> There would be enough typical constructs shared between two people (e.g. words, symbols, concepts, traditions) so that they could go beyond their individual biographically-determined situations and talk meaningfully about a common world. (Rose 1988:158–159)

More technically expressed, what Rose describes is "The idealization of the congruency of system of relevances" (Schutz 1953/1962:12),[25] which states that in the natural attitude "we" assume, until proven wrong, that the differences in perspectives that exist between the parts in an "us", are irrelevant for the purpose at hand. In other words, the knowledge of the world is common within a group that shares the same system of relevances.

In this case, if meaningful communication is the purpose at hand, the researcher will engage him or herself in dialogue, and will thus start to over-

---

25 It should be noted that Schütz discuss this in relation to the construction of "thought objects" among people in everyday life (in the natural attitude). The researcher gains access to this as a person among persons, and then interprets it according to his or her "scientific" attitude, and not the "natural" attitude (1953/1999:68). Nevertheless, as the discussion on positions below shows, the "scientific" attitude is encroached upon by the researcher's self. This, however, escaped Schütz and he was occupied with finding ways to the "objective" study of "subjective" systems of relevance (see 1953/1999:62–68, see also 1945/1999:125, cf. Bengtsson 1999:14).

come the differences in the systems of relevances between the researcher and the subjects of research. To succeed, the requirements are a common language and a certain amount of social competence. Merely observing would not take us very far, linguistic interactions and communicative action with other people are crucial.

Much of the understanding generated from participant observation is based on talks and informal interviews, and hence one has to have an understanding of not only the grammar and the words of the language, but also of that which Mikhail Bakhtin calls "dialogue" and "primary speech genres" (Holloway & Kneale 2000, Oinas 1999, Bandlamudi 1994). If we become engaged in communication we will, by necessity, learn, and be part of the local primary speech genres, and hence we lay the foundation to understand how meaning is generated dialogically in these. Thus, we also have the interpretative tools to grasp how most situations are signified locally. One consequence of this is that the main "material" one brings home from the field is not the notes, tapes or other texts or other "evidence". No, it is the cultural competence or interpretative capacity, mētis if you like, that one ultimately developed while learning to understand the local lifeworld-logic of the people in the place of study.

It should now be clear that in understanding how to become "insiders", we have to go beyond the body and its fears, its joys and empirical sensations, via linguistic encounters to the interpretative subject of our selves. Importantly, it is concerning these very issues that the critique of participant observation has been raised. In order to defuse this critique we need to tame the hermeneutic animal in us.

3.3   Critique and the taming of the hermeneutic animal

Methodologically speaking, studies based on qualitative methods in general and participant observations in particular have been questioned in terms of their scientific character. What this critique seems to disregard altogether though, is the role of controlled interpretation. To explain the importance of controlled interpretation – or what I think of as taming the hermeneutic animal – I will account for some general points of criticism that have been raised against this kind of qualitative method. In highlighting these points I hope to make clear how the method actually works. Below I treat in turn 1) the city as field, 2) theoretical interpretation, and 3) logical inference and generalisability. The first point of critique relates to participant observation and geography, whereas the next two are of a more general character of concern for qualitative ways of working at large. The account is inspired by Steve Herbert (2000), especially the two latter points.

3.4 The city as field

The first point of criticism of participant observation refers to how well the method suits studies of social life in cities, and thus also to my studies in Ligovo. If the ultimate goal of that fieldwork was to become an insider and learn Ligovo's mētis I think I managed to some extent, but not completely. Cities are open systems and in them several parallel social realities exist; life forms are specialised and everyday knowledge has certain social concentrations, i.e. it is not evenly diffused (cf. Schütz 1946/1999). These are mixed with each other into a complex urban whole. The critique lies in the fact that it is not possible to be an insider of all these realities simultaneously. This, however, does not prevent one from understanding places in a geographical way, when the places themselves are the concern of the study and not the communities that exist in them, although these in certain respects dominate the character of the place.

But let us discuss in more detail whether it is possible to answer the critique that participant observation is not a suitable method in cities. The critique starts by saying that it is impossible for the researcher to participate in urban life and follow the city as an ethnographic field; if by this term one means a society which is socially and spatially well delimited. These studies demand that there is a social community of belonging shared by the population, which one does not generally find in cities, except in certain districts with well-established populations. For the city at large, the community of belonging is imagined, and in most of the districts there is no socially based cohesion among the population.

It is thus difficult to situate oneself in a city or district that, for the researcher, is meaningfully delimited on these grounds, or so to say *by itself*. Usually, one solves this problem by separating a part to be studied through participant observation from the city, the part being a sports club, a place of work, a youth centre or the like (Arnstberg 1997:112–115). In these micro-places people not only share space, but also belong to a kind of social collective within which they must act as persons on a daily basis, and – most importantly for the participant observer – these micro-places form a coherent arena for the social life that the researcher wishes to study. The risk here is that the study will not deal with the city and the life of the city but with the arena itself.

One can also assert that to treat the city as a coherent field is a pseudo-problem. The city is an open and complex system for the city-dwellers too. They are also always interpreting and seeking to understand their environment. Since the city-dwellers, as with the researcher, cannot understand the city as one (1) system, one can say that their lifeworlds are constituted by fragments of the urban environment. The stories they have about the city are by necessity only parts of a greater context. Such is the environment of the city and the same conditions apply for the researcher and for those who live there. From a research point of view, the most important consequence is that it is more difficult to make an empirically based purposeful reduction of the interest at hand.

But except by shrinking the empirical parts of the studies to smaller units – micro-places – there are two other ways to respond to the critique. The first of these is to complement participant observation with other empirical methods. These could be mappings and other methods directed at spatial survey. The second way is to fill those parts where empirical participant observations of the city and city life are not possible with an understanding that is founded on theory. The sense of detail of social life provided by participant observations may hereby combine with geographical concepts of spatial overview. It is thus possible, by means of the theoretical scaffold, to understand the different phenomena that exist in the processes of development of individual places and landscapes.

3.5 Theoretical interpretation

According to another critique, the method is not scientific since the results cannot be repeated. This implies that the descriptions given by the researcher are "subjective" interpretations that cannot stand critical testing. This critique can easily be brushed aside since one cannot evaluate participant observation with the same rules as laboratory experiments as it is not based on positivistic and naturalistic epistemology. Nevertheless, in order to show how misplaced this critique is, I will emphasise the interpretative aspects of the method. It may also be remarked that upon closer scrutiny, laboratory experiments and other "science" in the making appear as contextual interpretations that are not at all separated from the subjects that perform them (Latour 1987). Interpretation is thus common with other sciences. The point to be made is that the interpretation itself is placed at the centre of both the method and the analysis, which – ironic as it may seem – guarantees that the arbitrariness of the results are reduced to a minimum. Science, in comparison, also deploys other techniques to avoid arbitrariness, e.g. repetition.

By interpreting speech, texts and actions, the researcher tries to elucidate the local structure of significances by learning them, and as discussed above, this learning builds the bridge. The researcher himself is the instrument and by constantly questioning and reflecting on the substance of his experiences, the researcher refines his or her interpretations. In the words of Steve Herbert:

> it is only through the interrogation of one's subjective experience within a milieu, and the subjective reactions it engenders, that one can glean the meaning structures that motivate everyday agency.
> (Herbert 2000:559)

But how is it possible to know that these interpretations are not subjective in the sense that they are arbitrary? How does one know that they are good interpretations? The answer is that if one goes beyond unproblemized descriptions to try to explain and understand, then one has to join theory and method and involve oneself in a hermeneutic process sometimes called "metaphoric dialogue" (Demeritt & Dyer 2002, see also Duncan & Ley 1993, Evans 1988). The following example may illustrate how this functions. One cannot see a system, e.g. a gender system, but one can see actions and hear words which are then interpreted in accordance with the existence of the system. To interpret means to relate to already existing knowledge and thus the theoretical concepts and instruments that we brought into the field will come to play a decisive role. "Theories in the field" should, in the words of James Duncan and Nancy Duncan, be regarded as tools for "interrogating commonsensical discourse" (2001:402) and in this they help to translate the local and specific into more general frameworks. Through the logic of these theoretical constructions we can assign behaviour and statements to the abstractions we already know that tell us how the society and space are built up and how they are functioning. We use those theoretical instruments that the research society has agreed upon, and this guarantees that the "subjectivity" of the researcher is not arbitrary, since by way of theory one refers to a common understanding of different problems in order to understand details. We tame the hermeneutic animal in us, interpreting within the frameworks of the scientifically acceptable.

3.6 Logical inference and generalisability

The same argument may be used to answer the critique which says that studies based on a small and sometimes a random (but not statistically representative) selection of subjects cannot serve as a basis for generalisation. This is correct insofar as statistical inference based on the representativity of the material is just not possible in many qualitative studies, which are often based on a small number of people, one case study or just one place. However, this does not mean that generalisation is not possible. Instead of statistical inference, qualitative studies draw generalisability from "logical" inference (Smith 1984, Jackson 1985, Herbert 2000). Logical inference is "the process by which the analyst draws conclusions about the essential linkage between two or more characteristics in terms of some systematic explanatory schema – some set of theoretical propositions" (Mitchell 1983, quoted in Smith 1984:359). Studies that do not use theory to inform the descriptions risk, as Loïc Wacquant (2002) shows in a critique of three recent urban ethnographical monographs, to naively parrot assumptions inherent in the moral categories of the researcher and his or her audience. Thus we get moralistic and, as such, bad social science. The hermeneutic animal was not tamed in these studies.

Moreover, it is the logic of an analysis, rather than the representativity or typicality of the material, that makes generalisation possible. Peter Jackson, following Mitchell (1983) writes: "The extent to which generalisation may be made from case studies depends upon the adequacy of the underlying theory and the whole corpus of related knowledge of which the case forms a part rather than on the particular instance itself" (1985:171). The logicality of the analyses, in turn, is to be judged in relation to how the wider social context is portrayed. It is in the relation to a trustworthy description of the wider context that the use of theoretical arguments can be made regarding how the categories and concepts stick together logically.

These descriptions start out with what the researcher wants to put forward as credible theoretical arguments. The difference is, however, that the bases of these descriptions can be agreed upon with certainty by several people. Many would have followed the general development, read the same books, seen the same films, and have similar experience of the broader characteristics of the field, and in relating the case presented by the researcher to this wider knowledge of the field, the logicality of the analyses can be assessed.

But to further answer the critique on the "un-generalisability" of studies of this kind, three additional aspects of the qualities of this methodology will be put forward. Two of these are concerned with supplementing the qualitative field studies with quantitative surveys and the like, and/or performing comparative analyses. These will not be discussed further as I did not apply them in this study,[26] but see Herbert (2000). A third aspect mentioned

---

26 Although I have not yet analysed the material, it could be mentioned that in 2000, I contributed a number of questions in a large survey based on a random and representative selection of the population of Sankt-Peterburg. The survey (supervised by professor D. Gavra and N. Sokolov, *doktor nauk*), was answered by ca 1100 people. The survey was made by *Tsentr sotsiologicheskikh issledovanii fakul'teta sotsiologii Sankt-Peterburgskogo gosudarstvennovo universiteta* (Sociological Research Center of the Faculty of Sociology of the Sankt-Peterburg State University). Also *Mezhregional'naia obshchestvenaia organizatsiia "Sotsiologicheskoe obshchestvo imeni M.M. Kovalevskovo"* g. Sankt-Peterburg, should be mentioned as part of conducting the survey.

by Herbert and by Agar (1996), and which is relevant for this study, is that the arena one chooses may be representative for other cases as well. Herbert writes:

> Dynamics in inner cities, in classrooms, on college, campuses or in corporate boardrooms are likely to be similar across locales. If an ethnographer can demonstrate that the dynamics he or she studies occurs elsewhere, he or she can confidently generalize.
> (Herbert 2000:560)

Anatolii Mikhailovich Rozhkov, one of my principal respondents, related to me during a discussion we were having about his move from the city centre to the suburb where he now lives, that it was unimportant in which suburb one landed, they were all the same. Several other respondents expressed the same notion in different forms. Several of them referred to an old, but still popular Soviet film – *S legkim parom* from 1975 – which makes fun of the "typicality" and similarity of the high-rise suburbs.[27]

The film is shown by the state television each New Year and is about a man who had just moved with his mother into a recently built flat in one of the *novoestroek*, or newly erected high-rise districts of Moscow. The man is about to get married and in the afternoon of New Year's Eve he goes with his friends to the public baths. The friends drink him under the table and put him, intoxicated close to unconsciousness, by mistake on a plane bound for Leningrad. As he finally wakes up at the airport he takes a taxi home, he finds his street, his block and his door. He opens the door with his key, enters and falls asleep. While sleeping, a woman enters the apartment. But she is not his wife to be, but another woman and they are not in Moscow but in quite another city – Leningrad. However, things were so similar to his circumstances in Moscow – the blocks, the street and its name, the fittings and the furniture of the flat etc. – that in his intoxicated state he did not understand that he was in another city. The woman is incidentally also waiting for her wedding, and the film then turns into a love

---

27 The full title of the film is *Ironiia sud'by, ili s legkim parom* (The irony of fate), Gosteleradio SSSR, 1975. The film is directed by El'dara Riazanova. The full title is not easy to translate since the second clause relates to an idiom. The idiom *s legkim parom* litterally refers to steam in a sauna, and implies the good feeling of being there.

drama which mainly takes place during New Year's night in a Leningrad flat – a flat that could have been located anywhere in Russia.

In this film, not only are the physical environments of Leningrad and Moscow almost identical, but the life stories of a number of people are also similar. The film plays with the general structures of the lifeworld, and people recognise their own stories in them. To the extent that the film at the time of its production reflected a greater social context, as I believe my respondents mean, one can be confident that my material, although it is based on studies of one suburb and a small number of people, also contains features common to large parts of Russia, especially regarding places on the outskirts of big cities.

To sum up, what the solutions to the problems of generalisability and of "subjective" interpretation have in common is that they refer to the analytical and synthesising capacities of the theories put to work in interpreting the empirical material. By "filling in" the field studies with theoretical propositions, it is possible to show how the local practice-related systems of signification are constructed and how they are interconnected with events on other scale levels. A side effect of this is that the method generates theory in the sense that one needs it to understand how categories and concepts stick (or do not stick) together in the particular case. Especially so if the theory used for interpretation does not fully map onto the situations encountered in the field (see the discussion on abduction below). The number of instances that the generated theory covers, as well as its longevity, denotes the force of its generalisability. Theories, in this sense, are thus primarily not true or false in a universalistic sense, rather they have limits of time and space extension, or applicability.

The process of controlled interpretation – of taming the hermeneutic animal – involves leaving the small world, centred on groups and individuals, in order to emplace them in the social, historical and spatial contexts of which they may, or may not be aware. This also means leaving behind naturalistic descriptions of what people say and do, and hereby other problems arise. Fundamentally, these problems emanate from the question of by which right the researcher leaves their world to create his or her own text. A text, or representation of them, which they can no longer control. Not even the researcher can be fully aware of its consequences. We encounter the problem of representation, and it presents itself mainly as an ethical question that grew into a critique during the 1980s.

3.7 Ethics

Ethics concerns, among other things, presentation, or re-presentation. It is about drawing portraits that are fair, and about selecting information to give a multifaceted picture of the place. The reason is that the ways we describe and represent the world to some extent also creates the world as we perceive it. The geographical metaphors we use have "normative power" (Minca 2001:xxviii) in that they generate (morally charged) allegories with the reader (Clifford 1986). From this follows that research should be "reflexive" regarding the role of the researcher in creating geographical re-presentations.

The reflexive shaping of the text puts the whole research process into perspective. Representations of the studied phenomena are not passive reflections but pictures that have been selected, filtered and actively brought forward by the researcher and the epistemological effects of this have been named the "crises of representation". The term was made popular by George Marcus and Michael Fischer (1986) and came to be used widely during the eighties, although the phenomenon had been known earlier (Gren 1994:13–20). The "crises" involved an awareness that there is no natural(istic) picture of reality which is independent from the researcher, or for that matter – absolutely true. Martin Gren writes: "Knowledge is invariably (re)presented in the form of *texts*, and a text is no longer held to be a passive mirror, but a creature of our own making (1994:36, *original emphasis*). As representations, and the politics of representation, become focused, it was possible to speak of geographical "poetics". This is a way of saying that the words matter and that we should think as carefully as the poets do in terms of the representation of the world. A concrete example of poetics (in the literal sense) is found in Allan Pred's poem about place (Pred 1986:56–57). Moreover, there are no descriptions, textual or otherwise, that are not constructed within the limits of language, and languages are not related to the "real" world in a one-to-one correspondence. Languages are constituted socially and have meaning only in relation to the (time and space bound) social contexts in which they appear.

Another way of expressing this is that knowledge also is time and space specific (Thrift 1985) or "situated"; a term coined by Donna Haraway in 1988. In connection to this, the researcher assumes a central role and the subsequent method have sometimes been called "reflexive". According to Gillian Rose, within geography it is mainly feminist researchers that have used this method and she writes that "[r]eflexivity in general is being advocated by these writers as strategy for situating knowledge" (1997:306).

But what should one reflect upon? The heart of the argument is that the researcher as a human subject is part of the creation of knowledge, and that he or she should not disregard his or her personal characteristics, social position and other "personal" factors in the creative process. It is thus necessary that the researcher not only reflects upon these aspects and on his or her "position", but also conveys an idea of these reflections to the reader. At this point it should be noted that this discussion is an intra-science debate and I do not want to push this self-critique too far. As George Marcus points out, too much reflexivity leads either to self-indulgence (the focus is on the self of the researcher), or to political correctness in explaining one's position in relation to the subjects of the study. Research hereby becomes a kind of identity politics (1992). Thus, although reflexivity is a relevant factor in understanding how knowledge is constituted, it may nonetheless lead the study away from the field and away from what is important in the lives of the respondents.

In a reflexive discussion about her selection of material from a high-rise suburb in the Stockholm area, Kerstin Bodström (2000:7–8) points out that the image of a place is always present, and that it colours both minor and major planning decisions, as well as everyday life. Since the researcher adds to the image of the place through his or her reports, and since this image may harmfully affect the residents, it is important that the researcher is reflexive concerning the implications the text might have when it leaves the desk. Following Claudio Minca, and the exaggerated post-modernist fear of power, descriptions could be turned into "violence".

To avoid researcher "violence", two ethical principles distinguish themselves above others in terms of importance. The first is to be explicit about who you are and why you are where you are – the respondent will then have the possibility to choose whether or not to participate in the research. The second principle is that respondents should not risk venturing their security by allowing the researcher to participate in their lives. Furthermore, the respondents themselves should be the ones in the first instance to decide what may or may not be detrimental.

As a consequence of the latter principle the researcher often tries to protect the identity of the respondents by distorting some of their characteristics that are not considered important to the general line of reasoning. Protecting identities might assume extra importance in certain places and countries, as with the case of Russia and its 20th century history, where the respondents have strong reasons to be suspicious of political power.

A related ethical question, and of special significance to geography, concerns withholding knowledge from the reader about the exact location of fieldwork. Even with the use of pseudonyms and other rewritings, e.g. changing the occupation, sex or varying the age of the respondents, it is fairly easy for people living in the same place as the respondents – and who thus know the micro-social context – to find out whom you are actually describing because their position in the social structure is evident. Protecting identities in these circumstances obviously fails, and this is the reason why its not uncommon in anthropological studies for the researcher to confuse the issue by stating wrong places. This also occurs in geographical studies, e.g. the places of homosexual communities and other sometimes stigmatised groups are not divulged as they might otherwise experience threats and even violence (England 1994:84). Obviously, the researcher cannot afford to expose respondents to such risks.

Thus there may exist strong reasons for not divulging the place of fieldwork. On the other hand, however, the study of places lies in the heart of geography, if not for any other reason than that a place is a part of "earth as the home of man". Moreover, according to the idiographic tradition, which is, or at least has been, fairly strong in geography, a place and its development are seen as unique in relation to other places. To then confuse the issue by not revealing the place would harm the very idea of earthwriting and would have epistemological consequences detrimental to geographic knowledge. In other words, it would be meaningless even to begin certain types of place research.

But there are other reasons for not confusing the name of the place of research. Researchers do not address themselves to other researchers only, but also to those people living in the place, now and in the future. To confuse the issue of where the research was conducted, would, in my mind, be ethically incorrect with regards to these people as this would more or less deny them the possibility to learn about their home district. In my case I received very good assistance from Anatolii Mikhailovich Rozhkov, a *kraeved* (local historian), who made great efforts to help me in my work.[28] To give the place – his place – a wrong name would be a blow to him, and to all of the other concerned citizens who are active for the sake of their district or those just eager to learn more about it.

It should be conceded, however, that the ethical necessity of protecting the identity of the respondents, and the similarly ethical question of stating where the fieldwork was carried out, might be in opposition to each other. In this study I have not confused the place name but use the correct one and try to protect the identities of the respondents in other ways; by using pseudonyms and other circumlocutions. I followed the principle of altering some characteristics of people, characteristics that are insignificant to the discussion, and I have also left out material that I know my respondents would not have wished me to use. The only key respondents whose real names are presented here are Anatolii Mikhailovich Rozhkov, whose book I discuss, and Anatolii Nikolaevich Grachev, who is a popularly elected politician in the newly established Municipal Circuit in Ligovo.

Both Anatolii Mikhailovich and Anatolii Nikolaevich were very helpful and took a keen interest in my work and I would like to believe that they would have been as helpful to any researcher interested in Ligovo. Having said this, one possible aspect of their kindness towards me and my work may have been that I was a foreigner, and the status that followed from this fact may have lent me a special "position" vis-à-vis the field.

---

28 He had e.g. written a book about the history of the place, see Chapter 5.

3.8 The position of the researcher as a foreigner

The question concerning reflexivity is thus not only about an ethical attitude in the text itself. It is also about the role and position of the researcher vis-à-vis the research context – in the field and at home. Concerning the latter, which is sometimes related to as "triple hermeneutics", the production of knowledge is considered in relation to what is considered epistemologically interesting in the researchers home society. Concerning the former, I will make a point of the fact that the researcher gets information from respondents in the field depending on whom they consider the researcher to be. It is the "perceived position" of the researcher that is important. However, in much of the general literature on positionality and the value of reflecting on this, it is rather the researchers own reflections on him or herself that seem to have assumed ascendancy (cf. Marcus 1992).

However, to reflect upon who one is, or what position one has, is to try to reflect upon things that we have no full knowledge of (Rose 1997:319, Ley & Duncan 1993:330). Neither as persons nor as researchers are we conscious about our whole being. Furthermore, neither can we gain full insight into who the respondents believe us to be. While not totally disregarding these issues and their role in the construction of knowledge, it is reflections on who the researcher is in the eyes of the respondents that ought to be in focus.

A related question is if the respondents change their behaviour just because there is somebody observing them. This, however, would only be possible for the respondents to do at the beginning of a fieldwork. In the course of time and as confidence and rapport is established between the researcher and the respondents, they will act in accordance with that social outer and inner world which they know and of which the researcher becomes a part (Herbert 2001).

As a researcher, one can instead use the reactions of the studied persons that one's very presence in the place evokes. The person of the researcher is placed into categories and treated according to the local categorical knowledge the respondents have. Some of the most evident of these categories concern age, colour, and sex. To each of these are coupled a range of connotations, and studying the reactions of the respondents in relation to these bodily facts may illuminate these connotations, and how they stick together in the locally constructed signifying systems. For example, from the bodily fact of my sex, it was possible to understand how parts of the gender system functions in Russia, as I was treated in accordance with the respondents perceptions of themselves as women or men, and of me as a man. In general, one is treated according to the respondents' perception of whom one is and this behaviour may be significant for their perceptions of the world. Below, I will account for the perception of me as a *foreigner*, which at the beginning of my fieldwork was a noteworthy characteristic for them. The fact of my foreignness in the eyes of the respondents had direct bearing on the research.

So, at the beginning of my fieldwork, one of the most prominent features was that I was perceived and considered a stranger. I was recognised as an *inostranets* (foreigner). The word is a compound of *inoi*, which among other things means "other", and *stranets*, from *strana*, which means "country". So in a direct translation *inostranets* means "person from another country". But there are foreigners and foreigners. Being from *zapad*, from "the west", I was usually met with interest paired with benevolence, whereas *inostrantsy* (pl.) from other parts of the world may have encountered a more unfavourable attitude. It should be stated that the reception was usually kind but, on some occasions, this was mixed with suspicion and fear – really, was I not a *shpion* (spy)? Why would a geographer otherwise be interested in suburbs? And *byt'* (everyday life) cannot be an interesting subject! What were the real reasons for being there?

To briefly describe how I was perceived in the field, the words; *interest, benevolence or kindness, suspicion* and *fear* would be prominent parts of the presentation. The interest in my person and the kindness I met were extremely important in making the work what it became and making it possible at all. The stories that arose during these encounters are first of all the ones related here. But to be *inostranets* in the field also implied problems. At the same time as fear and suspicion were talkative of the relations that people had to the political system, they constituted a hindrance to my work, delaying it and making it more difficult. For obvious reasons I had very little to do with those who were directly hostile to *inostrantsy* (because there are such people, too).

The following discussion is mainly based on my own experiences although these are by no means exceptional; other researchers have had similar experiences. Melinda Herrold writes that the villagers in the Amur region in Siberia in the years 1992–1993 could not believe that foreigners came to their villages to watch birds: "local people ... were highly suspicious. Foreigners, they asked, were doing *what* in a tick- and mosquito-infested marsh? Watching birds?? To veterans of ideological repartee, this explanation seemed neither candid nor likely" (2001:297, *original emphasis*). As Stephen Kotkin writes of his stay in Magnetogorsk in 1987, he often heard accusations that he was a spy "from all sorts of people, most of whom were unable to imagine how anyone 'permitted' by his own government to travel abroad could *not* be a spy" (1991:xvii, *original emphasis*). Even nearly ten years after the disintegration of the Soviet Union this suspiciousness remains. An example is provided by the travel book author Steve Kokker who, at a talk in connection with the publication of a travel guide, relates that in Russia it took two to three times longer to collect material than in the Baltic countries where he had also worked.[29] Even though the material he was interested in mainly concerned the location of the hotels, the restaurants, the museums, their opening hours, prices and so on, he found it difficult to get this information; people were suspicious although they were rather interested in his person. His own explanation for this situation included the fact that he used the phrase "I search for information" (*ia ishchu informatsiiu*), although he later understood that the word "information" was associated with informing the secret police, and that "to search" was considered a suspicious act in itself. I myself used the phrase "I collect material" (*ia sobiraiu material*), which I thought might sound a little less dangerous. This was a deliberate way to decrease the suspicions that followed from being an *inostranets*. Another strategy was to present myself as more of a sociologist than a geographer, as sociology is less associated with spying than geography is. It was also truer in the sense that this kind of social, or cultural geography is not mainly concerned with mapping resources, infrastructure and other sensitive objects. This would have been

---

29 The talk was held on 11 June 2000 in the English bookshop at Fontanka 40, Sankt-Peterburg, and concerned the publication of the second edition of *Russia, Ukraine & Belarus* (Melbourne: Lonely Planet. 2000).

the kind of geography that most people would have thought of had I said that I was a geographer; *where* things were located was a sensitive issue *to search* for in the Soviet Union – as discussed in Chapter 6, space was secret.

The suspicious attitude to foreigners is not surprising considering that during the Soviet era people were fed with the propaganda that alluded to foreigners as dangerous and a threat to peace.[30] The situation was and is somewhat different in Leningrad/Sankt-Peterburg compared to many other parts of Russia as people here are more used to foreigners. Already before the disintegration of the Soviet Union there were foreign students, tourists, companies and a number of persons belonging to the international research community. However, they did not usually live in suburbs and would not have been interested in the study of everyday life.

But besides the propaganda, it could be downright dangerous to be involved with *inostrantsy* during the Soviet era. Under Stalin, people could be sentenced to long periods of imprisonment simply for having contacts with foreigners. During the late Soviet era, contacts with foreigners could lead to unpleasant visits from the security police, to problems at work, with the schooling of the children or other things which are important in everyday life. A Swedish respondent who lived in Leningrad during the late sixties related how it was possible to ask for directions during sporadic encounters with people in the city, but added that if one asked what the name of a street had been prior to its renaming, then one had over-stepped the border of what was regarded as acceptable. "One should not ask questions", he said. There are many stories that relate the fear aroused by the possible consequences of contacts with *inostrantsy*. Klaus Mehnert has described it in *Sovjetmänniskan* (1959), Ryszard Kapuściński in *The Empire* (1996), Hedrick Smith in *The Russians* (1977), and for more analytical purposes Stefan Hedlund in *Öststatsekonomi* (1992). Common to all descriptions is that people were afraid of having contacts with foreigners. They knew it could lead to problems.

---

30 An additional factor that might have added to the suspiciousness, although I believe it to be of minor importance for my fieldwork, was the second post-Soviet war in Chechnya that started in 1999.

Even though the situation is much better now, and maybe especially so under Boris Yeltsin, the old times are far from forgotten. One example concerns the family with whom I stayed in Ligovo. Elizaveta, the daughter, is about to apply for some kind of higher education in the summer of 1999. Since the family does not have the means to pay for higher education it was crucial to act strategically and apply for such an education where there is a good chance of being accepted but which is also interesting for the daughter. The case is a matter not only for Elizaveta and her mother, Tania, but also Elizaveta's grandmother, Olga Nikoleavna is devoted to find realistic options.[31] One such option is to get help from one of the grandmother's friends who has many international contacts at her institute. The family devotes quite some time to the question and Tania tells me about the various options available to the daughter. I understand that the girl stands a good chance of being accepted at the institute thanks to Olga Nikolaevna's friend, and I say that it seems to be a good option, partly because she has a good chance of being accepted but also because, as she would be working with foreigners, this would most likely open the possibility for her to earn good money when she completed her education. Tania's answer is short and seems well thought-out: "Yes, that's now, but things may change".

One of the problems associated with the suspicion towards foreigners, and for me also the most disturbing events during fieldwork, was when I got to know people who, when they had understood why I was in the country, freely started to relate something interesting to me, but who would avoid getting into a formal interview situation. Sometimes they flatly refused, on other occasions they showed that they did not want to be interviewed in other ways. On one occassion, when a formal interview had been agreed to, the respondent said completely different things than in the preceding talks. The necessary confidence and trust had not been achieved to bridge the suspicions she harboured. After being refused formal interviews a couple of times I simply stopped trying to interview people with whom I did not have a relation characterised by trust, or which was not mediated by some-

---

31 To improve one's chances to be accepted in the Russian educational system it is not uncommon to get "help" from one's personal contacts. Concerning this case, see Borén 2003a:31. See also Ledeneva 1998.

one. I was grateful if people I met spontaneously talked freely and I did not interrupt this by bringing out my tape-recorder and formalising the setting, which I wanted to do at the end of the fieldwork, and also did with my key respondents.

These conditions gave me a kind of meta-understanding that every piece of information could be sensitive, although it was nothing special in itself. Rather, it was the context of giving information to a foreigner that made it sensitive. People have a real basis for being cautious, the earlier propaganda and the risks of having contacts with foreigners explain this cautiousness better than anything else does. But, certainly, there can be other reasons for people not wishing to be interviewed.

At the end of my last period of fieldwork, these questions were to be further accentuated. In January 2000 Vladimir Putin took over from Boris Yeltsin as President of the country,[32] and under Putin people became more cautious about what they were saying to strangers, especially foreigners. In some cases it was of direct significance for the people I met that Yeltsin had resigned and that Putin had taken over, and it is clear that this made the work more difficult, more so than the outbreak of the second war in Chechnya had done during the autumn of 1999. Even though the regime had already started to recycle the Soviet symbols during the Yeltsin era (from about 1995) and this development had come slowly, it was only when Putin took over that a radical break occurred from the freedom that had existed during the nineties. This was firstly noticeable in the way people were speaking about power. If the talk slipped into politics, under Yeltsin many people said that he was a boozer who had destroyed the country, while under Putin they became silent. They would prefer an embarrassing silence than express anxiety or commitment in front of a foreigner. If I knew the person well, he or she often lowered the voice and looked around before answering if the discussions touched upon the top political leadership in the country.

The question of trust is of course always of uttermost significance when conducting fieldwork, and with regards to the special history of the Soviet

---

32 Vladimir Putin was Acting President from January to March 2000, when he was elected.

Union concerning foreigners, this question has to be treated accordingly. When I was planning fieldwork I figured that the best way for me to find accommodation with a Russian suburban family would be to secure a place in a personal network – sometimes characterised as "survival" networks. I knew beforehand that "informal" contacts within these networks were the best means of getting things done and that these networks were based on mutual access to one another's contacts. I thought that since I might be a useful person to them, they would accommodate me in their network.[33] After some initial problems this strategy worked. My first attempt was through Aleksandr, a Russian relative to a close friend of mine whom my friend had helped during the first chaotic years at the beginning of the 1990s. I had met Aleksandr during the summers of these years when he came to work in Sweden and now I asked my friend to contact him on my behalf. Aleksandr promised to help.

We maintained contact and things initially seemed to turn out according to the original plans. However, when I made my initial visit to Sankt-Peterburg to study Russian and to arrange many of the practical arrangements, it transpired that he had not made the necessary arrangements. He mentioned something about a divorce in the family and, as I understood it, he regarded himself as having been disconnected from the Swedish line of his family. For me, this meant that I had to turn to plan B,[34] i.e. to spread by word of mouth that I needed a place to live in the outskirts of the city, and that I was going to study the life and landscape of that place. I did also say that whoever accommodated me would be an essential part of the study, and that the best arrangement would be if it were a whole family, preferably with three generations. It is common for three generations of the same family to live in one apartment in Russia and I wanted things to be as "usual" or

---

33 In short, I had planned to make these personal networks my "network 'in'". Michael Agar (1996:79–82) uses this concept and suggests that institutions that are in contact with the field, e.g. drug clinics if one is to study drug addicts, are useful as a network "in". These institutions would then act as intermediaries between the researcher and the field in the initial stage of the fieldwork, and if they are good, then the trust that the people have in these institutions would spill over to you. The institutions would thus function as a ticket of legitimacy making it easier to come close to the respondents.

34 Plan C was to get back to my parents' Russian friends from the time when we lived as expats in the Soviet Union.

as "common" as possible. After a week or so spent spreading the word, a course mate informed me that the mother of the family where she rents a room, had a friend – Olga Nikolaevna – who had relatives that might be willing to accept me as a tenant.

In fact it was in connection with Olga Nikolaevna that I first experienced the kind of positive interest that many people take in *inostranstry*. To be an *instranets* evoked a positive interest that was often of great help to the fieldwork. Sometimes this interest and assistance was really unbounded and people were prepared to help much more than I had ever expected. Olga Nikolaevna was one of these and she looked after me attentively and invested a great deal of her time showing Sankt-Peterburg to me. She took me to exhibitions and museums, to historical places and on walks, but also to the homes of people she knew and to the organisation where she was working on a voluntary basis. She tried to put me into contact with people of my age to help me get friends and fixed language lessons through a friend of hers, and finally she arranged my field place at Ligovo. Olga Nikolaevna soon became a matron to whom I could always turn for guidance. At a purely personal level I sometimes felt that she was a little too motherly, and also that she had too great a respect for me as a graduate student at the university; e.g. she doubted if it was appropriate for me to stay with people (i.e. her former daughter-in-law) who had no higher education, and were not *kul'turnye* (cultured) enough. Generally speaking, Olga Nikolaevna more or less adopted me.

So it was a great advantage being an *inostranets* and maybe coming from Sweden, too. Olga Nikolaevna had earlier hosted a Swedish student and they still kept in touch. He had invited her to Sweden and she had, on the whole, only positive experiences of Sweden and Swedes. But also more generally it seems valid to say that western foreigners have a high standing and that it is interesting to get to know them. Natasha, a respondent, explains that Olga Nikolaevna only met nice foreigners and that she therefore does not believe ill of any foreigner. She adds that Olga Nikolaevna herself becomes more interesting because of her contacts with foreigners. Tania, the mother of the family where I finally stayed, says that Olga Nikolaevna once told her that one should be in contact with just those foreigners that come to Russia. They are the well educated and *kul'turnye* people from their respective countries and they travel a lot, and for these reasons it is interesting to be in contact with them.

When Olga Nikolaevna heard of me I don't think she ever hesitated to help me find accommodation and she was the one who in many ways saved me during the initial stage of the fieldwork when my first "network 'in'" (Agar 1996:79–82) did not function as anticipated. Her networking capacity was tremendous and since networking is much about creating win-win situations, here was a chance to help me and at the same time to help herself and several people close to her. As I paid rent for the room her grandchildren and former daughter-in-law were materially provided for. But also, as I learned later, her son, the father of the grandchildren, was relieved of paying allowances for his children as Olga Nikolaevna had brought about the contact between his former wife and me. These kinds of material aspects of personal relations have their own logic in Russia, and it should be underlined that the material side of our relationships was not the only one. Although all the more infrequently, we still keep in touch and like each other as persons.

To sum up, being an *inostranets* was an advantage because one was interesting but also a disadvantage because there was often the thought – sometimes joking, sometimes not – that one was a spy. The details of these relations had to be decided upon from one situation to the next and one had to judge how it influenced the work as it proceeded. Finally, reflexivity in the field is about the researcher understanding who he or she is in relation to the field and how he or she is perceived by the people living there. So reflexivity is about understanding the inter-subjective processes of human relations – and the double hermeneutics of each situation – and how these processes influence the collection of material in the first stage, and then how they influence the re-presentation of the field. In the first place it is not about telling the story of one's own life before and during the fieldwork, but rather to be aware of the position one has in the eyes of the respondents – one's perceived position – and into which categories one is placed by them. By staying in the place for a long time, by continuously engaging in a discussion with oneself about whom one is in the eyes of the respondents, and by learning the local codes, one becomes less of a stranger and more of an insider.

3.9 Funnels, serendipity and abduction

The time aspect appears ever more central and the understanding of the production of knowledge should hereby be caught in some kind of time sensitive model. I have used a kind of funnel model, being inspired by Michael Agar's (1996) "funnel approach". In short, Agar's model – the funnel approach – treats fieldwork as a strategic process over time where one starts "with breadth and humanity in the beginning of the funnel, and then, within the context of that beginning, depth, problem-focus, and science at the narrow end" (1996:65). It is about selectively narrowing the problems: "You begin wide open to whatever you can learn, but within such a broad boundary, you are already bouncing between learning and checking what you have learned... Finally, as you approach the narrow end of the funnel, you begin some systematic testing. /.../ As the funnel narrows, your questions get more and more specific..." (1996:184). The attitude of the fieldworker is changed as the main focus shifts from learning to testing: "One first takes an involved, humanitarian position, striving for breadth of understanding in a student-child-apprentice position. As the fieldwork progresses, one in part takes a detached scientific view, focuses on some specific issues, and designs systematic approaches to formally document the experience from the perspective of a stranger" (1996:251–252). Somewhat paradoxically, the model means that the more of insider you become, the more like an outsider you have to act.

Another characteristic of the method is that one cannot know – at least not exactly – what kind of material one will get hold of. And one has to be ready to completely change the preconceived ideas one had when entering the field. A concept that captures this circumstance is "serendipity". Ulf Hannerz (1983:97) writes that serendipity is about finding one thing while looking for another. In the field one gets ideas about new connections and new threads to follow. But I would like to take the meaning of serendipity a step further in saying that during an explorative study the researcher cannot know what kind of material he or she will find. One has to work heuristically, continuously searching and making serendipity a principle. A reason for this is that fieldwork is about interaction with people and one cannot know in advance in which contexts one will be allowed to participate (to observe).

Since the material that one actually gets access to can be (radically) different than that which was preconceived when formulating objectives and problems at home, these may need to be changed in the course of fieldwork. These changes occur in relation to the social contexts in the place that are *researchable* in a practical sense, and to those that appear to be important and relevant when one has become established in the place. An example that well illustrates this widened type of serendipity is Nancy Ries' fieldwork carried out in Moscow in 1989. She went to study constructions of "Russianness" in relation to the cold war, which was a relevant question in the United States, but just wrong in the late Soviet Union. She found that there was in fact no Russian "cold war culture". And for the people she met, other questions were much more pertinent than nuclear apocalypse, and centred around perestroika and the dissolution of local worlds. She writes: "That was what people were talking about, and as ethnographers often do, I decided to let my respondents guide me to the heart of their concerns" (1997:7).

So, on one hand we ideally have a funnel in the field, a funnel to be narrowed as time passes. On the other hand the researcher always has to search and accept what he or she gets when an opportunity to participate arises. Funnel and serendipity, and the two are not that well-conformed to each other. What does one do if, at the end of the funnel, one runs across something new and important but for which one has no time to follow up systematically? In my fieldwork I adopted serendipity both as a principle and a strategy for the collection of material. I tried at all times to open up researchable tracks, most of which did not materialise, some were started but then became peripheral, while in others a deeper and better contact arose between me and the people I interacted with.

The funnel model was also used as a principle, but I was far from reaching the end of the funnel upon leaving the field. I had a serendipity material selected very much because there had been an opportunity to get it. In short, I tried to direct myself into social situations of different kinds, and once in a situation I would allow myself to be guided by the talk and doings of the people in combination with vague ideas of the contents of the final text. The funnel had to be narrowed when I was sitting behind my desk, at home. However, narrowing the funnel was not possible without working according to an idea of the contents of the *completed text*.

By applying the funnel model and a concept of serendipity in my own fieldwork one realises that the questions one puts to the material must be developed concurrently with the creation of the material. These are the conditions of explorative fieldwork and they place certain requirements on the general method. One of these is that the theoretical entrances (and exits) must be kept *open* during the course of the work – otherwise going to other places to experience other realities would lose its rationale. A scientific work method based on this openness is called abduction. Abduction is a way of doing research; it is a method of scientific work that "features the development of *new* theoretical propositions to account for material that the old propositions didn't map onto" (Agar 1996:35, *original emphasis*).

However, as was noted above, one does not start fieldwork without theory, and using theory as a reflective tool is inherent to the abductive way of working. Since theory is used as a reflective tool, one needs to have a critical relation to it. Abduction, Alvesson & Sköldberg (1994:47) argues, is to swing between a critical attitude to theory based upon one's own empirical observations at one end of the pendulum, and, at the other end, to interpret the empirical observations by a successively more precisely formulated theory (see also Agar 1996, Herbert 2000:552, Holt-Jensen 1999:67).

I myself could not start putting the material together into a whole without working according to some kind of a model. This model was completed after I had looked through the material at home and thus the abductive process was not finished with the fieldwork. The model, in the form of a drawing, is used to cut the material and bring forward the interesting aspects (i.e. interesting in relation to the model). In short the work proceeded as follows: I put questions to the material that were answerable in relation to the model. The model, which is rather general in its pure form, is adjusted and corroborated in relation to the answers, i.e. when filled in with "empirical" material the model is rearranged and recreated according to the local and time-specific circumstances valid when I was in the field. This generated theoretical propositions, such as the concept of serious enthusiasm, and to me this means working abductively, in a hermeneutic sense. Also, in this sense one keeps narrowing the funnel as one writes. Finishing the text becomes the end of the funnel and the process is based on ever narrower questions that, in the end, will make the text consist of the comprehensive results of a multitude of choices; choices made while writing, while the text is created. In a sense, this is the site where the production of knowledge actually happens. In other words, the final production of the text is the site of the creation of knowledge, as well as the end of the abductive process.

3.10 Conclusions

In geography, the issues of fieldwork and participant observation have not constituted a pertinent part in problemising the construction of knowledge, and literature on the subject has emerged only recently. Brought to a head, it may be said that the black box of geographic fieldwork is being opened up.

The main argument is simple enough: we have to control the interpretation of empirical material according to theory in order to be able to come up with new (geographically legitimate) knowledge – specific, as well as generalised – and in doing this we should reflect not only on who we are (what "position" we have), but first and foremost on who we are perceived to be by the respondents, i.e. what kind of "perceived position" we possess in the minds of the subjects of research. No information is given to the researcher without the respondent implicitly or explicitly reflecting on who the researcher is. It should also be mentioned that the interpretative capacity developed during fieldwork (the becoming of the researcher as an "insider"), and the use of theory, are crucial in avoiding moralistic accounts. Nothing is self-evident about "empirical field material" and it should thus be problemized and discussed, not only so the reader will be able to gauge the rigour of research, but also to integrate theory and method with regards to the hermeneutic aspects of the field researcher as a person. The following "empirical" chapters would not have been possible to write without the local knowledge and interpretative capacity gained during fieldwork.

In problemising fieldwork in this way, it may be concluded that the most important material one brings home from the field are not the notes, tapes and other "evidence", but an understanding, interpretative capacity or cultural competence, that makes it possible to interpret the material as an insider, from "within". Along with the procedures of abductive research, when this interpretative capacity is engaged in accordance with theory, it is possible to speak of controlled interpretation that draws upon logical inference for understanding and generalising the field material. One aspect of this approach is that theory may be generated while seeking to understand and make sense of the material.

Theoretically informed fieldwork in the form of participant observation may thus be used to understand how micro and macro factors co-exist over time in a given space and, with regards to the general purpose of this research, it is concluded that the method well suits and may be used to support the model with contextual and scale-sensitive empirical material. Using participant observation is, I argue, with regard to the fine-grained analyses it makes possible, one way to study the expressions of embodiment in people and emplacement in space of forces emanating from centres of power that exist at various scale levels, ranging from the level of the individual to the state and sometimes even further to the global level. As I have shown in the model in Chapter 1, this is theoretically imaginable, and through participant observations one is able to gain the empirical support for such a contextual and scale-sensitive model of place, space and everyday life.

4. A Soviet type high-rise housing district

Sankt-Peterburg, one of the largest cities in Europe, is world renowned for its splendid architecture, its canals and embankments, its grand palaces, museums, theatres and other cultural institutions. In the summers tourists flock to these, and for the inhabitants they are a source of identity and pride that they meet on an everyday basis. Their general value is hardly a contested issue and the whole of the historical centre of the city has received world heritage status from UNESCO. Not surprisingly, it is mainly the centre which is treated in the rather large and, as Elena Hellberg-Hirn (2003) points out, often elitist literature on Sankt-Peterburg. The fame and interest that the centre receives from visitors, scholars, and from the Sankt-Peterburgians themselves, contrast sharply with the lack of attention paid to everyday life and landscapes in the surrounding high-rise housing districts where the majority of the Sankt-Peterburgians live. One of these districts is Ligovo.

4.1 Ligovo – a background

Ligovo, or Uritsk, which is the Soviet name, is a typical example of Soviet spatial thought and practice regarding city planning from the years around 1970. At that time Ligovo/Uritsk was transformed from a small suburban town (*prigorod*) with low-rise and mainly wooden houses, into a high-rise housing district, which today is home to 54,000 people. It is located about 15 kilometres from the centre of Sankt-Peterburg along the road to Petrodvorets and Petergof, the famous summer residence of tsar Peter the Great. To the north Ligovo borders a large park, named after Lenin, that stretches towards the Gulf of Finland, and Iugo-Zapad, a high-rise area built in the 1980s. In the south the district border follows the Baltic railway. South of the railway is an area of private and rather small wooden houses, and areas of garages for private cars. Beyond these the sovkhoz farmland stretches out across the flat fields of the Baltic plain. To the west and east of Ligovo, similar high-rise housing districts form the wing of a continuous built-up urban landscape that reach in towards the Stalinist suburbs close to the centre, and outwards to the limit of the city (see Figure 4.1).

This stretch of continuous built-up urban land has been called the "southern wing of the city's seaside façade" (Lisovskii 1983:104, *my translation*). This wing, and other developments near the Gulf of Finland to the north of the centre of Sankt-Peterburg, and on Vasil'evskii Ostrov, was a way for Soviet planners to conceive of the city's early history and Peter the Great's original intentions of an "exit to the sea", i.e. the establishment of a coastal city (Shaw 1978:189).

The name Ligovo is mentioned in writing for the first time in 1500, but the area had been inhabited for a long time before that. In the 1850s Ligovo, then a village, was relocated to its present position, and it assumed the borders that is retains to this day. In the latter half of the 19th century Ligovo was conceived of as a rather wealthy summer resort (*dachnyi poselok*). In 1918 Ligovo was renamed Uritsk after the revolutionary leader Moisei Solomonovich Uritskii, who died in that year. In 1925 Uritsk received the status of a town (*gorod*) (Rozhkov 1997).

Although renamed at the beginning of the Soviet period, the historical name was retained both as the name of the train station and of the geomorphologic terrace in the north of the district. Moreover, when the local library opened in around 1980, it was named Ligovo on the initiative of the librarian. In addition to this, one of the district's Soviet shopping centres, built around the same time, uses the historical name. Today, if you ask for the place, both Ligovo and Uritsk may be used, and on maps from the 1990s one might find either one of them, although the latter is the official name. Uritsk is used in the name of the Municipal Circuit of local self-government. However, as most people in the district used Ligovo in popular parlance to refer to the place in a general way, I will also do so throughout the text.

MEETING PLACES 111

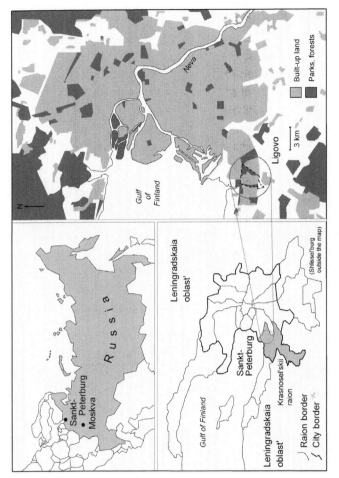

Figure 4.1 Map of Ligovo and Krasnosel'skii raion in Sankt-Peterburg

During the Great Patriotic War (1941–1945), the front of the siege of Leningrad went right through the eastern part of Ligovo. The small town was destroyed when the German Army advanced, and then again as they were forced back. After the war, the remains of the rather wealthy type of two-storey wooden buildings (Figure 4.2) that had been located along the main streets of the small town were replaced with simpler wooden structures and a smaller number of low brick buildings (Aminov 1988, 1990).

Figure 4.2   Historical Ligovo, wooden houses at Nikolaevskaia Street (Rozhkov 1997:120)

In 1963 Uritsk was administratively annexed to the city of Leningrad, and in 1973 it was incorporated within the newly created Krasnosel'skii raion (Riazantsev 1987, *Sankt-Peterburg, Petrograd, Leningrad* 1992). Hereby the city of Leningrad grew and room was made available for developments designed to solve the large housing deficit that had plagued Russian and Soviet cities since the beginning of industrialisation and urbanisation. Krasnosel'skii is the largest (in area) of Sankt-Peterburg's administrative districts (*raiony*), and it contains, apart from the high-rise housing areas in direct connection to the city, also a few detached towns and villages. Agricultural land, smaller woods, a few industrial areas, large areas of garages for private cars, and dacha-areas separate these from the built-up cityscape of Sankt-Peterburg. According to the official statistics in *Raiony Sankt-Peterburga* –98, & –99 (1999, 2000), Krasnosel'skii had a population of slightly more than 300,000 at the end of 1999. In Sankt-Peterburg at large, the official population figure was 4.7 million. In both the city and the raion at large, the official population figure decreased during the 1990s.

Along with the other high-rise housing districts on the outskirts of Sankt-Peterburg, Ligovo is colloquially conceptualised as *"spal'nyi"*. *Spal'nyi* is an adjective derived from the verb *spat'*, which means to sleep. The term signifies, (stereo-)typically, a place from which people commute to work and return home to sleep. But *spal'nyi* also connotes a certain type of district; the typical houses – machines for living – have nothing but right angles, all look the same, there are no colours and there is nothing to do. This, at least, is one of the stereo-typed popular pictures that is locked in the term *spal'nyi*. Another is that these areas are *"zelenye"* (green), with possibilities for recreation, clean air and good health. In popular thinking, Ligovo conforms well to both of these images. These kinds of areas are also recognised colloquially as *"novye raiony"* (new districts), which is a general, although somewhat fuzzy, term for housing districts built from about the 1960s and onwards. A more official term for these areas is *"raiony novostroek"* (newly built districts). Ligovo, built around 1970, is now in its thirties and is established as one of many similar housing areas in Sankt-Peterburg.

In most of these areas, the historical places were more or less totally restructured when the *novye raiony* were being built. Churches and graveyards were no exceptions, and neither were the street names and other things that might have been saved to remind one of the local history. The Soviet authorities, however, had no interest in doing so and in Ligovo the only houses to be saved when the area was developed as a modernistic high-rise housing district was a hospital and a small district of brick buildings that had been constructed after the war. Apart from these buildings, some of the major lines of transportation, a few historical names and part of the street pattern, are about all that remain from the time before the area was developed. Along the small rivers that flank the district a few old apple trees still stand, and in Polezhaevskii Park there are craters of WW2-shells, as well as some other historical relics. Otherwise, the history of the district is expressed in monuments, most of which relate to the Great Patriotic War 1941–1945.

4.2 (War) history inscribed in public space

The Great Patriotic War was generally considered not only as the victory of one country over another, but also and maybe more so, as a victory for the socialist system. As the war had concerned all Soviet citizens, as had the revolution, their symbolic power was used by the central authorities as a uniting historical factor in forming a supposedly Soviet identity. The monuments and names are part of this and they are thus not only memorials to the horrifying human losses of the war, or of the revolution, but also the Soviet authorities ideological stamp on urban space. (Figure 4.3 & 4.4.)

Figure 4.3   A war monument to Alexander V. German, who has given his name to one of the main streets of Ligovo. (Photo: Thomas Borén)

Figure 4.4 A war monument to mark the front (2000).
(Photo: Thomas Borén)

Taken together, the names and monuments, as well as works of art and other public signs that have been placed in the districts, form a certain cultural landscape that is talkative of what it meant to be a Soviet citizen in Leningrad. At the very least, this landscape is talkative of what the Soviet authorities wanted Soviet identity to look like. A special position in Leningrad's war history is given to the blockade (1941–1944), and a large number of monuments are accordingly dedicated to this.

One of the more important of these is the "Zelenyi Poias Slavy" (Green Belt of Honour), a part of which also runs through Ligovo. The whole belt stretches for 200 kilometres along the defence-line of the Leningrad blockade, and consists of an uninterrupted line of forest parks and woods in which almost 60 monuments have also been placed (Bylinkina & Riabushina 1985:156). In the Ligovo part of the green belt, one finds Berezovaia Alleia Slavy (The Birch Alley of Honour). This is a birch alley esplanade that runs through Polezhaevskii Park along the same line as the front did during the siege of Leningrad. Moreover, the alley's 900 birch trees correspond with the total number of days the city was under siege (Figure 4.5).

Figure 4.5   Berezovaia Alleia Slavy in Ligovo (1999). (Photo: Thomas Borén)

In addition to the monuments, the name of one of the most central buildings – the cinema "Rubezh" ([defence] line, or front) – also relates back to Ligovo's war history, as do the names of all the major streets. The naming of various objects lends them a sense of what they have been named after, and explicitly situates them within a certain historical context. Prospekt Veteranov (Veteran's Avenue), named in honour of those who took part in the war, is just one example.

Other street names that relate to the Great Patriotic War are: Ulitsa Partizana Germana (Partisan German's Street), Avangardnaia Ulitsa (The Street of the Vanguard), Ulitsa Dobrovol'tsev (Street of the Volunteers), Ulitsa Otvazhnikh (Street of the Courageous), and Prospekt Narodnogo Opolcheniia (Avenue of the Home Guard). Some of the names relate to the war only in a general way, whereas some do have local historical significance attached to them. The front passed close to Ulitsa Avangardnaia, and at the beginning of the war the home guard was active in defending the area close to the railway, along which the Prospekt Narodnogo Opolcheniia now runs (Gorbachevich & Khablo 1998).

4.3 Thinking big – planning big

When the Soviet authorities were planning cities they thought big – Soviet style big – and the subsequent urban landscape must be seen as a result of the political priorities of the time. This not only concerned the scale and numbers of monuments and so forth, but also the Soviet solution to housing and city-building. One particular feature of the Soviet city was that market forces were not free to balance supply and demand. The solutions to the urban questions, such as housing, were very dependent on political decisions concerning how resources within the planned economy should be allocated, i.e. what priorities should be made. In general terms, the political and economical processes under these conditions resulted in a specific type of urban landscape – in "landscapes of priority" (Sjöberg 1999). The conceptualisation of these landscapes covers the specific geography of city building in socialist countries on a *national* and inter-urban level. The concept is not originally intended for the urban landscape of individual cities, but seems to also apply to the building of districts and a city's inner structure, as these too were the result, within the urbanised frame of the planned economy, of political decisions and intentions of what should constitute a Soviet city and a Soviet way of life (Borén 2003b, Gentile 2003, 2004a).

Generally speaking, the urban landscape of priorities resulted in the large forms and the monumental scale of high-rise housing districts like Ligovo. Speaking in more practically oriented terms, the development was directed by the Leningrad general plan of 1966, which had the legal status of a law (Shaw 1978, Lisovskii 1983). Concerning the physical landscape, the contemporary planning norms were organised around certain concepts. One of the most central of these during the final years of the 1960s and at the beginning of the 1970s was the *mikro-raion* (micro-district, or microraion). Depending on the size of the city, the *mikro-raion* was built for between 6,000 and 15,000 people and they were centred on municipal and commercial services of various kinds (Bater 1980, 1996, Shaw 1978, Lisovskii 1983).[35] Within the *mikro-raion* are "living complexes", or "super blocks", i.e. a group of apartment blocks placed within a radius of 50–100 meters and designed to house 1,000 to 1,500 people. Between the houses there would be a yard, often with a football ground, a green space or some other facility in the middle. In direct connection to the blocks of flats there would be schools and day-care centres. Above the *mikro-raion* in the hierarchy of planning concepts was the *zhiloi raion* (residential district). This would contain several *mikro-raiony* and could have a population of 25,000 to 80,000 inhabitants. At the centre of the *zhiloi raion* further specialised service would be located, e.g. a cinema and specialised shops. One of the founding principles of Soviet planning at this time was that everything that was needed in everyday life (schools, day-care centres, shops etc.) as well as green spaces and medical facilities should be easily accessible and within a short walking distance of one's home. Only in exceptional cases would journeys to the city centre be needed. The original idea with the *mikro-raion* was that there should also be industries and workplaces in the close vicinity and the Soviet authorities hereby tried to decrease the time and distances involved in commuting to and from work.

This general description fits Ligovo well. As part of an urban landscape of political priorities, each of the *mikro-raiony* in the district have schools, day-care centres, clinics, and play- and sports grounds situated in the yards between the mainly five- and nine-storey houses (Figure 4.6, see also Figure 6.3).

---

35 The general descriptions of the *mikro-raion* as a planning concept differs slightly (e.g. concerning numbers) among different researchers. For a review of Soviet urban planning practices, see Borén 2003b.

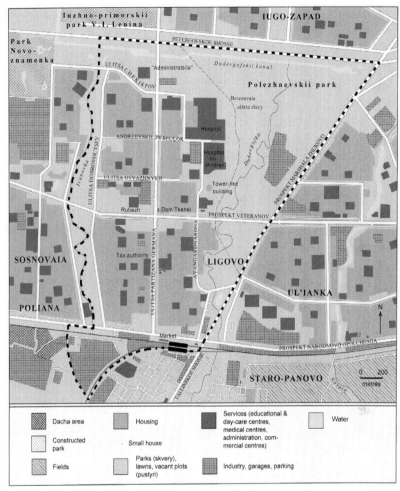

Figure 4.6   Map of Ligovo (based on *Sankt Peterburg atlas goroda*, 2002:64–65)

There are green areas and commercial centres within easy reach of all of the inhabitants as well as good access to public means of transportation. There are no large factories nearby, but within the *zhiloi raion* there are two hospitals (one of them for children), a medical college, a health committee, an ambulance station, a fire brigade, a heating station, a department of the tax authorities, and the police department of Krasnosel'skii raion, as well as the administration of Krasnosel'skii raion.

The eastern part of Ligovo comprises Polezhaevskii Park, in which the vegetation in large parts is more or less wild (Figure 4.7). Through the park runs the small river called Dudergofka, along the course of which are a couple of spontaneous bathing-places. At the northern end of the park the river is channelled into the Dudergofskii Canal, which leads the water away. At the western end one finds the line of the former front, demarcated in the landscape by the above mentioned Berezovaia Alleia Slavy. Apart from the planned foot-paths, the park is criss-crossed by beaten tracks, and dotted with spontaneous barbecue-places. During the summer months one can see a number of plumes of smoke rising up from the park towards the sky. Inside the park there is also something that looks like a small industrial area where companies engaged in park and garden maintenance are located. According to Daud Aminov (1988, 1990), there are plans to landscape the park with ponds, fountains, monuments and other facilities.

Figure 4.7   Polezhaevskii Park (2000). (Photo: Thomas Borén)

Some of the buildings add architectonic variation to the district. Of particular note among these is the "Rubezh" cinema (Figure 4.8). Although close copies of this building are to be found in other parts of Sankt-Peterburg, people talked of this as an important landmark of the district. Rather close to "Rubezh" is a high, round tower-like building with flats. Visible from afar, this building really is a physical landmark, but it was seldom talked about in this way. Another distinctive building, although neither the building nor its landmark-qualities were talked about as much as the cinema, is the "Administration". This building formerly housed both the local branch of the communist party (*raikom KPSS*) and the Executive Committee of the district soviet (*raiispolkom*). Nowadays it houses the post-Soviet administration of Krasnosel'skii raion, and is in popular parlance simply called the *Administratsiia* (administration), denoting both the local government and the building itself (Figure 4.9).[36] The building, and the steps leading up to it from the Dudergofskii canal, is terrace-shaped and is thus aligned in form with the geomorphologic terrace found here (Lisovskii 1983:112–113). The terrace is called the Ligovo terrace, and it can also be mentioned that apart from the rise in the ground level here, and the gullies of the small rivers that flank the district, the relief of the area is totally flat. One of the hospitals was built shortly after the Second World War and thus differs in style from the rest of the district, as do the small district of brick houses. The former is situated at the northern end of Ligovo, and the latter at the southern end.

The *mikro-raiony* are separated by two main thoroughfares; the 90 metre wide Prospekt Veteranov and the equally broad Ulitsa Partizana Germana. And the point at which they intersect is the very centre of Ligovo. The Rubezh cinema is situated here and on the other side of the Ulitsa Partizana Germana one finds Dom Tkanei, a ten-storey apartment house with a shopping centre on the ground floor. The shops are rather specialised with products such as textile fabrics, clothes, cameras, watches etc. The fire brigade is also situated close to the central crossing, as are two of the war monuments and a little further along one find the round tower-like building. All of this is situated on the northern side of Prospekt Veteranov.

---

36 The local government of Krasnosel'skii raion should not be confused with the local *self*-government of Ligovo, see Chapter 7.

On the southern side, however, no city-centre functions are to be found. Up till 2003, there was only a *pustyr'*.

Figure 4.8 The "Rubezh" cinema (1999). (Photo: Thomas Borén)

Figure 4.9 The building of the administration of Krasnosel'skii raion (2000). (Photo: Thomas Borén)

4.4 The *pustyr'*, and the houses

The *pustyr'* is to be found in several parts of Ligovo and it is also a fairly common phenomenon in other parts of Sankt-Peterburg as well. The plural form is *pustyria* and literally the word means vacant plots. Generally speaking, the *pustyr'* has resulted from a lack of co-ordination in time between planning practices and building practices, and the outcome of this is that within an otherwise densely built-up area certain premises are not yet developed. On these plots the land is not carefully maintained, and bushes and high-grass grow more or less unchecked while the plots wait to be developed according to the intentions in the plans.

In the case of the centrally located but undeveloped *pustyr'* across the street from the cinema and Dom Tkanei, the idea is that it should be developed with extra-ordinary and individually designed buildings, with the intention of giving this part of Prospekt Veteranov "a monumental scale and the necessary representativity" (Lisovskii 1983:113, *my translation*). A general effect of this planning practice, which pertains also for other parts of the city, is that ordinary housing districts acquire magnificent frontages, or façades, facing on to the main streets. For those passing-by on the main avenues and thorough-fares, the area will look more attractive and often also newer than the houses hidden behind these façades would otherwise have allowed. This effect is clearly visible when driving around in the city, although in Ligovo it has until recently only concerned one side of the main street, as Dom Tkanei was built as one of these façade houses in the end of the 1970s. The duration of time between planning and actual development may however be very long. The actual building of the houses on the *pustyr'* on the south side of Prospekt Veteranov, one of the most central sites in Ligovo, only started in 2003. Other *pustyria* (pl.) in Ligovo will have to wait even longer. One of them is situated near the train station, and this site is reserved, it would seem,[37] for a subway station that is to be built when the subway lines are extended to the outermost districts of Sankt-Peterburg.

---

37 According to the general plans, the subway station will be built in connection to the train station (Komarov 1988:4), but I have not seen any detailed planning solutions.

So, some of the houses in Ligovo and in other similar suburbs are given individual architectonic form, or are lavishly fitted out in some way or other. The bulk of the houses, however, are not. The "ordinary" buildings, placed inside the *mikro-raiony*, were constructed in large numbers according to standard series, and variation among the series is not their most distinguishing feature. Ligovo represents well the mainstream architectonic forms for the years around 1970, when straight lines and right angles dominated the picture. See Figure 4.10.

In addition to the characteristics of the architectonic ideals, the living practices of people have, with time, added to both the appearance and the function of the houses. On the façades, outside the kitchen windows, quite a number of residents have attached boxes. These function as refrigerators or freezers during the cold months of the year. (See Figure 4.11.) The balconies, many of which are glassed-in and from which some residents have hung flower-boxes, often function as storeage areas or as places for drying washing. Some people have put up satellite dishes on the façades.

Figure 4.10 View of Ligovo from a 14-storey house, the Gulf of Finland in the background (2000). (Photo: Thomas Borén)

MEETING PLACES 125

Figure 4.11 Façade with "freezers", glassed-in balconies, flower-boxes, antennas and satellite dishes (2000). (Photo: Thomas Borén)

Other details of the houses are not the result of individual practices but of neighbour collaboration. In some stairwells and houses, the neighbours have united to install front-doors of iron (fitted with code systems) at the entrances, and in some houses, where technically possible, iron doors have been fitted on single floors between the stairwell and the common corridor to the individual apartments. Apart from initiatives like these, there are only sporadic signs of a communal sensibility concerning the houses. One of these occurred in direct connection to the bombing of apartment blocks in Moscow in 1999, when the neighbours gathered for a couple of meetings in the yard to try to arrange a schedule for guarding the building. The organisation failed, but shortly hereafter, and as a result of political initiative, all of the houses had locks fitted to every door leading to spaces that had earlier been open (these locks and doors had long been broken), such as the roof, the basement, the garbage room, and other such areas. One collaborative initiative among neighbours that did work in the house where I lived, however, was the installation of cable-TV. Some neighbours joined together and collected money for the installation and now all residents can watch these channels, even those who did not pay.

Individual efforts and neighbour collaboration aside, what is clearly neglected is the maintenance of the buildings. The façades, the front-doors and the stairwells are deteriorating. The glass in the front-doors and in the stairwells is often broken and, in some cases, these have been replaced with pieces of wood. In the stairs, almost all of the banisters are damaged, and many of the wooden post-boxes, which hang together on a wall in the stairwell on the bottom-floor, are in a similarly sorry state. The paint on the walls is flaking and worn and has often been scribbled upon, and the façades are worn and sometimes cracked. Notwithstanding these problems, in general the houses "work" and people can live in them without any major problems. If the lift is broken it will usually be repaired within a day, the garbage is collected and the stairs are swept regularly, the heating functions and there is hot and cold water in the taps. The standard inside the apartments is fairly high with large windows, parquet floors, bathtubs, gas-ovens, refrigerators, and balconies. Washing machines and freezers are not standard, but are nonetheless fairly common. The larger flats, which have windows on both sides of the building, often have balconies on both sides.

4.5 The greenery, the benches and other spatial details

One of the first impressions of districts like Ligovo concerns the yards and the special character of the greenery. When high-rise districts of this kind were developed, the plans included services, transport and other facilities, but as these had lower priority than the actual construction of living quarters, they were not completed at the same time as the construction of the buildings. People, however, started to move into the apartments as soon as the houses had been built, and they therefore found the area essentially devoid of any such infrastructure. Except for the houses, the infrastructure (services, transports etc.) and other facilities were not yet ready, as was also the case with the greenery. Nevertheless, people took things into their own hands and did what they could to solve the problems, and greening the yards were among the easier for them to solve. People acted independently and planted what they liked where they liked. The result of these practices is still clearly visible as the yards and spaces around the houses lend themselves to be described as growing wild. In Figure 4.12, an overview is given, and in Figure 4.13 an example shows how this looks in extreme cases. To some extent, however, the original plans for greening the area were later at least partly fulfilled. Professionals arrived and took away some of what the residents had planted themselves, and replaced this with planned vegetation. However, not everything was taken away and some of the older residents in the district can to this day point at certain trees or brushes and say: "I planted that, and that one was put there by the neighbours on this or that floor."

Figure 4.12 The greenery as a mix of planned and spontaneous plantation, and a football ground. Note the brusches. (2000). (Photo: Thomas Borén)

Figure 4.13 An extreme example of the "wild" character of the greenery in the yards (2000). (Photo: Thomas Borén)

The yards in districts like Ligovo are large and spacious, and as has been mentioned above, they often contain primary and secondary schools, and day-care centres. These are generally situated in two- or three-storey buildings. (See Figure 4.14.) In addition to schools and day-care centres, a few other types of buildings are to be found, such as garages where people with disabilities can park their cars, but otherwise the intention was that the yards should be functionally separated from the lines of transport and points of commercial services. Nevertheless, people drive their cars along the many footpaths into the yards so that they can park as close to their front doors as possible. In general, the paths in the yards are in poor condition and full of potholes.

Almost all the yards contain football grounds, and in some cases basketball courts or other types of sports grounds. Most of these would once have been illuminated with spotlights in the evenings, although I never saw any of these actually working. Most of them were broken and seemed to have been so for a long time. Nevertheless, the football grounds are frequently used, mainly by boys and younger men. In the winter, if the field (or other open areas) is covered in newly fallen snow, it happened that older women used the crystal clean new snow to clean their carpets. Apart from sport grounds the yards contain playgrounds for children.

Figure 4.14 View over a yard, to the left is a school located in-between the houses (2000). (Photo: Thomas Borén)

During my stay in Ligovo the playgrounds were among the few public facilities that were actually attended to in such a way that it made a large difference. When restored the bright colours of the new playground equipment, and the orderly appearance, immediately attracted large numbers of children accompanied by young mothers or older relatives.

Another distinct feature of the district is the benches that are placed just outside the front doors. Here, during daytime, mostly in the warmer periods of the year but also in the winter, mainly elderly women sit and talk, and sometimes also older men. Young mothers accompanied by their children represents another group that uses the benches. In the summer nights, the benches are used by youths of both sexes, sitting calmly talking, smoking cigarettes and often having a few beers. The benches fulfil an important and multifaceted social role as it is on and around them that neighbours meet, talk, and in a sense also supervise the area. If seen as a social institution, it is socially situated among neighbours, and thus in-between the strictly private sphere of friends and close relatives, and the sphere of formalised public relations. Its very site is also in a sense in-between the public and the private as the benches are most often located at the very entrances to the houses. Unfortunately, this social institution was not open to me, and seldom could one see men in my age-group (early 30s) sit on the benches. Actually, where I lived the only man of my age who regularly spent time sitting on the benches was regarded (by Elena Alekseevna) as slightly retarded. I tried sitting on the benches a few times, but always felt extremely uncomfortable and had to leave. Clearly, the bench-institution has its own social rules of access and appropriate behaviour.

Another detail of the yards is the large number of loose dogs, and some cats. The dogs are of all sizes, shapes and colour, and are as familiar a picture in the yards as are the trees, the parked cars or the old ladies sitting on the benches. The dogs may be described as half-tame, and people put out food for them, or toss scraps and left-overs directly out of the kitchen window. If it is cold, it happens that people take the animals home, or let them sleep in the stairwells. In addition to the dogs in the yards, a familiar sight is un-leashed dogs going for walks with their owners. The dogs are often big and fitted with muzzles. As a rule these dogs are well looked after and when the temperature drops to around zero-degrees many of the owners dress them to keep the dogs not only warm but also clean. Some of the dogs are dressed in special dog-coats, but many are dressed in ordinary jumpers, with the forelegs in the sleeves and the head through the collar. One aspect of animal life that is sometimes mentioned in the literature on Sankt-Peterburg, concerns the mosquitoes. In Ligovo, however, these and other insects (with the possible exception of occasional cockroaches), were generally not considered a problem. Otherwise the animals of the district mainly consist of birds. Pidgins and crows are common, there are small birds and one may occasionally see or hear a seagull fly by.

4.6   A *spal'nyi* raion?

So, what else is there to do in Ligovo aside from playing football, sitting on the benches, walking dogs, or the fairly common practice of going for promenades? The area is well supplied with services of various kinds. There is a post office, banks (with black-market exchangers standing right outside the offices), a library, clinics, hair-dressers, shoe-repair shops and the like, public youth clubs (one with a sports centre), computer game centres, a small casino with gambling machines, restaurants, coffee shops, *shaverma*-boots (a kind of fast-food), a night-club, petrol stations, and a large number of stores of various kinds. Some of these are located in special shopping centres built during the Soviet times, others have been established in the 1990s. The latter are smaller and built with iron-sheets and glass, and not with concrete as their Soviet equivalents were (see Figure 4.15). Other shops are to be found in the cellars and in similar spaces of the apartment blocks. At the train station there is a larger market and in yet other places people sell things; either holding a bunch of goods in their hands or in a bucket or box placed directly on the ground, or from a wagon, a car-boot or a kiosk. Additionally, in the immediate proximity of almost every bus-stop there is a kiosk where beer, sodas, cigarettes, sweets and similar goods are sold. In general, all goods needed in everyday life can easily be found and most people seem to do their shopping in the district. As can be seen in Figures 4.16 and 4.17 the market and other places for shopping can be as busy as any city.

Even if the district is called *spal'nyi* it does not give a very sleepy impression; the district is more city than high-rise suburb and there are cars and people on the streets around the clock. During the daytime the traffic is heavy and during rush hours the air at the central junction is filled with thick grey and black exhaust fumes. There are a number of buss-lines along which buses, trolley buses and minibuses shuttle, and there are rail-bound trams and commuter trains, but as yet no subway. After midnight the public transport system is more or less non-existent, but it is always easy to find an informal taxi (*chastnik*). Pulkovo International Airport is nearby and large passenger planes intermittently thunder by, which – if the wind is in the right direction – make the car alarms in the yards go off, creating a loud symphony of toots, hoots and sirens echoing between the houses. Moreover, the night-club is open everyday (until six o'clock in the morning), and there are 24-hour shops and liquor kiosks. The small casino is also open around the clock.

Figure 4.15 A post-Soviet shopping centre, and a Soviet shopping centre in the back to the left (2000). (Photo: Thomas Borén)

Figure 4.16 The market at Ligovo train station (2000). (Photo: Thomas Borén)

Figure 4.17 Small scale traders outside Dom Tkanei (1999). (Photo: Thomas Borén)

Another typical urban phenomenon is the open street prostitution at Prospekt Veteranov. The women stand at the central crossing, men in cars stop, negotiate and drive away. Drugs in various forms are not uncommon. In the house where I lived there was traffic of people to an apartment on the ground floor, where – according to bench gossip that Elena Alekseevna had snatched up – a pusher lived. The grape-vine also reported that in the last year only (1999–2000), three young men (the pusher not included) had been arrested for drug related crimes and that a fourth young man had died from a heroin overdose. All this happened in Elena's apartment block alone. Concerning other criminal activity, my hosts tell me that three times in only a couple of months thieves had tried to steal their handbags. One of these occasions happened in the stairwell when Elena's daughter Tania had acid thrown in her face. Only by sheer luck had her eyes been saved, and the foul burns left no serious scars. On another occasion burglars broke into the apartment, but did not find the valuables. In spite of these examples of the darker side of city life, and more could be related, the district is not a slum. While there are tendencies of it deteriorating into one, and the neglected state of the houses and the yards might be a contributive factor to such an impression, it is not crimes, drugs and prostitution that characterise the district. The character is set by all of those people who are not part of that, but who live "normal" lives.

4.7 Conclusions

From the descriptions of Ligovo presented here, it is possible to elucidate several clear-cut examples of how a place is created as a meeting-place. Two of the more salient are found in the greening of the yards, and in the appearance of the façades. In these, as well as in the other descriptions of Ligovo, people's practices of living one's environment, and the formations created by the planning and building practices of the spatial competence of the Soviet period, mix and together form the urban space. The description of Ligovo, one of many of Sankt-Peterburg's high rise districts, is but one example of what the urban space of areas like these might look like. And, as with any area, it has some place-specific characteristics, such as its history, or special buildings. In many respects however, and as is also discussed in relation to the film *S legkim parom* in chapter three, the general description of Ligovo would in many ways be valid also for other areas dating from the same period. The houses would be similar, and they would be laid out according to similar planning practices. Newer and larger façade-houses would front the main thoroughfares, and there would be *pustyria* where they had not yet been built. The greenery in the yards would be as wild, and there would be benches outside the front doors. Moreover, similar living practices in a similar type of space would give rise to similar types of spatial details. There would be dogs in the yards, boxes outside the windows, cars parked by the front doors, and so on. Apart from the material similarities, the other areas would, like Ligovo, also be popularly conceptualised and understood as *spal'nyi*, *zelenyi* and *novyi* in the general geographical imagination of people in Sankt-Peterburg.

So, the identity of Ligovo is not unique, or even particular when compared with similar housing districts. The war and the heavy exploitation of the district spared very little of historical Ligovo, and thus left little of that kind of material for identity construction. But history is nevertheless present in the district. In the form of names and monuments, Soviet and Leningrad history is put on the very front page of what Ligovo is. Or rather what the ones who gave the names and put up the monuments wanted Ligovo, or Uritsk, to be. In short, they wanted the place and the inhabitants to be part of the Soviet master narrative of the building of communism. The raising of monuments and naming the district, the streets and so forth, was a way for Soviet authorities to inscribe the Soviet master narrative in local space, i.e. the local was used for larger purposes. When the Soviet Union collapsed, this story obviously lost momentum. In the next chapter, I analyse how Ligovo and Sankt-Peterburg at large are being re-thought, and how Ligovo is contextually replaced into another master narrative, as a new total action-space evolves.

5 Symbolic landscapes and Ligovo's genius loci

> So earthly life can be opposed to heavenly life as temporal to eternal, but there is no opposition in the spatial sense. Morover notions of moral value and of locality fuse together: places have a moral significance and morals have a localized significance. Geography becomes a kind of ethics. (Lotman 1990:172)

Cities are full of stories, some rich in detail and with a complete and intriguing plot, as well as with clear connections and tight bonds to the constantly repeated master narratives with which we understand where, when, who and why we are. Sankt-Peterburg has many such stories and the inhabitants, who love their city, are constantly reminded of them and the greatness they tell when they move along the prospects, canals or the embankments of River Neva. These are the stories that are often repeated, inscribed as they are in architecture and monuments, in other texts and in the very heart of being Sankt-Peterburgian. Moreover, these are also the stories that visitors first encounter. It is the Sankt-Peterburg text which ultimately consists of the proud stories of Peter the Great, Catherine the Second, of Pushkin, Gogol and Dostoevskii, of Lenin and the Revolution, and many, many more who (are fixed points of reference for who) made, built and wrote Sankt-Peterburg into the city we know today. One more thing; these are all stories of the centre.

But there are other stories as well, not so great and not so central for what it takes to be Sankt-Peterburgian; stories that are local, stories that have died or simply fallen into oblivion, stories that have been consigned as marginal, stories that are distant in time and space. These could be the stories of Nyen, the Swedish city that preceded Sankt-Peterburg on the riverbanks of Neva. They could be the stories of high-rise suburbs, places outside (written) history or better, without formulated *genius loci* – nonsacred places. These could be the stories of ordinary men and women. Ordinary people whose spatialities nevertheless empower and nourish with actual practice the spatialities of the great stories, of the great maps, of great power and of the great festivities. What are these small stories like in Sankt-Peterburg? Just because we do not usually hear them does not mean they do not exist.

This chapter takes the history of Ligovo as such a story and, besides telling parts of Ligovo's history, analyses the writing of that history as a part of the change of the total action-space in Sankt-Peterburg. I will show that in writing the history of Ligovo, the author whose book I use draws upon codes in what I take to be the master narrative of the new meta-project. Obviously, in Russia something has happened to the total action-space that prevailed during Soviet times. Constant planned-economical progress along modernistic lines of thought and the building of communism no longer constitute a relevant societal meta-project. When this withdrew, something else could emerge and a new master-narrative could start to be written. This was a time when people driven by serious enthusiasm could make themselves heard and begin to formulate the new master narrative and meta-project, thus filling total action-space with new ideals and goals for action. In Sankt-Peterburg the ideas that took this place are related to the city's pre-Revolutionary history.

These ideas, however, would mean very little for Ligovo if it were not for the fact that this new meta-project has started to penetrate into the understanding of what Ligovo is, or should be, and this is the subject of the first part of the chapter. The analyses are based on a post-Soviet book on the history of Ligovo and Krasnosel'skii raion named *Na iugo-zapade Sankt-Peterburga* (In Sankt-Peterburg's South-West), that was first published 1995, and in a revised edition 1997. It is written by the war veteran, *kraeved* (local historian) and director of the local war memorial museum Anatolii Mikhailovich Rozhkov, and is the only post-Soviet book that deals with the history of the area. The time periods he covers in his book concern the Great Patriotic War and the history of Krasnosel'skii raion from the 16th century up to the First World War. Ligovo's history goes back to at least the year 1500, when the name appeared in writing for the first time. However, apart from the name, only shattered remnants are left of the landscape as it was before the Great Patriotic War and the large scale building program of the 1960s and -70s. A few remnants and the stories connected to these. By making use of these stories the book becomes part of the place-making processes; it is an attempt at placial identity politics and an explicit intervention in Ligovo's social life to give its lingering Soviet urban landscape new meaning.

In the second part of the chapter I explicate, in line with the semiotic theory of the Moscow-Tartu school, some of the codes the author uses to create this new meaning. Based on semiotic theory, I argue that it is possible to move from the specific case of Ligovo to a generalised understanding of Sankt-Peterburg, as the study of the Ligovo text reveals codes used in the understanding of Sankt-Peterburg. By using the codes of the new master narrative of Sankt-Peterburg developed in the 1990s, Rozhkov's history receives the force of conviction and thus becomes an important course-relation affecting the lifeworlds of people in Ligovo. In writing Ligovo's history in the medium of serious enthusiasm the author attempts to create a new picture of Ligovo. In doing this he also juxtaposes Ligovo in time and space, and this is the subject of the third part of the chapter. The textual technique of juxtaposing creates a sense of continuity with the past, and with other places in Sankt-Peterburg. In the fourth section, to further support my argument in the chapter at large, I triangulate the results of the textual analysis against other aspects of my fieldwork experiences and other research results.

I started to read Rozhkov's book merely to get a kind of historical background to the place, but immediately reacted to the frank purpose of his book. Such a patriotic disposition would be impossible to declare in most of the books I read, not to mention how a book with a similar attitude would be received if were a book to be used in Swedish schools. But Rozhkov obviously could and the book was positively received, and it is used in the local schools. I understood that here was a difference – a rich point of difference – and it puzzled me. Why could he write like that? What was the difference really about? I mean a book is not just a book but a cultural production produced and received in a certain cultural context. Since the reason for me to be in Russia to a large extent concerned that very cultural context, the book seemed central.

But to find the clues to a cultural contextual understanding of the book, it had to be read and understood not word by word and sentence by sentence as history, but as a myth. Lévi-Strauss (1979:45) suggests that to understand the meaning of a myth, we have to read it in its "totality", as one reads music as bundles of events. I do not know if I read Rozhkov's text as one can read music, but I certainly started to see, or read off its pattern; when going up and down in the text, reading it over and over again, translating parts of it to different languages until the text was fragmented and then reconnected around five categories. In the end I did not read it as a history book, but as a myth which meant to intervene in the world we live in; to solve the paradoxes of the lived experiences, as well as a guide for behaviour, or map if you like. I was hunting for its social causes, its cultural context, or in short, its reason.

Of the five categories I found by doing this, three relate to codes in the spatial artificial language of Sankt-Peterburg, and two to juxtapositions of Ligovo in time and space. These codes and juxtapositions are not just linguistically oriented abstractions of the spatial language, but also relate to post-Soviet life. Actually, it is part of the creation of that life. The book, which is used in the local schools, represents one of very few popularly written – and scientifically sanctioned – accounts of the district, and as such it is one of the most powerful geographical re-presentations of the district. It's metaphors are full of normative power, not only telling history but also shaping the present. However, to do exactly this is the explicit purpose of the book and Rozhkov writes that the book aims to strengthen the "spiritual" bond between the "excellent" past and the establishment of the present everyday existence (*zhit'em-byt'em*).

5.1 Rozhkov's history of Ligovo

The literature on Sankt-Peterburg almost exclusively confines itself to the central parts of the city, or to the nearby towns with beautiful palaces and excellent parks. Very little literature concerns the outskirts of the city. With the exception of Rozhkov's book, this is true also for Ligovo.

In the preface to the book, the author points out that the historical place of south-west Sankt-Peterburg, which is described in beautiful terms, was destroyed in the Great Patriotic War, and a couple of decades later subject to a massive phase of reconstruction that again heavily changed the characteristics of the landscape. He writes, in a tone that I find melancholy, that buildings, place names and traditions have disappeared, that events are forgotten and that the "bond with the past disappears" (1997:4, *my translation*). In connection with this, the photographs and historical maps included in the second edition are given a pertinent role:

> Включенные в книгу фотографии воспроизводят пейзажи, сооружения и события, имевшие место на земле нынешнего Красносельского района Санкт-Петербурга. Знакомство с ними, можно надеяться, будет способствовать укреплению любви к родной земле, а издание этой книги можно считать еще одной попыткой усиления духовной связи между замечательным прошлым и утверждающимся нынешним житьем-бытьем. Она должна способствовать восстановлению уважения к минувшему, воспитанию чувства неразрывной связи с ним. Другими словами, воссоздать то состояние, свойственность которого русскому народу так прекрасно высказана А. С. Пушкиным:
>
> *«Два чувства дивно близки нам*
> *В них обретает сердце пищу:*
> *Любовь к родному пепелищу,*
> *Любовь к отеческим гробам...*
> *На них основано от века*
> *По воле Бога самого,*
> *Самостоянье человека*
> *Залог величия его».* (p.5) [38]

---

[38] In my translation: "The pictures included in the book recall the landscapes, buildings and events that took place on the lands of the present-day Krasnosel'skii raion of Sankt-Peterburg. Familiarity with them, one may hope, will further strengthen the love to the native land, and it is possible to consider the publication of this book as yet another attempt to reinforce the spiritual bonds between the remarkable past, and the present establishment of an everyday way of life. It should promote a renewal of respect for the past, and breed the sense of the in-

This exclamation of purpose includes a range of factors that cultural historians since long have argued are crucial to understand Russia. Pictures are given a central place as intermediaries, and through these – and the text – people of today and their everyday lives are interwoven with space, its history and its (high) culture with a bond founded on love, spirituality, and to some extent, also personal responsibility. In the exclamation man and place are seen as part of an almost absolute totality that stretch from the doings of everyday life via the nation and the poetry of the national bard to the will of God in the Russian cosmology. In the introductory quote to this chapter, Yurii Lotman writes about Russian medieval space in which places on earth were connected to religious values. Places were then connoted either to heaven or to its opposite. In today's secular society the religious aspects are not as central as they used to be, but the logic of place and ethics, as judged by the purpose of the book, still are.

The author, who I came to know well over the course of time, took good care of me. He was very interested in my research and he offered his help in all imaginable ways, sometimes for a consideration and sometimes not. We met regularly during fieldwork and he became a key respondent thanks to his prodigious knowledge of the history of Ligovo. Since 1980 he has collected material on Ligovo and Krasnosel'skii raion, which he keeps in the local war memorial museum. The museum is situated in the former Dom Pionerov, which in the 1990s changed its name to Dom Detskogo i Iunosheskogo Tvorchestva (DDIuT), or House of Children' and Youths' Creative Work. DDIuT is a youth centre where the local youth can learn and practice dance, music, acrobatics, electronics, model building, and

---

dissoluble bonds with it. In other words, to reconstruct that condition, the characteristics of which were so excellently stated to the Russian people by A. S. Pushkin: 'Two feelings amazingly close to us/ In them the heart is fed:/ Love to the native hearth,/ Love to paternal graves.../ From a century on them is based/ On the very will of God,/ The free will of a man/ Is where his greatness is secured'". This is my own translation of the poem, I am not a translator and it does not aspire to be a professional translator's interpretation of Pushkin. Rather, it is Rozhkov's use of Pushkin and the patriotic inclinations of the poem that is interesting. I have looked for, but not found an English translation of the poem, which is published in full under the title *Nabroski* (Drafts) in *Polnoe sobranie sochinenii Pushkina v 6 tomakh* (Berlin, 1921). Rozhkov, who quotes about half the poem, does not refer to the source, and my limited knowledge of Russian poetry was not to any help in finding it. That great knowledge had instead Sanna Witt. Many thanks!

several other leisure time pursuits under the supervision of professional teachers in each respective speciality. The museum, which specialises on Krasnosel'selskii's role in the Great Patriotic War, is visited by school classes, new military recruits and other interested groups and individuals. The museum was created and established here on Rozhkov's initiative in 1985, and shortly after I finished my fieldwork in 2000 he retired as its Director at the age of 75.

Regarding the book, it should be added that Anatolii Mikhailovich Rozhkov is a conscientious author. It is important to him that the factual information is correct and his basic attitude is that the representation of history is rather unproblematic; historical events are facts and the author is not a part of their construction as facts. His text also closely follows the other texts on Ligovo that I have read, mainly those written by Daud Aminov (1988, 1990, 1996), Valentina Lenina (1993), and M. Riazantsev (1987). Anatolii Mikhailovich is as far away from a post-modern text-theoretician as one may be and he would probably not have imagined that his text could be used as source material for this kind of place analysis. I once tried to tell him that this is how I use it, but I don't think I got the message through. It ended with me saying that his text was important for my discussion of Ligovo.

The book is used in schools in the district and consequently its presentation of Ligovo's history is the one that the growing generation learns and brings with them into the future. The book, however, was not intended as school material. Anatolii Mikhailovich relates to me that the reason for him to write the book was that he thought a book about Krasnosel'skii raion was needed since everything else that is published about Sankt-Peterburg deals with the centre. I ask Anatolii if the publisher "Liki Rossii" is a local company in order to find out if it had been commissioned by the local administration, if they had ordered it, or if someone else had been involved in the book's creation. Anatolii replies that the book had been his idea and why he had felt that such a book was needed. When I asked about the publisher, he went to his bookshelves and took down several large volumes to serve as examples of the quality of the publisher. The books concerned various scientific topics and he empressed upon me that Liki Rossii is a large professional publisher with first class publications. Earlier, Anatolii had shown me the pre-print reviews of the manuscript that had been written by two professional historians. These were equally positive and hereby the book is also given scientific sanction. I believe that if one were to ask if Anatolii's book related the "truth", I am sure that the answer would be yes. The author is serious, the publisher is established, and the text has been refereed by external reviewers.

Nevertheless, Anatolii's book is an excellent example of how mindscapes are formed and how a certain historical place consciousness is created. In my analysis, the image of Ligovo – as presented in the book – is examined on the basis of the idea that it adds a non-experience based consciousness among the population, which augments their own experience based perceptions of the place. Almost none of the people living in Ligovo today have their own lived experience of Ligovo as it was prior to the large-scale construction of the time-typical buildings that characterise the area today, and even fewer from the time before the place was destroyed in the war. The book thus fills this void of history with a narrative consisting of stories from different time periods. Taken together the stories form a history created in accordance with the author's purpose with his book. And it is a purpose that has to be understood in terms of its social implications and consequences; as an attempt to come on the social life of today.

Hereby the text becomes a map created for orientation in the post-Soviet landscape of the not-so-taken-for-granted. As any map is a construction of its creator it involves performative and creative aspects, involving choices concerning how to set the available codes at work. It is the creative aspects of map making that cause Denis Cosgrove and Luciana Martins to talk in terms of performative mapping. Performative mapping refers to the ways in which genius loci are "actively made and remade" (2001:170). In the original Roman meaning of the term, genius loci accentuate the sacredness of a place, but in later uses the concept has been taken to denote the special qualities or the "spirit" of a place. The genius loci is often seen as a result of historical processes in which mythical, artistic, ethnic and aesthetic aspects enter and blend with the forces of power, both in the making and the understanding of a place (Loukaki 1997). Performative mapping thus enters these historical processes to shape the genius loci and is thus an active intervention in the world. The places on the map are used to portray not only what they are in terms of history, materiality and so on, but also in terms of what they should be (Cosgrove & Martins 2001). Thus, the making of genius loci is part of the making of a place; to performatively map a place is to find, invoke or create its "spirit", and to map its spirit will contribute to the making and remaking of its genius loci. In other words, performative mapping becomes a kind of placial identity politics concerned with where, when, who and why we are.

The objective in Rozhkov's personal and local version of identity politics is to weave together the spaces of Ligovo's past with those of the present everyday life, and in concentrating on the excellent, the magnificent and the extra-ordinary aspects of the historical cultural geography of Ligovo, Anatolii Mikhailovich gives the population reasons to regard their place as something special, something to be proud of. In short, he gives them genius loci.

Judging from the purpose of the book, this is intentional. What Rozhkov does not make explicit, however, and what he himself is probably unaware of, is that he uses some of the codes in the artificial language of Sankt-Peterburg as text to convey his message. It is an advantage that Rozhkov is not a trained researcher because if he had problemized the history of Ligovo the following analyses would have been more difficult. His descriptions are not part of a larger theoretical problem but can be taken to represent what is important for him to uphold. Since he is the first to write a book on the history of Ligovo, by choosing the stories he did, which emphasise certain aspects of history, he also tells us that these are the aspects that he finds most important. Moreover, the messages he conveys in doing this should, to be meaningful, correspond to categories in the master narrative of Sankt-Peterburg. Hereby it is possible to conclude that the categories of meaning, into which I divide Rozhkov's text, relate to codes of an artificial language of Sankt-Peterburg that underlie communication about space.

As a comment on the method used to identify these codes, the centre does not automatically include the periphery in its story-telling. The centre would, I believe, take the periphery for granted, and it is the periphery that needs to inscribe itself in the stories of which it wishes to be a part. Therefore it might be useful to investigate texts from "marginal" areas, as it is such areas that would need to more forcefully motivate their inclusion in any historical rendition. If Rozhkov endeavours, consciously or not, to identify and relate the history of Ligovo (the periphery) with the history conveyed in the texts on Sankt-Peterburg (the centre), then the strategy would logically be to allow his history of Ligovo to treat similar objects and events as treated in the texts on Sankt-Peterburg. In doing so he will use the codes that are found in the text in the master narrative. In the case of Ligovo, it is also somehow gratifying that there only exists one main text (Rozhkov's book), since in this text it would be necessary to employ the most fundamental codes in the narrative of which it wishes to be a part.

5.2 The artificial spatial language of Sankt-Peterburg as text

The text on which the analyses are based is the section about Ligovo (pages 117–125) in the chapter entitled "From the history of the populated localities" (*Iz istorii naselennykh punktov*) in Rozhkov's book.[39] I have grouped the text into three categories, each of which – I will argue – refers to a code in the artificial spatial language of Sankt-Peterburg as text. Apart from these three categories, the close reading on which the categorisation is based also exposed how Ligovo is spatially and temporally juxtaposed.

It should also be mentioned that the codes I identify here are by no means the only codes that exist in the spatial artificial language of Sankt-Peterburg, and in other parts of Rozhkov's book he draws on other histories concerning what the city is. Most important of these relate to the Second World War and to the siege of Leningrad. Stated concisely, these stories relate to the city of Lenin, as opposed to the city of Peter (Brodsky 1987, Hellberg-Hirn 2003), and are thereby also included in the place-making process. These stories were, however, already used by Ligovo's Soviet place-makers, and were given physical and symbolical expression in the form of monuments and names in Ligovo (see Chapter 4).

---

39 The descriptions of the other five localities in Krasnosel'skii raion (pages 110–150) largely follows the same pattern, as do the rest of the pre-Revolutionary parts of the book. There are a few exceptions regarding Krasnoe Selo, in which fairly large space is also devoted to workers and industry.

So, how does Rozhkov describe Ligovo? The geography as presented in the text may be divided in three categories; 1) location and status, 2) cultural heritage context (persons), and 3) stories of modernisation. These categories are emphasised in the text and in the photographs while other aspects of Ligovo's evolution are suppressed. A further note on the categories is that they are "fuzzy", i.e. they are interwoven in each other, and in one and the same paragraph several of the categories may be represented, sometimes overlapping in the same sentence, sometimes in different sentences.

5.3   Location and status

The first category concerns geographic rudiments, such as where the area is located and what status in the order of places it has historically had. The larger part of this is concerned with the early history, and the fact that the place was given the status of a town (*gorod*) in 1925 is quickly passed over. The time of this change is, however, outside the time-period that Rozhkov concentrates on.

The historical village of Ligovo is placed in the regional context by Rozhkov. It was situated "in the 13th verst" from Sankt-Peterburg along the Narva Road. At the end of the 19th century, the village consisted of 38 peasant houses (*krest'ianskikh domov*) which, during the warmer months of the year, were let to summer guests. To these should be added the 116 dachas that could also be found in the vicinity of the village. "In general", Rozhkov writes, "the settlement created a fairly pleasing impression: to the east were the pine woods of P.G. Kurikov and Il'ina, to the south – fields and Kurikov's park, to the west – ploughlands, the small river Ligovka and meadows, and to the north the hay-fields stretched almost to the Gulf of Finland." (p.125, *my translation*)

The description is – aside from the clearly normative "pleasing impression" – a naturalistic and rather "objective" geographic account of an historical place, but in the following it is more manifest that Rozhkov's selection of material is interesting from the point of view of place-making. The following quote, which Rozhkov has chosen from a contemporary account of Ligovo by A.P. Verlander from 1883, shows the relative (wished-for) location:

> Лигово, конечно, не столица, но его трудно признать и деревнею: оно так близко от Петербурга и так хорошо соединено с ним, сто это, скорее, форштадт столицы, а не село в обыкновенном смысле этого слова. Отсюда такое заключение: с одной стороны, Лигово не может удовлетворить ни истинного поклонника всероссийской столицы, ни завзятого любителя деревянного захолустья; с другой же – Лигово как пункт оседлости может сделаться прекрасным источником дешевого и здорового комфорта. Под Лондоном, Веною, Парижем, Берлином – Лигово давно обратилось бы в самую цветущую колонию небогатых чиновников и многочисленных служащих. Ведь места заманчивые, и уже столько дач! (p.122, 125)[40]

Hereby Ligovo and Sankt-Peterburg are placed on the same map of Europe as the largest, most beautiful and significant capitals of the continent. Ligovo, Sankt-Peterburg and Russia are being written into Europe and into the status that follows from this placement. This category relates to a code in the artificial language that treats Sankt-Peterburg as a European city, and it is in the light of this that the remaining topography of Ligovo, as described by Rozhkov, should be understood. That the description of Ligovo can be related to the code "Sankt-Peterburg as a European city" is more palpable when put in relation to the category concerned with the stories of modernisation. It should also be noted that one of the larger intellectual discussions in Russia during the 19th century was formed around the European question. Two camps evolved, the slavophiles and the zapadniks whereupon the description of Ligovo's location may also be seen as taking

---

40 In my translation: "Ligovo, of course, is not the capital, but it is also difficult to recognise it as the country: it is so close to Petersburg and so well joined with it that this, rather, is a forshtadt of the capital and not a village in the usual meaning of this word. Thus, the conclusion from this is that, on the one hand, Ligovo may neither satisfy a true admirer of the all-Russian capital, nor an inveterate lover of a dull out-of-the-way place. On the other hand, Ligovo as a residential place may become a first-rate source of cheap and sound comfort. Ligovo would, in the environs of London, Vienna, Paris and Berlin, long ago have turned into the most prosperous colony of numerous office workers and functionaries of modest means. The places are very tempting, and already so many dachas!"

a stand for the west-oriented zapadniks, both by Verlander, and by Rozhkov.[41]

5.4 Cultural heritage context (persons) – the Heroes

Another salient feature of Rozhkov's text is that prominent persons in the history of Ligovo are emphasised. For the most significant of these, any connection to the place is sufficient enough reason to include them in the account. One example of this is that the house where Anna Pavlova lived as a child is portrayed in one of the photographs. Anna Pavlova (1881–1931) was a well-known ballerina. One person that had a tremendous influence on the development of Ligovo is Peter I (1672–1725), who moved the capital of Russia close to it. Ligovo came to be positioned between the city and Peter I's summer residence Petergof, and in 1710 he decided to develop the coast-line between the city and his summer residence. The coast was divided into plots that were distributed to people who had been taken into his confidence. They were obliged to preserve the wooded areas and to build "seaside estates" (*primorskie dvory*). Peter I spent time in the close vicinity of Ligovo and in January 1716 he ordered that a dam should be built whereupon an artificial lake was created. This pool, which was referred to as a lake, existed up until the Second World War when it was destroyed by the Nazi-forces during the blockade of Leningrad. Traces and remains of the dam and the earlier shores are still evident in Ligovo today. It can also be mentioned that three of the eight photographs in Rozhkov's account include the lake in one way or another. He also mentions that during the early 18th century, court servants (*dvortsovye sluzhashchie*) settled in Ligovo.

A further sovereign, Catherine II (1729–1796), is mentioned in the text and it is related how in 1765 she gave extensive estates (*pomest'ia*) to her favourite earl G.G. Orlov (1734–1783) as a gesture of gratitude for his par-

---

[41] For extensive accounts of Russia's relation to the rest of Europe, see Bodin 1993, Neumann 1996. For an artistic account of these questions see also *Russian Arc*, a film directed by Alexander Sukarov (2002). The film shows that these questions are as pertinent today as ever.

ticipation in her palace revolution. Ligovo was included in these estates, and it thereby became private property. In the same year, the Free Economic Society (*Vol'noe ekonomicheskoe obshchestvo*) was founded and Orlov and his summer residence neighbours A.V. Oluf'ev and R.I. Vorontsov were part of its management.[42] A Councillor of State (*statskii sovetnik*),[43] C.V. Drukovnov, is also named as one of Orlov's collaborators in his and the society's work to develop Russian agriculture. Moreover, Orlov's palace is pictured in one of the photographs where it is situated in a park close to the banks of the Ligovo Lake. The park is said to have been created by Giacomo Quarenghi, a well-known architect working in Sankt-Peterburg at the time.[44] The park, Rozhkov writes, is typical of the other 18th century parks located along the road to Petergof, which had been constructed during the reign of Catherine II.

Following Orlov's death an illegitimate daughter, who Rozhkov names only by her christian name of Natal'ia, inherited the estate. She subsequently married earl F.F. Buksgevden, and they owned the manor from 1783 until 1811 when their son, P.F. Buksgevden, took over. In 1840 Buksgevden sold the Ligovo estate (*myza*) to earl G.G. Kushelev. Kushelev employed the Englishman MacLatling, and together they continued Orlov's work of developing agricultural methods, techniques etc. At the beginning of the 1860s, following Kushelev's death, his widow E.D. Kushelev became insolvent and the estate deteriorated and was sold to "some" (*kakoi-to*) merchant. This is the first of two instances where Ligovo is connected to something negative in Rozhkov's text. In total, the number of "negative" sentences in his text amounts to four, of which three concern this case.

Among the final owners of Ligovo; the merchant of the 1st guild P.G. Kurikov, the technological engineer K.M. Polezhaev and his son B.K. Polezhaev, K.M Polezhaev is given most space in Rozhkov's account. K.M.

---

42   The Free Economic Society was designed specifically to help improve agriculture (Hooson 1968:253).
43   *Statskii sovetnik* was a title of rank in tsarist Russian civil service.
44   Giacomo Quarenghi (1744–1817) was an Italian architect and an advocate of classicism, who worked in Russia from 1780. He constructed a number of well known buildings in Sankt-Peterburg and its environs (BES 1998:515). Quarenghi was one of Catherine II's favourite architects.

Polezhaev was Chairman of the Board of Directors of S.-Peterburgsko-Moskovskii kommercheskii bank (Commercial Bank of S.-Peterburg-Moscow), and Polezhaevskii Park was named after him sometime around 1900. The park is mentioned as having earlier been called Ligovskii Park, or with the name of its owner. It should be mentioned that none of the last three owners of the Ligovo estate owned the village of Ligovo-Novoe mesto (for the history of the name, see below) as peasant serfs – "souls" – could redeem their land from the middle of the 1860s.[45] The Ligovo estate was, however, still large: 1422 *desiatin*, or 1550 hectares.[46]

What all of these people have in common is that they may be regarded as high-class and distinguished, they are tsars and tsarinas, earls or other wealthy notables, or successful individuals in some other way. Two foreign western professionals are mentioned, which further supports the idea of the code "Sankt-Peterburg as a European City". To the analysis a few exceptions should be added. One is the short passage concerning the deterioration of the estate, and another is Rozhkov's account of a farmer named Fedor Kirillov, who built a small unusual looking house that was used for amusements. These exceptions do not, however, detract from the main impression of the text which is that the history being told is the history of people who in some way or another belong to the Russian elite. Several of these are already a part of a common Russian historical consciousness. Most people know of the tsars and earl Orlov, and many know of Anna Pavlova the ballerina and Giacomo Quarenghi the architect. Other persons presented in the text are locally distinguished and the readers maybe learn about them for the first time. But nevertheless, these persons occupies prominent positions and the contrast is striking with how seldom the account discusses "normal" people – farmers, artisans, shopkeepers and such like. Women are hardly mentioned at all, and maybe it is symptomatic that three of the four sentences that touch upon things that are "bad" in Ligovo's history, concern women. A couple of times

---

45   In 1861 the legal ground of serfdom was abolished in Russia, but the freeing of the serfs was not realized for some years (Kropotkin 1962). This is often overlooked when the Russian serfdom is discussed, and more correct would be to date the emancipation of the serfs a couple of years into the 1860s. Moreover, in some provinces serfdom was abolished several decades earlier.

46   One *desiatin* equals 1.09 hectare.

farms and summer houses are mentioned by Rozhkov, and sometimes also "souls", but "ordinary" people are otherwise more or less erased from his history of Ligovo.

This follows a wider pattern in Russian consciousness: it is the heroes that count, and everyday life (*byt'*) is uninteresting. It would probably also be correct to assume that Rozhkov's readers would not principally be interested in stories of everyday life, but instead prefer stories about the heroes, and perhaps even expect them. Moreover, the heroes would act, in Rozhkov's presentation, seemingly independently of the processes and structures in society at large. Although these are treated to a certain extent in other parts of Rozhkov's book, the result of the heroic poetry is that Ligovo is placed in a context of Russia's cultural heritage. Ligovo should, justifiably, be a place of this Cultural Heritage, and this is one important aspect of Rozhkov's place-making efforts. The code that this category refers to in the spatial artificial language on Sankt-Peterburg may be formulated as "Sankt-Peterburg as the City of (Male) Heroes".

Rozhkov's use of a poem by Pushkin in the introduction of his book should also be seen in this context. Alexandr Pushkin is Russia's foremost national poet, and just one example of his greatness is that in 1999, during the celebrations to mark the 200th anniversary of his birth, at least one radio channel in Sankt-Peterburg broadcast only material that in some way or another was related to Pushkin throughout the entire day. At home in the flat, Elena Alekseevna followed the programmes and accompanied the recitations of the poems aloud. Another example on the significance of the poet is that Rozhkov has written a whole book on Pushkin and his relation to Krasnosel'skii raion. It is still (2002) in the form of a manuscript and not yet published.[47] To relate Krasnosel'skii raion and hereby also Ligovo to Pushkin, is an additional way to make use of the code "Sankt-Peterburg as the City of (Male) Heroes".

---

47 There are more examples of Pushkin's importance to the national and regional self-definition of Russia, e.g. from film (Sandler 1994), and for the cultural elite in Sankt-Peterburg (Hellberg-Hirn 2003:81–87).

5.5 Stories of modernisation – Ligovo's main functions

The third of the categories are the stories that relate to what may broadly be defined as modernisation. Most of the issues that Rozhkov has chosen to treat are concerned with a development towards something "better". These are events that, as in the case of the Russian elite, extol the district and make the history of the district remarkable in one way or another. The driving agents behind these events are the elite, whose role as a textual category is hereby strengthened – the categories strengthen each other. An additional aspect of the modern is that it is domesticated or civilisationised nature which is described, and not the wild or pristine.

Earl Orlov took over the estate in 1765, and his work in the Free Economic Society, which was directed at improving and developing methods to increase the outcomes and profitability of agriculture, promoted Ligovo and its surroundings. During the time of Orlov, Ligovo became a sort of experimental field for the development of new high-yielding varieties of agricultural produce, such as grass and herbs (*trava*), and new sorts of root crops. Rozhkov also connects Orlov's efforts in agriculture with a park ground that is given extensive space in his further account. He writes that as a result of the concentration on agriculture a small palace park was established to the west of the lake.

The stories of modernisation are, however, first and foremost about persons that take part in the development of agriculture. Rozhkov writes:

> В 1840 году мыза Лигово была продана графу Г.Г. Кушелеву. С этого времени Лигово стало славиться своим образцовым сельским хозяйством. Кушелев не только продолжил сельскохозяйственные эксперименты Г.Г. Орлова, но и стал уделять им большое внимание. При этом новый владелец перепоручил управление имением англичанину Мак-Латлингу, который вложил много сил и энергии в совершенствование имения и его хозяйственной деятельности. (p.122)[48]

---

48 In my translation: "In 1840 the Ligovo farm was sold to earl G.G. Kushelev. From this time on, Ligovo became renowned for its exemplary agriculture. Kushelev not only extended the agricultural experiments of G.G. Orlov, but also devoted greater attention to them. During the era of this new owner the management of the estate

This resulted in what might be understood as a fantastic landscape. Rozhkov refers to a contemporary observer who in 1852 wrote that it was not possible to see enough (*naliubovat'sia*) of the "excellently (*prekrasnyi*) cultivated fields, meadows, parks and hedges" (p.122, *my translation*), and the milk cows and sheep are said to have been perfectly (*otlichno*) kept. At this time a book was published about Ligovo and "all our landlords (*sel'skie khoziaeva*)" (ibid., *my translation*) travelled here to study. The Free Economic Society awarded MacLatling with a number of decorations and rewards for the agricultural successes achieved at Ligovo.

When Rozhkov comes to the end of the 19th century in his descriptions, it is no longer the development of agriculture and the rural landscape that are in focus, but Ligovo's new "main function" is as a place of summer amusements. Also here it is the advantages of Ligovo that are emphasised, and that the landscape is well adjusted to this new function. And, as I have already noted, the settlement gives a "pleasing impression". Everything in Ligovo is always good, irrespective of whether it is agriculture or summer tourism that is the main function of the place. Rozhkov continues in this respect to refer to Verlander (from 1883), who noted that there is a public (*obshchii*) park to walk in, a special garden with an apiary, an orchestra that performs twice every week, boats to rent, and beside a few other amusements that it was free of charge to angle for fish and to hunt at the coast.

The code in the spatial artificial language that this category relates to may be denominated "Sankt-Peterburg as a Functional Node of Development". In the descriptions of Ligovo it is the instrumental significance of the place that is underlined. The code, in summary, relates to a fundamental feature in the development of Sankt-Peterburg: the city was established to open up Russia to impressions from the outside world in order to modernise the country (cf. the code "Sankt-Peterburg as a European City"). Sankt-Peterburg as a place was hereby given an instrumental function and became part of a sequence of events that should point forward into the future and to something better and more "modern".

---

was turned over to the Englishman MacLatling, who invested a lot of effort and energy into the improvement of the estate and its farming activities."

5.6 Time-spatial strategies of continuity – the creation of continuity

Two additional aspects of the place-making processes should receive special mention. The first of these is about juxtaposing geographic phenomena over time, and the second is about juxtaposing Ligovo with Sankt-Peterburg and its environs. Both aspects fulfil the function of creating what Edward Relph has called a "perceptual unity" (1976:4), the first over time, and the second in space. Relph does not use the concept over time, but as a way to tie together places in space. Here, I borrow the concept and show how it may also be applied to a place over time. In both cases, the perceptual unity is about constructing continuity.

5.7 Juxtaposition in space over time

Juxtaposing in space over time is, in principle, about the fact that about all of the historical phenomena that Rozhkov treats in his text either still exist as remains in the landscape of today, or, if no traces of a certain phenomenon remain, it is placed in and related to the locations of spatial objects that do exist today. This not only makes it possible for the reader to orient him or herself in historical Ligovo, but this textual strategy also has the result that historical phenomena are weaved into the present *through* the spatial consciousness of today. This happens when you know where the historically important places are. This is true, with only a few exceptions, for all the phenomena that are not directly connected to Ligovo's main functions. Ligovo has had two main functions: as a place modernisation of agriculture, and as a place for summer amusements. When surfaces and objects directly connected to these functions are mentioned, their emplacements are not as exact and they are placed in Ligovo as a whole, e.g. by referring to important persons of the place. This is fully logical as it is the main functions, first the agricultural development and then tourism development, that in Rozhkov's account "carries" the whole of Ligovo through time – and as the main functions cover the whole surface of Ligovo, it would hence not be necessary to juxtapose these to specific places in Ligovo.

Concerning the other spatial phenomena that Rozhkov treats in his text, almost all have a direct connection to the space of Ligovo today. An impression of *longue durée* is hereby created, and the impression is strengthened by the fact that Rozhkov returns to some of the spatial objects at different moments in history. This also strengthens the perceptual unity over time, as the Ligovo of the past becomes concretely and more tightly connected to the Ligovo of today. Helped by Rozhkov, it is possible for people to point at a "there" in the present and tell what was there before, without the objects needing to have anything in common apart from their absolute location.

The first example of this may also be related to the first textual category and is thus concerned with the location of Ligovo. Actually the village has been located at different absolute locations under different names, although it has always been situated close to the small river that runs through the district. This river is consequently given a prominent role in creating the perceptual unity. At the time that the river, which still runs through the district, is first mentioned by Rozhkov, the village of Ligovo is placed close to it.[49] The transport arteries are also used in this way. In the year 1759, the village is placed close to the Petergofskaia Road, which also still exists today. The mention of Ligovo in 1840 is an exception to this, and the author only numbers the different villages that fall within the rule of the estate of Ligovo. However, later in the text he returns to this year and mentions that sometime between 1783 and 1840 the village had been moved to a location near the Krasnosel'skaia Road and for a while had been called Novoe mesto (The New Place). The road still exists although part of it is today named Tallinskoe Highway.[50] For the year 1850 there are two references: Maloe (Small) and Bol'shoe (Big) Ligovo, and Maloe is placed close to the Krasnosel'skaia Road and Bol'shoe at the shore of the lake. Although the lake no longer exists, there are clear traces left in Ligovo today of the gully in which the lake was dammed, which Rozhkov also men-

---

49 The small river has changed name twice (first from Ligi to Ligovka, and then to Dudergofka), and its shape has been transformed, first when it was dammed (the damm was destroyed in WW2), and then in connection with the construction of the canal, built just to the north of the Ligovo terrace.

50 What Rozhkov mentions as roads (*dorogi*) have in many cases been upgraded to highways (*shosse*), or avenues (*prospekta*).

tions later in the text. At the end of the 19th century Ligovo is located by the Narvskoe Highway, which is today called Tallinskoe Highway.[51] In 1918 Ligovo was renamed Uritsk, and when Uritsk was given the status of a town (*gorod*) in 1925, Rozhkov describes that it was planned at the junction of two main roads that "existed already in the pre-Petrine era: Narvskaia and Primorskaia (later Petergofskaia – A.R.) Roads" (p.117, *my translation*). The Petergofskaia Road still exists today and the junction of the roads is where Prospekt Marshala Zhukova becomes Tallinskoe Highway.

The lake as a trope in Rozhkov's text occupies a place apart to create the sense of historical continuity. As I have already mentioned, it is pictured in three of the eight photographs, and is centrally placed in a fourth photograph showing a historical map from 1901. The photographs strengthen the argument of Rozhkov's text in which the lake is also given fairly large space. Concomitantly, the lake is thoroughly emplaced in the Ligovo of today. He explicitly writes that traces of the lake "have remained intact to our time. This deep, winding gully stretches from the Baltic Railway along Prospekt Marshala Zhukova to the edge of the Ligovo terrace. This gully intersects at present with Prospekt Veteranov." (p.118, *my translation*). The railway as well as Prospekt Marshala Zhukova and Prospekt Veteranov exist today, under these names.

Earl Orlov's efforts to develop agricultural methods are also connected to the lake as this development resulted in the establishment of a Palace Park. In the description of the park, two moments in time merge – the 18th century passes almost imperceptibly into the 20th century and is connected to what is left of the park today. Historical Ligovo becomes one with the Ligovo of today and historical continuity is fully established. The lake frequently recurs in Rozhkov's descriptions; for example in 1830 when it is mentioned in connection with a new road – the Pulkova Road – the extension of which is also present in the space of Ligovo today, although the road itself no longer exists.

There are more examples of the strategy of emplacing spatial historical phenomena at spatially distinct locations that exist today. The "seaside es-

---

51 The Narvskoe Highway, although I have not seen the name on any maps, should be the same as Tallinskoe. Since it leads to Tallinn via Narva, I take it to be one and the same.

tates" from the Petrine era are placed at the Gulf of Finland and along the Primorskaia Road. The Gulf still exists, as does the road under the name Petergofskaia Road. The palace park is said to be typical of the parks that were placed along the Petergofskaia Road, and so it continues with other objects that no longer exist, such as a hotel, a tavern and a mill which are also emplaced into today's space. In Rozhkov's text, there are only a few exceptions (e.g. a smithy) of mentioned objects that are not emplaced into the present in this way.

A special position for the creation of continuity is held by the name Ligovo, which is mentioned in writing for first time in the year 1500. The exact location of Ligovo has, however, varied over time, although it has always been situated close to the mouth of the small river Ligovka (today Dudergofka). According to the research that Rozhkov refers to, the name Ligovo originates from the old name of the small river – Ligi. What this word means is, however, rather unclear. Rozhkov refers to different researchers, and one suggestion is that it stems from the Finnish word "*lika*", which means puddle, mud, or slush. Another suggestion, and one that Rozhkov argues is more likely, is that it stems from the Finnish-Ugric "*lige*" meaning wet, or "*ligi*", which means close to or near, and he adds that this may denote a position close to the Gulf of Finland. The most spectacular suggestion that is referred to is that proffered by researchers of "Baltic morphology" who suggest that the name may stem from "*Ligo*", who, Rozhkov writes, was the pagan goddess of joy and love.[52]

By around 1840, the name Ligovo denoted a farm (*myza*), as well as one of the seven villages that belonged to the estate. At this time, the total population of farmers and serfs in all of the villages was 347 "souls" (women were not counted), and the farm incorporated approximately 2,750 hectares (2,555 *desiatin*) of land. According to a map from 1850 there are two farms (*myza*) named Ligovo: Maloe (Small) and Bol'shoe (Big) Ligovo. The area that is today known as Ligovo was established shortly after 1850 under the name Novoe mesto (The New Place) and was a village. What had happened, according to Rozhkov, was that the village had been moved

---

52 According to BES (1998:643), *Ligo* is ancient Latvian. It is a holyday (*prazdnik*) connected with the summer solstice. According to Rozhkov, *Ligo* is equal to the Russian Lade in pagan belief.

and he writes that Novoe mesto was later to be called Ligovo. The borders of Novoe mesto are the same as those that demarcate today's *zhiloi raion* and Munitsipal'nyi okrug No 40 "Uritsk" (see Figures 4.1 and 4.6).[53]

Concerning the name Ligovo, it is obviously still in use today although it was replaced with the name Uritsk in 1918. Moreover, with regards to the name, Rozhkov not only uses a time-sensitive strategy of juxtaposition, but also a spatial strategy. This is part of the second aspect of Rozhkov's juxtapositionings of Ligovo.

5.8 Juxtaposition of Ligovo with Sankt-Peterburg

The second aspect of juxtaposition works in two ways. The first of them is more concrete and directly relates to the name Ligovo as Rozhkov also accounts for other names in the city that derive from, or in other ways are connected to Ligovo. This concerns Ligovskii prospekt (earlier named Ligovskaia ulitsa) which, up to 1914, followed the city part of the Ligovo-canal. The Ligovskii prospect is today a large avenue in the city, whereas the city part of the Ligovo-canal no longer exists. At Ligovskii prospekt, there is also a small street named after the canal – Ligovskii pereulok. Parts of the canal are, however, still to be found in the environs of Ligovo. The canal was constructed between 1718–1725 to channel water from the small river Liga to Letnii sad (The Summer Garden), a park in the centre of Sankt-Peterburg, and Rozhkov points out that this was the first canal of its kind in the city.[54] This canal physically links historic Ligovo to the city, and the use of derived forms of Ligovo in the names in the city act to mentally connect Ligovo to the centre as an integrated part of both the historical city, and the city of today.

The second type of juxtaposing Ligovo is done by connecting Ligovo to other parts of Sankt-Peterburg in a less direct way. This concerns juxtaposing Ligovo with Sankt-Peterburg and places in the city that are "distinguished" and of a high status, in an approximately similar manner as he

---

53 See Chapter 4 and 7.
54 The water was taken a bit upstream from Ligovo.

concentrates on the elite. Rozhkov focuses these descriptions, which may be regarded as a kind of place poetry, on constructions of various kind. But also more common and mundane objects are used to juxtapose Ligovo with the city, and the reader gets to know that the mill at the dam was to become "widely known (*shirokuiu izvestnost'*) in Sankt-Peterburg" (p.118, *my translation*). A tavern – Solomennyi kabachok – is similarly mentioned as having been rather well known. Concerning the first case of more or less poetic place descriptions of high-status constructions, the following example retells how Rozhkov represents the summer palace of earl Orlov and the typical 18th century park that was created by Giacomo Quarenghi:

> Большой двухэтажный каменный графский дворец с бельведером стоял в окружении фруктового сада, недалеко от озера, к которому от дворца вела широкая аллея, обсаженная вязами. Могучие дубы, клены, сосны, ели подчеркивали неповторимые ландшафты. Парк и озеро украшали декоративные сооружения в духе того времени: грот, остров любви с храмом Амура, павильоны, беседки. На аллеях среди зелени белели античные статуи. Остатки так называемого «былого величия» были заметны до начала Отечественной войны. Берега озера окаймляли кусты белого и розового шиповника. На зеркальной поверхности плавали белые лилии. В окружении вязов и кленов у самой кромки лиговской террасы на берегу озера, рядом с плотиной стояла водная мельница. Рядом с застывшими мельничными колесами стремительно сбегал вниз, к Бабьей речке, водопад. (p.121)[55]

---

[55] In my translation: "The earl's large two-storey palace with a belvedere was situated in the surroundings of a fruit garden, near the lake, towards which a wide tree-lined path with planted elms led from the palace. Mighty oaks, maples, pine and spruces emphasised the unique landscape. In the spirit of the time, the park and the lake were decorated with ornamental buildings: a grotto, a love island with an Amor temple, pavilions, and summer-houses. Along the tree-lined paths, in the middle of the greenery, white classical statues showed up. The remains of the so-called "grandeur of the past" were prominent until the beginning of the Patriotic War. [The war against Napoleon's invading army in 1812] The shores of the lake were edged with white and pink dogroses. On the smooth surface white lilies floated. Surrounded by elms and maples on the very edge of the Ligovo-terrace, next to the dam was a mill. Alongside the frozen millwheels, a waterfall ran swift

What is described is a superb landscape fully concordant with the 18th century parks and palaces that have been preserved in other places in Sankt-Peterburg. Hereby the text is connected to the preconceptions that the reader, according to the Sankt-Peterburgian historical consciousness, is expected to have. These other parks and palaces are a great source of pride in Sankt-Peterburg, and a constituent part of people's identity. The underlying message in Rozhkov's text is that Ligovo is also a part of this legacy, and by creating a perceptual unity of Ligovo with the centre of Sankt-Peterburg and the prominent places in the city's environs, e.g. Pushkin (Tsarskoe selo) and Pavlovsk, he constructs a new image of Ligovo, a Ligovo that must have been as beautiful as these other historical places. These historical, high-culture places have been cared for by the system and make up an important part of the real action-space in Sankt-Peterburg. Also during the Soviet times these places were an important part of the cultural landscape of the city, but their significance were placed in a different context by the then prevailing master narrative.

Technically speaking, in terms of the creation of the perceptual unity, a spatial-semiotic interpolation occurs between these high-culture places, which are to be seen as mental fixed points for what Sankt-Peterburg is. In this interpolation, that which is situated in-between these places often disappear. That which is semiotically highlighted is what is regarded as valuable (in relation to a master narrative), while places and objects without this value are toned down so that they eventually became invisible, even though they might be socially or materially more important. This process is an important part of spatial semiosis, i.e. the process whereby a sign of a spatial phenomenon comes about. In the case of Sankt-Peterburg, to most people the name would signify a European city with beautiful palaces and great parks, but to whom would it signify the city's many high-rise districts? In spatial semiosis – the creation of maps of meaning – generalisations are made that include certain parts of space, but exclude others.

---

into the small river Baby." *Baby* means women, especially old peasant women and this colloquial name of the small river stems from the fact that women used to wash cloths here (Rozhkov, personal communication).

5.9 Triangulating the results

I have argued that the three codes I explicated exist in the artificial language of Sankt-Peterburg, and supplemented the analyses with time-spatial aspects (juxtapositions) concerning Ligovo in Sankt-Peterburg. The analyses are based on theory and on one text, which is thoroughly analysed. However, the understanding and interpretation of that text would not have been possible without fieldwork. As I argued in Chapter 3, the main "material" one brings home from the field is not the tapes, notes or other records, but an *understanding* of the field. It is the cultural competence needed *for* that field that has been trained and developed by living close to the people from that place. In this case, I had learned the codes in the field, and this enabled me to see them in the text as well. Inductive empirical over-kills are thus not necessary, but rather, in line with the argument of logical inference, one should *point* at what else is known about the field, to make ones theoretically developed argument grounded. (And when this is not enough to comprehensively understand a phenomenon, one creates theory.)

The interpretation presented here is thus related to my fieldwork experiences. One of the most central of these concerns the many places of high-culture that, among others, my first key respondent, Olga Nikolaevna, suggested that I should visit. We went to these pre-Revolutionary places – museums, parks, statues, cathedrals, castles, and the like – together, and she obviously took pleasure in showing me the great history of Sankt-Peterburg. Firstly I thought of these visits as something that we did to get to know each other, and that I would later be able to do the same kind of visits in the high-rise districts where life was "really" lived. Although I did a number of interview-walks[56] in Ligovo and other high-rise districts, visits to "common places" like these were, however, harder to arrange, and people seldom spoke with enthusiasm and affection about them. My main impression was that to most people, they were simply not interesting.

---

56 Interviewing while walking in the milieu that was the concern of the interview (see Cele 2004 for an account of this method).

However, determined as I was to let my respondents be my guides I came to understand that the places of high-culture which I was shown were a significant part of what it means to be Sankt-Peterburgian, and visiting them was a way to practice the meaning of being Sankt-Peterburgian. Overtime, I also came to appreciate these places – although I had not at first found them interesting for my study – and thought that to know Sankt-Peterburginess, I had to know these places. The places of high-culture and the stories they reflected of the by-gone pre-Revolutionary days were essential to understand the city and its inhabitants, and the warm reception of Rozhkov's book and his history of Ligovo, make all the more sense in the light of this.

Moreover, as I was an *inostranets* and new to the city, it was also important to Olga Nikolaevna and other respondents to show me who they really were. That is, they had to show that they were not the human correspondences of the Soviet urban landscape in which they lived, but Peterburgians. Thus, they better related to what was left of the pre-Revolutionary landscape formed during and after Peter the Great's modernisation of Russia. The places of high-culture that evoked this landscape thus become popular symbols to identify with, not only for the cultured elite but for all who wanted to construct a not-Soviet identity.

Words of caution, no doubt these places were visited, and a played a role during the Soviet times too, but then the (semiotic) context was different. Just one example is that, with a few exceptions, churches and cathedrals were closed, and if they were not used as warehouse or the like, they were made into atheistic museums. Moreover, tsarist history was also used in Soviet propaganda. In the 1990's, however, there was nothing left of Soviet ideology to balance the impact of tsarist history.

In contrast to the high-cultured pre-Revolutionary places, for people to visit Soviet places, and thus in practice value them, was not as interesting among my respondents. One young man in Ligovo likened the *administratsiia*, i.e. the modernistic building of the local political administration (Figure 4.9), to a medieval castle, and we, he continued while pointing at the high-rise buildings surrounding it, are the local peasants subsumed under it. This building as a symbol (of the Soviet times) was something that one should avoid when navigating in post-Soviet space. New culturo-spatial points of reference were in the making.

But the local interest in pre-Revolutionary Sankt-Peterburg did not only concern visits to the places of high-culture. These places are also used in the marketing of a diverse range of products. Brand names relate to them or to other relevant pre-Revolutionary phenomena and pictures of city symbols are shown on a range of packages. At home I still have bottles of vodka named Petrovskaia and Sankt-Peterburg, to just name just two examples. On the first bottle is pictured Falconet's statue of Peter I at the Senate Square, and on the second bottle label is a picture of the spire of the Peter-Paul Cathedral between an opened bridge. This label thus plays, apart from the name, on two historic symbolic buildings as well as on the "white nights", which is an additional symbol of the city.

Beside the market actors, the spatial codes of post-Soviet pre-Revolutionary Sankt-Peterburg are also used by public institutions. In Ligovo, the school in which the children of the family were I lived study, the photo-albums for the school classes formed but one means of establishing the codes of the spatial language of Sankt-Peterburg as the picture of each class is situated next to pictures of pre-Revolutionary buildings, statues or other monuments. Another example of how the growing generations are firmly placed in the pre-Revolutionary history of Sankt-Peterburg through acts of schooling comes from the DDIuT. Here school-classes come to play a "city game", in which they compete in teams on their knowledge of the historical city.

A third local public institution is the Ligovo Library. The name, which is reminiscent of pre-Revolutionary times, was suggested by the present superintendent who has worked here since the library opened in around 1980. She tells me that she wanted the name to remind one of old times now that the district had been completely rebuilt. The library, which is also used for exhibitions, meetings, lectures and public reading by artists from all over Sankt-Peterburg, is a small cultural centre of Ligovo. The library material concerning Ligovo is, however, rather limited and when the librarian shows me the photo album with pictures from historical Ligovo, it turns out to include many from Anatolii's personal and museum collections which I had already seen. The photos concern the period before the Great Patriotic War and then mainly before 1917. But I make a short note that this is what the children learn in the library, and the library thus became interesting in another way than I had first anticipated, since also here Rozhkov's material and the spatial codes to understand the district is made available. One last example, in the stairs to the local Ligovo library, the visitor is met by wall-paintings showing city symbols, historical persons and events.

So, the results of the study of the Rozhkov text match with other results from fieldwork. The codes relating to Sankt-Peterburg's pre-Revolutionary history are found in a range of different situations, and people make use of them in practice by talking, reading, using and visiting things and places that are associated with these codes. But what then of other research? The only larger study in this field is Elena Hellberg-Hirn's (2003) work on the cultural identity of post-Soviet Sankt-Peterburg. She argues that the identity construction oriented towards the city's pre-Revolutionary history and away from the Soviet history, started already during the Soviet times as a kind of resistance to Soviet power among the cultural elite, as well as among what were perceived as subversive elements – the dissidents. Her account of Sankt-Peterburg as the city of Peter, as opposed to the city of Lenin – Leningrad – shows the role *of* the city centre and its stories in the construction of a post-Soviet cultural identity *for* the city.

Hellberg-Hirn pinpoints the pre-Revolutionary *Imperial imprints* of the city, especially the city's cultural history that is related to the city's first and last tsars, Peter I and Nikolai II, in this construction. In the post-Soviet setting these parts of history became especially valued references in the myth about the city and hereby the codes in use for understanding the city were again being replaced. She writes:

> First, the new Petrine capital negated Moscow's cultural code; then socialist Leningrad negated Imperial Petersburg; and finally, since 1991, St Petersburg has been negating Soviet Leningrad. On each occasion, a profound re-evaluation of Russian history and culture has taken place. Issues of Petersburg's identity in the post-Soviet era are intimately connected with the political disenchantment and anti-Soviet power shift of 1991. (Hellberg-Hirn 2003:160)

After the collapse of Soviet power, cultural elements of the pre-Revolutionary period were more or less free to blossom, underpinned as they became by the Sankt-Peterburg authorities who had an interest in de-Sovietising the city, and Hellberg-Hirn calls the current dominant discourse "retro imperial". The resistance that some groups made, for example concerning the name change in 1991 from Leningrad to Sankt-Peterburg, was not sufficient to stop the process. Leningrad became Sankt-Peterburg, not only by name, but also by way of the cultural politics pursued by different official institutions.

Hellberg-Hirn amply discusses how elements in the Imperial history of the centre of Sankt-Peterburg are used by the post-Soviet cultural institutions of Sankt-Peterburg today in much the same way as Rozhkov makes use of historical events and places in Ligovo's history. By doing this Rozhkov emplaces Ligovo in the history of Sankt-Peterburg. Of methodological importance here is that the respective studies are made independent of each other.[57] In Hellberg-Hirn's study, a corresponding picture of Sankt-Peterburg's city centre is drawn to what I have explicated as codes in the spatial artificial language used by Rozhkov. This (type of) history of pre-Revolutionary Sankt-Peterburg is also presented in a range of scholarly works, as well as in tourist oriented maps, guidebooks, brochures and the like, and is as such well established as the Sankt-Peterburg text.[58]

5.10 Anti-codes

A short comment on what is not in the Rozhkov-text, and the role of anti-codes, may be important. Concerning the suppressed aspects of Ligovo's history, four salient historical phenomena are conspicuous by their absence, namely; 1) the period of Swedish rule, 2) everyday life, 3) people other than Russians, apart from west-Europeans, and 4) "bad" things that

---

57 See Borén, Thomas *Urban Life and Landscape in Russia in the aftermath of Modernity: Ligovo essays* (Draft manuscript, 133 pages, 2003-08-06). Hellberg-Hirn's study was published fall 2003.
58 For works on the city's history, see also Bater 1976, Berman 1990, Brodsky 1987, Hellstedt 1988, Jangfeldt 1998, Lindgren 1990, Olsson 1967, Varis and Porter 1996, Volkov 1996.

could be connected to Ligovo. These elements may be said to correspond to "anti-codes" in the artificial language, and would be central to the creation of meaning in that they are "non-culture" and would as such not be ascribed any value, but would nevertheless be buoyes of orientation (to avoid).[59] Briefly put, the meta-texts on these issues say that: 1) the Swedes were occupants of historical Slavic lands, 2) everyday life is uninteresting, 3) Russians are the norm to which others should conform, and that they view themselves as on a par with Westerners, and 4) those things that stall, break, or do not contribute to development are considered "bad".

That these are not dealt with may be understood with regards to Rozhkov's objectives with his book – his accounts concern the exclusively "excellent" and an exclusively Russian history (disregarding the non-excellent and the non-Russian). According to the purpose, the book should consider aspects that make the population of today form close bonds with the historical lands and then the ordinary, poor peasant life is not seen as an important source of inspiration.

Apart from these, it should be mentioned that other types of discourses on the history of Sankt-Peterburg also exist, and have at times been of historical importance. One of these is the way the "old-believers" viewed the city as something foreign, strange to the Russian body and as a sign of the end of time (see especially Bodin 2003, Lotman & Uspenskij 1984b).

5.11 Conclusions

Ligovo is a high-rise residential district on the outskirts of the city that lacks the aesthetic and narrative qualities connected to, and highly valued in, what it means to be Sankt-Peterburgian. However, when Ligovo is performatively mapped by Rozhkov, these qualities are invoked and connected to the grand cultural geographies of Sankt-Peterburg. The codes and the juxtapositions in his text fits the purpose of his book well, i.e. to create a story of the place that the population of today may be proud of, and the greatness of which they may embrace as they share the same space (as

---

59 Cf. also Lotman's notion of boundary (1990:131–142).

the history of the place). By writing Ligovo's history the way Rozhkov does, by way of juxtapositions, a perceptual unity in time and space is created, firstly with the high-culture of the tsarist era (he constructs continuity) and, secondly, with the prestigious and for the Sankt-Peterburg identity so valuable historical architectonic heritage that exist in places other than Ligovo (he mentally transposes other Sankt-Peterburg spaces on Ligovo).

In sum, Rozhkov's history forms a semantic whole that may best be regarded as a "myth" as it strives to fulfil the purpose of his book and in doing this includes certain aspects, but excludes and tones down others. This way of writing history should be seen as a part of the transformation of society from communist-times until today. The book is part of the formulation of the new meta-project, and is hereby also part of the formation of the post-Soviet total action-space. With the help of the book, it is possible to understand parts of this new meta-project and the aims and directions for society that it schedules.

The specific shape that these formulations give Ligovo is in several important respects the genius loci of Sankt-Peterburg, which thus also becomes the genius loci of Ligovo. The codes in the artificial spatial language of Sankt-Peterburg as text are central for the creation of such a text. Moreover, Rozhkov's text can be regarded as a "performative map". As with the case of all maps, it is used to give directions on how to orient oneself in the landscape of the not-so-taken-for-granted. This is the landscape devoid of clear landmarks after the fall of the communism. Hereby it is also an example of how the cultural geography of Ligovo is used in a local version of identity politics.

However, unless the new meta-project is related to the lived experiences of people, it would not be successful. For a new total action-space to be formed it would have to relate to not only changes in the system and the real action-space but also to changes in the lifeworlds and the actual action-space. In this conclusion, I will show the social consequences of the book, describe its reason and its relation to 1) the Soviet urban landscape, 2) the identity of Sankt-Peterburg and 3) its role for Ligovo.

The first conclusion is based on Claude Lévi-Strauss' argument that a myth is a response to a need to try to solve a paradox that cannot be solved (Doniger 1979). As the description of Ligovo has mythical properties, we might ask what is the paradox that this myth is created and driven by. What conflict or major question among the population made them receive Rozhkov's book so warmly that it was printed in two editions, both of which sold out, and that schools started to use copied versions of the book?

The answer, I argue, relates to the end of communism, when whatever was left of the ideals of that ideology vanished more or less overnight. In what followed, Leningrad became Sankt-Peterburg, and the identity that started to develop largely drew on the history of the pre-Revolutionary city for material for that construction. The materials were found in the grandeur of the times. However, the high-rise suburb of Ligovo – as with most Soviet high-rise suburbs – does not have these qualities. It was apparent to everyone that Ligovo did not possess the qualities that had now become central to what it means to be Sankt-Peterburgian (and not Leningradian). Still, they are Sankt-Peterburgians, they live within its bounds and see the images of the fantastic city on an everyday basis; images that do not accord with their own lived experiences. Exactly here, I suggest, lies the paradox that cannot be resolved unless they move from the district. The myth that Rozhkov created deals with the obvious difference between the new post-Soviet ideals and the Soviet spatial reality that the majority of the people still found themselves in. In doing this, he also creates the genius loci of Ligovo, and reveals to us three codes in the spatial language of Sankt-Peterburg.

The second conclusion is that the three categories spelled out above are meaningful to the readers and they, in Lotman's thinking, thus relate to codes in the language of Sankt-Peterburg. The performative map approach is similar to Lotman's view of the creative aspects of languages, i.e. performative mapping involves writing meta-texts and, to do just that, you have to use the codes at your disposal. The relevant codes are primarily found in the spatial language, and they are put to work in line with the intentions of the mapmaker. The artificial spatial language of the Sankt-Peterburg text (and of the Sankt-Peterburg landscape) is translated into the language of a map or of a literal text to treat an area, and hereby you enter the historical processes of creating the genius loci of that (specific) place. As I have argued above, using codes this way makes it possible to transcend scale-relations. Rozhkov, who has a specific purpose with his book, uses an artificial language to communicate the messages in accordance with his purpose. He does not want the message to be conceived wrongly, and therefore makes use of the artificial language, rather than develop a language of his own. Beside this, he also uses specific linguistic strategies to place the history of Ligovo in the Ligovo of today, and in the regional spatial context of Sankt-Peterburg. The codes are thus useful to understand not only Ligovo, but also Sankt-Peterburg, and especially how Sankt-Peterburg is a meaningful place to belong to. If every Sankt-Peterburgian knows these codes, which I believe they do, the study has revealed some general traits of the identity of Sankt-Peterburgians, and we now know a few aspects of what it means to be Sankt-Peterburgian, as well as the meaning of Sankt-Peterburg itself. In addition, we also know a part of the performative cartography and the performative mapping practices that are connected to the construction of identity.

The third conclusion relates heavily to the second as, in telling the stories of Ligovo's history, Rozhkov uses the codes in the artificial language of Sankt-Peterburg. To sum up, these kinds of stories that bring historical remnants to life and which focus on beautiful high-culture and the historical heroes, are part of the performative mapping that creates Ligovo's genius loci. Rozhkov's accounts, however, do not replace the stories of the district based in lived experiences, but – and here is where his project of identity politics concerning the strengthening of the everyday existence of today is most powerful – they are written in such a way that they resemble and connect to the stories of Sankt-Peterburg. Thus the local cultural geography of Ligovo is presented in such a way that it feeds upon the pre-understanding of what the city really is, i.e. great parks, beautiful buildings, etc., used as tropes in the stories of the city. Ligovo, in Rozhkov's account, is in itself not only worthy of being proud of in itself, but also becomes part of a much larger and more important history. Whether the creation of Ligovo's genius loci and its connections with the city centre will actually strengthen the everyday existence in a practical sense remains to be seen. However, what can be concluded with some certainty is that the stories in Rozhkov's book give the inhabitants of Ligovo a broader spectrum of possible interpretations of where, when, who and why they are. Hereby they can more easily connect their biographies closer to the great 300-year history of Sankt-Peterburg, i.e. the history of Sankt-Peterburg as it is formulated in the new meta-project of the post-communist total action-space.

6 Secret space, mental maps and stiff landscapes

To the detriment of many a geographer, maps were no exception to the general rule of security thinking under the Soviet regime. Maps were classified, and if they were not, they were falsified. To this can be added that the falsified city maps that did exist were in short supply, and difficult to find. Even though the peculiar Soviet policy regarding maps makes the study of maps from different time-periods worthless as a method of gaining insights into processes of urban change, the policy towards maps and spatial representation says something of Soviet spatial thought.

In this chapter, I will critically review Soviet and post-Soviet maps of Ligovo and pair this study with two theoretical notions developed to interpret the consequences that Soviet map policy had on everyday spatialities. The first of these is that people had better mental representations of space as a result of the lack of correct maps, and the second is that Soviet urban space may be understood as a "stiff landscape". These notions would also be examples of how the method discussed in Chapter 3 generates theory to account for things that would otherwise not make sense. The main questions approached in this chapter are: What can explain the Soviet authorities' fear of accurate representations of space? What expression did this fear have in Ligovo? What are the social consequences? The chapter starts with a scrutiny of Soviet map policy and a study of map material from Ligovo. This is then contextualised in terms of how the Soviet authorities, with maps, tried to protect their idea of the total action-space (the building of communism). In this chapter, maps are seen as part of the medium of power and as a course-relation that plays a part in forming time-space. The chapter ends with a discussion on how people related to this in their actual action-spaces, and on Soviet urban landscapes as "stiff".

6.1 The semiotics of maps

That maps affect the way we perceive the world goes without saying in geographical communities, and so does the fact that maps are orchestrated – hundreds of choices concerning symbols, colour, form, projection, size, scale, positioning, etc., are made by someone for specific purposes. In democratic societies, most often this is politically rather unproblematic (with the exception of military installations) and for most people, maps are practical devices for orientation. A map uses taken-for-granted categories and as long as it works, it is not questioned.

This fact is exploited in persuasive cartography, i.e. a cartography that provides maps of the world with a certain, explicit or implicit, goal in mind. This kind of cartography, as D.J. Zeigler (2002) shows, was used in the post-communist states in Europe as they started to propel themselves out of Moscow's field of gravity. Their new maps challenged the established wordview of them as Eastern and communist, and provided the countries with a new image and a new place in the world, in which their recent political history did not determine the perception of their geographical position. This was done by rather innocent means, and did not spill over into propaganda cartography, in which map symbols are used deceptively. Exactly what difference there is between persuasive cartography and propaganda cartography is open to discussion. Following Judith Tyner (1982), I take it that there is a difference in degrees of persuasiveness based on the intent of the mapmaker.[60] Persuasive cartography uses a cartographically accepted tone of voice and, as Zeigler (2002:672) writes, communicates in whispers, whereas propaganda maps shout.

Soviet true maps neither whispered nor shouted. They were silent, locked in and guarded by the KGB. Soviet cartography and especially public maps have to be treated differently – Soviet maps were false and signified little of what they were said to portray in the "real" world. The referents

---

60   See also John Agar's (1978) statement that cartographers of propaganda maps seek to be *convincing* and his discussion of "non-cartographic" maps. Further material for comparison is Tommy Book's (1991:161–167) account of the intriguing "big politics"-cartography of Berlin, and Alan Burnett's (1985) study of maps relating to the cold war and nuclear weapons.

were just not there, and what was left was a "terror of signs", concealing more than they revealed, or at least that is what the Soviet authorities aimed at. The representation of space was a highly sensitive issue and this is best understood as a politics of the sign.

The general reasoning pursued here is in line with the semiotics explicated in the preceding chapters. Here it should be spelled out that a critical review of maps requires that one needs to be aware that they represent not only the spatial referents or the "real" world pictured in the map, but also what the mapmaker wants us to believe about the world. To understand why he or she chooses to represent or display space in a certain way, we need to understand the map-maker's intentions and view of the world, as well as the values, the culture (in the broad sense of the term) and the semiotic subsystem(s) the map-maker acts within. The mapmaker in this context is seen as a person working within a knowledge-based and politicised institutional framework, and the map is a device both to decode and to write the larger text of society (Zeigler 2002, Casey 2002, Pickles 1992, Harley 1988, cf. Harley 1989/1997).

Regarding Soviet maps, an additional problematic is added. As with so much else, Soviet authorities treated space as something secret, and information on space became totally politicised. The politics of the sign, of which maps and spatial information were a part, was part of the semiospheric war that the Soviet authorities initiated and then waged after the revolution. Such a war makes the semiotic strategies of the actors very active and inventive. The result of which could be paradigmatic changes to one or several of the warring languages, or maybe the extinction of the language as a semiotic entity, and hence its institutions as well.

This is what the Soviet communist regime in several respects aimed at after the revolution. There were thousands of name changes, and literature, science, maps and other means of expression were censured. Sergei Medvedev puts it in the following frank terms:

> The new authority, unable to practically control the space [of the Soviet Union] in accordance with ideology, translated its revolutionary ambitions into a symbolic sphere, deploying a self-sufficient Soviet discourse. Everything external to this discourse was driven out of life. In retrospect, the Soviet power could have

written on its banners the maxim of Jacques Derrida: "There exists nothing beyond text" – because everything actually became text. /.../ Within the USSR, the inherent geographic determinism of Russia turns out to be semiotic determinism, a terror of signs. (Medvedev 1999:26)

This pertained to a great deal of Soviet rhetoric, there were few "real" referents behind the official picture of the USSR – the "richest country on the earth" had no groceries in the shops – and this is what Medvedev means by the terror of signs: Signifiers without referents. That the official rhetoric of the state is a political language cannot be doubted, neither can the fact that there is a politics of representation. The example of Soviet maps provides a telling example of this, and it is one that turns out to be a politics of the sign.

6.2   Soviet maps

The politics of the sign – the terror if you like – constituted one part of the Soviet power strategies. In the case of maps and map-making, the politics meant that strict security control applied.

Four groups of classification existed: 1) public maps; 2) maps for authorised use only; 3) secret maps, and 4) top-secret maps, depending on the information they contained (Jagomägi & Mardiste 1994:84–89). The regulation of the handling of secret maps was published in sets of instructions called "Secrecy of Topographic and Geodetic Material". All topographic maps were classified as secret maps or top-secret maps, and extracts would only be allowed from the secret maps if they did not show any secret objects. Both secret maps and maps for authorised use only were kept in special storage. Admission to them was "extremely" restricted, and all map-users had to be registered. The KGB was responsible for regulating access and, as reported by Jagomägi and Mardiste (1994:87), some post-graduate students were unable to finish their theses because they were not able to obtain permission to access maps. Robert Gohstand writes that the restrictions surrounding access to large-scale maps "for all practical purposes"

(1993:654–655) excluded their use by urban geographers (see also French 1979:74, Book 1996b:17–19).

Moreover, in the Soviet Union the publication of maps was extremely difficult (the unfalsified maps were printed in extremely small editions) and even scientific publications suffered from inaccurate maps, if they were included at all. In many respects, it seems as though geography had to do without maps. Anu Kull, for example, writes that cartography was not taught at the Department of Geography in Tartu for the reason that there was no demand for cartographers (1990:28). In addition to this, and as Jagomägi and Mardiste point out, since the persons who had access to the maps were so few, it was unlikely that any mistakes in the maps would be found since there were very few people to double-check the material.

Public maps could be used freely, but adding information to them had to be approved. Furthermore, permission from Glavlit censors was required before such amendments could be printed. Starting in the late 1930s, when the NKVD had assumed control over map-making (from 1935), Soviet mapmakers and the appurtenant cartographic bureaucracy started to falsify the information in maps and atlases sold for public use. These practices increased during and following the Great Patriotic War since Germans had gotten hold of correct maps from the 1930s and used them during Operation Barbarossa. Even synoptic (weather) maps were banned from being printed and in other public maps the distortions were extreme. Later, after the war and after Stalin's death when things somewhat normalised, maps for authorised use only could be moderately distorted although the falsification practices mostly concerned public maps. However, the security regulations concerning topographic maps did not change after the Second World War, and it was only in 1989 that correct topographic maps started to be published for public use. These had the scale 1:200,000 or smaller. Previously, all public maps had been based on the map of the Soviet Union with a scale of 1:2,500,000. These were then merely enlarged to a scale of 1:600,000 but still contained only the most general data. In the 1970s even the 1:2,500,000 map was impaired as a projection was created that implemented random distortions in distances, co-ordinates and directions on maps using the projection (Postnikov 2002:249–251). Throughout this period, however, detailed maps were nonetheless produced, many at a much larger scale (1:10,000 and 1:5,000) (Salishchev 1989). The falsifications in public maps were rather large. Some cities, especially "secret" cities, were totally left out and not marked on any public map. In general, they were also left out of classified small-scale military maps (Gentile 2004b:264).[61]

Another type of falsification was the distortion of position. The article *Soviet Cartographic Falsification* (1970)[62] compares maps from different time-periods and shows falsified maps of the Leningrad area, the coast of the Gulf of Anadyr and of Logashkino, a town at the mouth of the East Siberian River Alazeia. Logashkino "shifted" location from the west to the east of the stream, and from the inland to the coast, in the span of 30 years (1939–1969). Other towns changed position from the east to the west of a meridian and, in some cases, the shift could be in the order of 40 km. The article mentions one case where a lake was displaced 80 km but goes on to argue how such practices of falsification were unlikely to have deceived foreign states, which already had the earlier maps.

Not only position was distorted but also the form of the mapped objects, e.g. coastlines, rivers, railroads, etc., were subject to similar practices. This cold war tactic peaked in the 1960s, but continued at least up to 1988, even though this strategy had long been made redundant by the development of spy satellites (Bond 1989, Book 1996a: 36, Kotkin 2001:67). Worthy of note, however, and as I will show below, is that several post-Soviet large-scale maps from the 1990s still contain false information. During the Soviet times, large-scale city maps, which would have been the most interesting for the general purpose of this thesis, were also falsified and heavily distorted.[63]

---

61   Michael Gentile (2004b) classifies Soviet cities into seven categories according to their degree of closure. "Secret" cities are cities with the highest degree of closure.
62   No author of the article is stated. Some of the cases the author discusses, are easily available in Monmonier's reader (1996).
63   After WW2, Soviet cartographic policy also applied to the newly formed communist states in Eastern Europe, which obstructed geographical research in these countries too (Book 1996b:17–19).

6.3 Historical maps

In Western Europe, as in other parts of the world, maps and cartography have historically been a "science of the princes" (Harley 1988:281, see also Karimov 1999). Knowledge of space had to be restricted and maps were not intended for the everyday usage of "ordinary" people. This also applies to tsarist Russia and Alexei Postnikov writes that long before the Soviets came to power there were "draconian restrictions imposed on the compilation, publication and use of large-scale maps" (1996:169). Maps in general were treated confidentially and were accessible only by authorised persons. Actually, not only maps but also map-making methods were classified in pre-Revolutionary Russia. This affects the map as a historical source, and as Postnikov points out (1996:168–172), the maps that were published and made available to a larger audience during tsarist times did not reflect the geographic knowledge of the country at the time of production and publication.

During the Soviet times the historical maps were treated with similar security measures as new maps, i.e. historical maps from the 17th and 18th centuries with a map scale of 1:1,000,000 or larger were classified, and maps with a scale between 1:1,000,000 and 1:2,500,000 were for official use only and kept away from the public. Only fragments of large-scale historical maps would occasionally be allowed to be published during the Soviet times (Postnikov 1996:7–8).[64]

However, as N.N. Komedchikov writes, the *Russians: Historical Ethnographic Atlas* was published in 1967 and this was the "first time a detailed study made possible map representation of such important elements of the material culture of the Russian people as land cultivation methods, peasant residences, and traditional clothing" (2000:32). Although the Soviet Union stepped up map falsifications during the 1960s, it was most likely easier to get maps published at this time. The timing of this publication and other at-

---

64 Today, the restrictions on historical maps have been removed (Postnikov 1996). It could also be noted that some of the historical maps of the western part of today's Russia are Swedish from the time of Swedish rule in the area. The maps where given as war tribute to Russia after the Great Nordic War. However, the originals were often kept in Sweden (Ehrensvärd 2000:234–236), where they have for a long time been open to the public to study.

lases and recently de-classified maps reported by Andrew Bond (1989:161) coincides with the "thaw" – initiated under Khrushchev – in internal as well as external Soviet relations. Soon after the fall Khrushchev, these were classified again.

However, the Soviet authorities did not only falsify new maps and classify old maps. When Estonia lost independence after World War Two, all major cartographic and geodetic archives were shipped away and a campaign was started to collect and destroy printed material, including maps. Destruction peaked in 1949 and altogether about 22 million publications were destroyed during the 1940s and early 1950s. However, also in 1973, during the Brezhnev era, maps dating from Estonia's former period of independence were destroyed. The remaining unfalsified maps were kept at special places under the direction of the Central Board of Geodesy and Cartography (GUGK), a military institution (Jagomägi & Mardiste 1994:86).

6.4 City maps

City maps were also falsified during the Soviet times and it was with some delight that some of my respondents pointed out the former KGB (now FSB) headquarters on Liteinyi Prospekt in Sankt-Peterburg, and told me that the building had not been demarcated on earlier maps. Actually, in the summer of 1998 one of my first "discoveries" in the field was that the new post-Soviet map I had bought was false and that several houses were simply missing. I had not yet moved to Ligovo and ventured out alone to Primorskaia on Vasil'evskii Island, and even if the example does not concern Ligovo, it shows that false maps were still in circulation.[65]

The larger the scale of the maps, the less accurate the maps would be. The director of GUGK, V.R Yashchenko, has, according to Bond, intimated

---

65 Also in other places I ran into problems with maps. In Severodvinsk at the White Sea there were no maps at all and not even post-cards with city views to buy. The city had recently re-closed (it was closed during the Soviet times) and it had no official city map. After the dissolution of the Soviet Union the city opened and a private person had produced a city map on his own. Unfortunately it was out of print. In Kaliningrad, another formerly closed city, I was able to buy a city map, but I found it very difficult to use for orientation.

that the level of distortion was directly proportional to map scale: the larger the scale and the more stringent the requirements for geometric accuracy, precision, and detail, the more pervasive the intentional distortion and elimination of information. (Bond 1989:160)

A study of Soviet cartography and public urban large-scale maps has been carried out by Tommy Book (1996a). He writes that Soviet city maps were, in several respects, in "exceptionally" short supply. First, only the most popular tourist cities would be represented in large-scale maps. Even fairly large cities with populations of between one half and one million inhabitants, not to mention smaller towns, would have printed public city maps only in exceptional cases. Second, for the case of cities that had public city maps, these were usually printed in small numbers and would thus have been difficult to find. Moreover, even when one could find such maps they were falsified.

Two types of city map falsifications are discussed by Tommy Book – *elimination/selection* and *distortion* (1996a). Book exemplifies the first type with maps from Vilnius, which show a significantly simplified street pattern. In a housing district in which there are nine streets on the pre-Soviet map, the Soviet map shows only three – the rest have been eliminated. A further example of elimination concerns the lack of differentiation between land uses of various kinds on city maps, i.e. many surfaces are coloured the same irrespective of whether they picture housing or industrial areas. Another aspect of elimination/selection is that political objects, such as statues of celebrated communists, monuments raised in honour of the Red Army and other things related to socialist ideology, are given a disproportionately large space and prominent place on the maps. Objects of strategic importance, e.g. railway stations, ports, industrial areas, and "politically incorrect" objects (monasteries, churches and the like), on the other hand, were represented with map symbols in only a vague manner or were completely left out of the picture. Important buildings in terms of state security (e.g. KGB offices) were left out too and, according to Monmonier (1996:117), the maps often omitted a scale as well as failed to identify principal thoroughfares.

The second type of falsification – distortion – endeavoured to camouflage phenomena whose physical form would reveal their function. Ports and wharves were, if they were not totally emitted from the map, often given the form of a natural coastline. Distortion also relates to scale. Raymond Hutchings (1987:76) reports from a visit in 1971 to the outer districts of Moscow how he found that angles and distances were distorted on his map after comparing the map with the terrain.[66] He also noticed that the map was constructed at different scales; a larger scale at the centre and a smaller scale in the periphery. According to Jagomägi and Mardiste (1994:86), all large-scale maps such as city maps and tourist guides, were prepared on a specially distorted base, which had been prepared by the GUGK.

In addition to the falsification practices employed in the production of public city maps, the following case provides a telling example of how spatial information was also distorted in scientific papers as the use of map type and map symbols was ideologically governed. The case in point identifies and illustrates what I argue is a third type of falsification. The map example used here shows socio-economic segregation (Figure 6.1) in Kazan' from a study made by V.O. Rukavishnikov (1978a, Russian original 1978b).[67] A second map in the same article is a choropleth map showing ethnically based segregation, and is produced according to high cartographic standards.[68] This shows that the choice of map type and map symbols in the case discussed below are not made because of a lack of cartographic knowledge. Both maps concern the city of Kazan', the capital of what was formerly Tatar ASSR, with a population of about one million people.

The map in Figure 6.1 uses dots of various sizes to symbolise *qualitative* differences between categories. Aside from this being a somewhat peculiar cartographic practice, the result is that the bigger symbols tend to "take over" the map. In this particular case, the "worker" category (in the Soviet ideological rhetoric the favoured group) dominates the picture creating an impression that "hides" the "intelligentsia" category, which is symbolised with very small

---

66 Ukazatel' k skhematicheskomu planu Moskvu (1971) is the name of the map.
67 When comparing selected areas of the English map with the Russian original I detected that in one case it had one too many of the smallest dots and in another area one too few. This does however not change the analysis persued here.
68 Both maps are easy accessible in James Bater's reader (1996:131).

dots. This also hides the segregated conditions in the city and gives the reader the impression that the socio-economic segregation is limited since the worker category, which dominates the picture, is rather evenly spread in the city.

A perusal of the map, however, shows that the intelligentsia is concentrated to certain districts and absent in others. This kind of class- or socio-economic group-related segregation was against the official urban policy and it would have been politically sensitive to publish a map that clearly showed such segregation. V.O. Rukavishnikov, the author of the article in which the map is published, compares segregation in the pre-Revolutionary era with the situation during Soviet rule and concludes, on the basis of the map, that for the latter period "[n]o rigid relationship between an individual's status in society and his place of residence is to be found" (1978a:68), whereas such a relationship had existed before the revolution. This is not the place to engage in polemics on what should count as segregation or not, but what is absolutely clear is that if Rukavishnikov had not needed to take the politics of the sign into account when producing maps, the social composition of Kazan' would be better shown with proportional symbols related to quantity and degrees, and not to quality. Better still would have been the selection of another type of map, e.g. a choropleth map as was the case regarding ethnic segregation. Of course, this only applies if the map is meant to be easy to read. As it was, the actual conditions had to be suppressed for ideological reasons, which, as a side effect, also must have made it more difficult for the Soviet authorities to fulfil their intention of fighting class-based segregation.

If the Rukavishnikov map represents a third category of Soviet falsifications of city maps, probably many more could be added if the problem was studied thoroughly. The two types of falsifications concerning "distortion by ideological choice of map symbols" and "distortion by ideological choice of map type" which have been discussed in this case could suggestively be grouped under the common label "distortion by ideological choices".

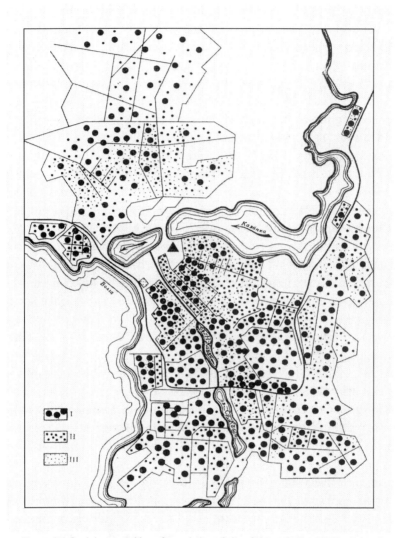

Figure 6.1 Social composition of population of city of Kazan in the 1970s: I – workers; II – clerical personnel [i.e. white-collar workers, office workers, *sluzhashchie* in the Russian original]; III – professionals and paraprofessionals (intelligentsia). Discontinuities in the built-up territory (industrial zones, dikes, etc.) are not indicated and are covered by the same symbols as the adjacent residential areas. (Rukavishnikov 1978a:70)

In relation to this, I would like to point out that although all maps are made within some kind of ideological framework, not all cartographic practices distort to the extent that they falsify the content of the maps. Not being able to freely discuss spatial inequalities due to ideological restrictions, as is suggested with the case in the Rukavishnikov map, is to give free range to rumours and prejudices.

6.5 Maps of Ligovo

The public city maps of Soviet Leningrad closely correspond with the notions made above and these maps cannot be used to study processes of urban change. Most of the maps are extremely simple and do not cover the outer parts of Leningrad but are directed to tourists who were neither expected nor supposed to visit the outer housing districts. According to Tommy Book (1996a:36–37), the intention of Soviet authorities was that tourists should keep to the approved tourist attractions, preferably accompanied by guides.

A couple of examples of the extremely simple maps that tourists would have had to make do with are found in *Leningrad and its environs*, an otherwise lavish travel guide from 1979 which, aside from the English edition, is also published in several other languages, including Swedish, and *Leningrad: A guide* whose second edition went to print as late as 1990. It was not that the simplified and falsified maps found in these publications were made simple and easy to read in order to facilitate for tourists. Also the maps in the similarly expensive and supposedly scientific urban atlas *Leningrad: Istoriko-geograficheskii atlas* (Leningrad: Historico-Geographical Atlas) from 1981 picture the city in ways that fit well with Book's two types of falsification. Many of the maps in the atlas, however, do also cover the outer districts of the city.

The Soviet maps stand in stark contrast to the new Russian maps now available.[69] The map that I used most frequently during the fieldwork is

---

69 Today even detailed Soviet topographic military maps are on sale. With the end of the cold war the CIA also made their secret map of Leningrad available (AN 1993).

named *Sankt-Peterburg 98* (1998) and had every house marked on it, as well as other details, and when I compared the accuracy of the positions, forms, angles and distances of the houses on the Ligovo-part of the map, they corresponded perfectly with the terrain. However, the map does not contain the smaller roads inside the *mikro-raiony*. The most detailed public city maps of Sankt-Peterburg that I found were from 2002 (*Sankt Peterburg atlas goroda*, 2002). I came across this atlas only after I had left the field and, at least for Ligovo, it accurately represents, apart from objects such as hospitals, schools, markets, petrol stations and the like, also the fine grained pattern of smaller roads inside the districts.

In Figure 6.2 and 6.3, the difference between Ligovo as pictured in the city atlas from 1981 and in *Sankt Peterburg atlas goroda* (2002) is shown. Especially of note in the 1981 map is the simplified street pattern and the land use symbols. The land use symbols only specify parks and built-up areas, whereas the third category is unspecified. Apart from the false street pattern, the excerpt includes one area marked as built-up land that is not likely to have contained any buildings at the time the map was drawn.

The scale of the base map used in the atlas of 1981 is also distorted in accordance with Hutching's above related notion – i.e. the scale is larger at the centre than in Ligovo. It could also be noted that none of the maps in the atlas with this distorted base denote scale. The only city maps in *Leningrad: Istoriko-geograficheskii atlas* from 1981 where scale is given are those produced at a scale of 1:600,000 or smaller.

During the 1990s false maps were still in circulation, *and were still* being produced. The problem is clearly seen when comparing Sankt-Peterburg city maps from the 1990s with the terrain. Maps picturing Ligovo give a confusing picture; streets are left out, built-up areas are not marked and green areas are marked as built-up areas (maps *Turistu o Sankt-Peterburge*, 1995 and *Osnovnye magistral'ye proezdy g. Sankt-Peterburga, Sankt-Peterburg i Leningradskaia oblast'*, 1996). An example of a map with this kind of problem is pictured in Figure 6.4.

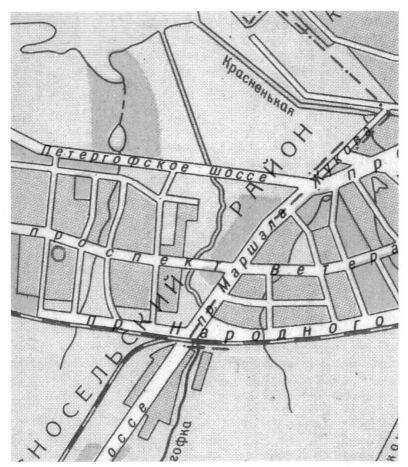

Figure 6.2 Ligovo map from 1981. Detail of a Leningrad map (*Leningrad: Istoriko-geograficheskii atlas*, 1981:89).

But there are more examples. In the map *Sankt-Peterburg universal'nyi plan* (1998) the birch alley called Berezovaia Alleia Slavy (Birch Alley of Honour) for park promenades is pictured as a road. In this map, other non-existing streets have also been added. In a Ligovo map printed in *Uchebnyi geograficheskii atlas Leningradskoi oblasti i Sankt-Peterburga* (1997), which is said to picture, among other things, water arteries and parks, the small river Ivanovka in Ligovo is not included. Besides this, the map shows a totally inaccurate street pattern in Ligovo. The map is included in an atlas intended for school use.

Of the maps I purchased during fieldwork, some of which have been discussed here, only the map *Sankt-Peterburg 98* (1998) corresponds with the terrain in a cartographically acceptable manner. That cartographic praxis should be somewhat confused after decades of Soviet map policy comes as no surprise, but while people in general knew that Soviet maps were inaccurate, the problem now may be that people may expect the new maps to be cartographically correct. This is, however, not the case for many maps, although good maps are available. Some maps, it should be mentioned, can be seen as state of the art expressions of cartographic knowledge, e.g. *Sankt-Peterburg 98* (1998), *Sankt Peterburg atlas goroda* (2002) and *Sankt Peterburg atlas goroda dlia zhitelei i gostei* (2003).

It may also be mentioned that not only was every house in the housing district in Ligovo accurately positioned in the maps in *Sankt-Peterburg 98* (1998) and *Sankt Peterburg atlas goroda* (2002), but so too were the objects lying outside the district (e.g. garages, the nearby sovkhoz and the like) that can be seen from regular air-flights over the district. Such objects were not included in the Soviet maps. The area is close to the Pulkovo airport and the new maps seem to match with the terrain as judged by the photographs I took when flying in or out of Sankt-Peterburg (see Figure 6.5 and 6.6).

6.6 End note on Soviet maps

The falsification of maps and restrictions to the use of accurate maps was part of a cold war strategy to confuse the enemy. Mark Monmonier writes (1996:115–118) that the distortion practices constituted part of a cold war tactic that was employed for state security reasons and was meant to confuse eventual attackers and cruise missiles. At least this is what is often said, but as F.J. Ormeling writes:

> The purpose of these apparently deliberate errors, which must have been very costly in the remaking of printing plates alone, is not entirely clear because foreign powers who require maps of the

Soviet Union for military purposes will probably have made these for themselves by using photographs taken from surveillance planes and satellites. (Ormeling 1974:49)

The Soviet map policy also hampered the country's own population and its civil servants. The geographer Iu. N. Golubchikov (in Bond 1989:161–163) numbers a range of situations in which the lack of maps and remote sensing imagery proved problematic for geographic research and society in general. The lack of maps led to a kind of "hyperopia" (reverse myopia) since only small-scale maps were accessible. Higher education suffered as students could not study and use the latest techniques, as did the mapping and understanding of natural hazards. The economy suffered as Golubchikov claims that the lack of large-scale maps led planners to underestimate the cultivated areas that would have been needed to meet the targets of agricultural production for certain crops. One additional point is that the lack of maps also made public participation in debate and decision making more difficult during glasnost.

One of the major problems of having falsified maps in circulation is that correct maps have to be kept somewhere if society is to function smoothly in relation to areas such as physical planning. One example is that in Riga the city's planners had access to only one (1) correct map, which hung on an office wall well covered behind a cloth (Ulla Berglund, personal communication). Besides the extra costs involved in having to store double sets of maps (correct and false) and to control who should have access to what spatial information, these kinds of procedures also increased the risk of mistakes and misunderstandings in general, not only by planners and other practitioners but also within geographic research.

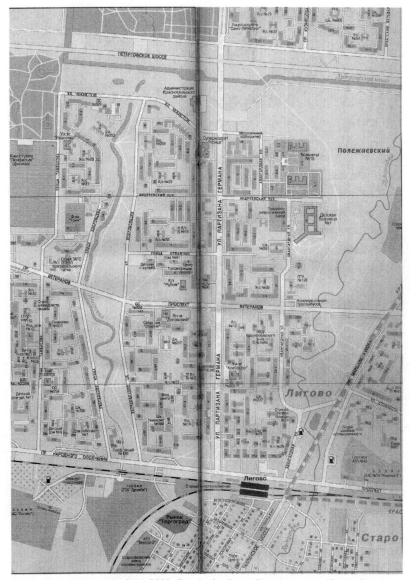

Figure 6.3   Ligovo map from 2002. Detail of a Sankt-Peterburg map (*Sankt Peterburg atlas goroda*, 2002:64–65)

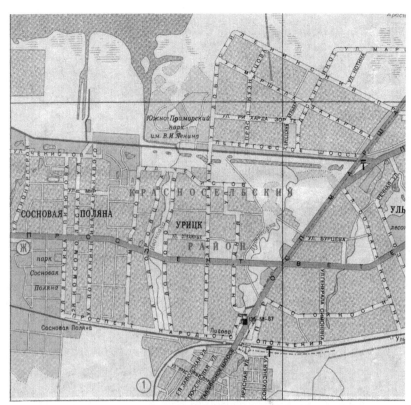

Figure 6.4 An inaccurate cartographic representation of Ligovo in a map from 1996. Detail of map of Sankt-Peterburg (*Osnovnye magistral'ye proezdy g. Sankt-Peterburga, Sankt-Peterburg i Leningradskaia oblast'*, 1996)

Figure 6.5   Aerial photo of Ligovo from late autumn 2000. Ligovo is pictured in the centre of the photo. In the distance is the Gulf of Finland. The photo is taken from the south-east. (Photo: Thomas Borén)

Figure 6.6   Aerial photo of Ligovo. Farm buildings at the sovkhoz are pictured in the foreground. Ligovo is in the distance. The photo is taken from the south-east in the summer (around 2000). (Photo: Thomas Borén)

As false maps are still in circulation one important task would be to sort out, describe, classify and catalogue all of the false maps.[70] Of equal importance, at least for geographers interested in spatial change, would be to catalogue all the correct but classified maps and make them easily accessible to the public. It should be mentioned that the Soviet Union carried out extensive mapping projects over various parts of the world and, to the extent that the resulting maps do not suffer from falsifications, these would constitute a very rich source of knowledge.[71] Until the correct maps have been sorted from the falsified maps, it remains problematic to trust any information in any of the Soviet maps.

It may also be discussed to what degree the problem with falsified maps is scrutinized in the Russian society of today. In an otherwise lawful account of Soviet maps and cartography by Komedchikov (2000), no mention is made by the author of the falsifications. The article primarily deals with small-scale maps and atlases of physical geography and the closest he comes to a discussion of the political aversion to correct spatial representations for public use in the Soviet Union is that he mentions that certain maps did not get imprimatur, or that the maps were only printed in an extremely small edition.[72] Although V.R. Yashchenko, director at GUGK, disclosed already in 1988 that Soviet maps were deliberately distorted (Bond 1989), it seems that Russian cartography has not yet fully cleared with its Soviet history.[73]

---

70 If for no other reason that they may finally be consigned to the bin for Soviet geographical curios.
71 For accounts of Soviet achievements in cartography, see Kamedchikov 2000, Salishchev 1988, 1989, Ormeling 1974.
72 Komedchikov mentions an economic map of the "Federal Republic of Germany" (1973 & 1979) which was printed in only 14 copies, an atlas of the Amur oblast' (1976–1980) which, apart from a few hydro-climatological maps, was not published at all and a map of vegetation that was not given imprimatur (Komedchikov 2000:25, 27, 34n2).
73 Cf. K.A Salishchev's (1988:183–186) critique of GUGK. The article is originally published in Russian in 1987, and the author does not elaborate on the falsifications although he mentions the lack of topographic maps, and that GUGK delivered maps that had their bases deliberately constructed improperly (p.184). In a later article (1989:15, 18, originally in Russian 1988) he spells out the problem a little more.

6.7 The Soviet fear of accurate information

In this section, I aim to hypothesise the Soviet Union's suspicious attitude towards maps, and I understand this attitude to mean that space as a category was supposed to be secret. Why then, was the Soviet state so afraid of accurate representations of space? According to the research literature, the reason is connected to the cold war, but as falsifications of large-scale city maps, as well as small-scale maps, continued well after satellites made this tactic redundant, this explanation can hardly be considered to suffice.

Part of the answer is to be found in the fact that correct maps are like glasses that make contours and details sharp even from long distances. Maps give map-viewers an extended range for seeing, and thereby also a sense of having more control over the spatial aspects of being in and experiencing the world. This applies not only to foreign powers, which were perceived as a threat by Soviet authorities, but also to the general public and citizenry of the Soviet Union. That only the KPSS (Communist Party of the Soviet Union) should have such control was in line with Marxist-Leninist ideology, which among other things stated that the party should take the leading role in all aspects of social development (towards a communist society).

The concentration of initiative to party members can be understood as a result of the party's perception of the vulnerability of communist state formation. Soviet state security thinking applied to much more than just hostile foreign powers. According to its own rhetorical logic, the state was still under formation, as it had not reached its final goal of achieving the communist stage of society. For the process of communist state formation to be successful, the determined road to that goal based on Marxist-Leninist philosophy was not to be criticised. To ensure that subjects were unable to question that formation, secrecy in general became a tool of power and as a means the state created the politics of the sign.

In the background to this politics lie, I believe, the special relation to the sign. As has been discussed in Chapter 2, the sign has a special position in the Russian cultural tradition, and for the state to then disclose the geography of the Soviet Union by naming and mapping referents in a cartographically correct way, may have been perceived as a threat with regards to the citizenry's capacity to question the communist state formation. Everyday actions and spatialities were instead covered with a terror of signs, irrespective of whether people actually believed in the information or not. The politics of the sign included not only maps, but all kinds of displays and representations – popular and scientific, novels as well as statistics – were censured and subject to informational control.

However, I would like to take the analysis a bit further and connect Soviet map policy not only to the politics of the sign in a representational approach showing Soviet power strategies, but also to a socio-spatial sphere of everyday practice, i.e. to the spatialities of lived experience.

6.8   Maps, people and the stiff landscape

Somewhat paradoxically, a consequence of the Soviet politics of the sign and its attendant map policy was that instead of relying on maps in their everyday whereabouts, people learned and memorised the spaces of their everyday lives better than they would have had accurate maps been accessible. During fieldwork, I was surprised how much people my age and those who were older knew about their city. They were like living directories and on occasions when I asked for information about where I could find one kind of shop or other, it seemed to me that all of them could instantly rattle off a number of names and addresses. At least names and addresses of shops from Soviet times. I thought a bit about this and wondered why I could not do the same in Stockholm, my home city and also a smaller city than Sankt-Peterburg. It was only later that I connected this to the lack of maps and (spatial) information in general. Instead of maps as stores of spatial information, people would have to learn where everything was located. As simple as that? Well there is at least one more component; in the planned economy, shops stayed put.

In a market economy shops work in conditions that constantly change. Rents are renegotiated, the clientele living in the surrounding areas change, competition puts firms out of business and other aspects connected to the dynamic aspects of capitalism affect the establishment of new shops or relocation of old ones. The Soviet planned economy did not have these characteristics and once a shop had located somewhere it moved to new premises only in exceptional cases. The general principle of location in the economic geography of Soviet shops was that once in place, the shops stayed put. I proceed from this thesis to pursue the argument that the planned economy, with its lack of (re-)location dynamics regarding firms and service establishments, gave rise to an economic urban landscape that can be described as stiff. And obviously, in a stiff landscape it is easier (and worthwhile) to memorise where shops are located. The shops are likely to keep their locations and still be in place when one returns.

An additional reason for shops being clearly marked on the mental maps of ordinary people is that everyday consumer goods were often in short supply, not to mention more durable goods such as books and furniture, and people talked and discussed on an everyday bases where and when certain goods would be available. These discussions also relate to scale: out of necessity to live what was perceived as a "normal" life with regards to the provisioning of goods and services, the peculiarities of the Soviet system of distribution made, or perhaps forced, people to be interested in knowing about shops in other parts of the city, since a good may be available in a shop in another district but not in one's own. On the basis of these talks and the practices connected to shopping, people thus developed knowledge of economic urban geography not only of one's own residential district, but also of the city at large. This knowledge was applied in practice and turned into a certain spatiality as the customer would need to move about and travel in the city to find the shop. Moreover, the practical application of one's geographical knowledge of the urban economic landscape would further strengthen the accuracy of one's mental map of the city.

In sum, in a stiff landscape the location of the shops in other districts could be taken for granted once they were known and the overall system of distribution of goods and services made, or maybe forced, people to be acutely aware of the details of the stiff landscape; to find the needed goods you would have to know the city well. The implications of this are rather far reaching. On the one hand, the state's politics of the sign did not work when it came to urban public large-scale maps – urban space could not be kept secret. On the other hand, the politics of the sign caused people to socialise and develop spatialities of mutual interest to interact, but this interaction was not directed at communist state formation but to consumerist ideals. A further and more speculative implication is that spatial representations in maps, and representations in general, do not have the impact that the map-makers themselves intended them to have. The lived experiences of everyday life of the acting subject seem to far outweigh representations made by authorities, thus also making theories of power shake at their linguistic foundations. People are not obedient, but pragmatic.

6.9 Conclusions

The first conclusion to be drawn from this chapter is that the general problem with Soviet cartography is still evident in many maps produced in the 1990s. The second is that Medvedev, Book, Monmonier and others are correct in their assertion that Soviet public maps signified little of that which they were said to signify. The third conclusion is that because of this people constructed mental maps that were more accurate than the printed maps. Moreover, in a stiff landscape, it is both easier and more worthwhile to memorise the details of the urban landscape. It would also have been crucial to have a good knowledge of city space since the goods and services needed to live a "normal" life were in short supply.

The theoretical propositions relating to both the notion of stiff landscape and the notion that people's mental maps were better than would have been the case had the correct spatial information been available elsewhere, have been developed to understand the consequences of Soviet map policy for everyday life. It can also be noted that although these propositions are partly based on my empirical findings from fieldwork, here it is the logic used in the analysis (see Chapter 3) that is used to support my claims, and not a large empirical body of field-material. However, testing these propositions empirically will become all the more difficult as memories of the Soviet urban landscape and everyday life fade.

To summarise the results in relation to the model, the chapter has shown an aspect of how the action-spaces relate to each other. The state in real action-space produces falsified maps in order to protect and support their meta-project of building a communist society. In the actual action-spaces of the everyday, people corrupted this strategy by creating better mental spatial representations than the state allowed for in printed material. The course-relations from the system were not able to outweigh the impact of people's spatialities and the course-relations stemming from the lifeworld. In this case it may thus be concluded that the spatial rethorics of the system had to give way to the practices of the lifeworld.

7 Political structure and communication

> In democratic settings, the locality is the main locus of "bottom-up" public participation in government affairs for the vast majority of the citizenry. In authoritarian or totalitarian settings local government is often the mechanism for "top-down" control of society by the state. (Lankina 2002:1038)

If the falsified maps in the previous chapter represent part of the official Soviet spatial thought and politics that was pursued from above to control the action-spaces of people, then the *idea* of the newly created municipalities in Russia is its opposite. In Sankt-Peterburg, the municipalities started to be implemented in 1997, and they represent the political level that is closest to people. The municipalities are also the smallest political territories in the political administrative structure, and contrary to the political system of the Soviet Union, they are based on the idea of *self-government*. The potential dynamics of this represent a change at the local level that marks a major qualitative shift in the Russian political system.

The question is then, does it work? The answer, based on my study of Ligovo and what the municipality has actually accomplished, is that local self-government in Sankt-Peterburg has not realized its potential. In this chapter I analyse the political system at the local level in Sankt-Peterburg and how it has changed from the Soviet times with regards to the political structure and to the political communication in the local media. The chapter aims to understand how the local politics and the political communication in Ligovo play a part in forming the place, and how the place as a meeting-place works with regards to the political course-relations that jostle in this space. Within this also lies a possibility to understand how the real action-space is constructed. The main (empirical) question asked in this chapter is whether the new system of self-governing municipalities has moved the power over the construction of space closer to the local population.

In theoretical terms, the question is how the system and lifeworld are integrated in the place as a meeting-place, and whether the courses that stem from the self-governing municipalities constitute a strong enough force of change to alter the balance between the course-relations that existed in the place before the municipalities were implemented. I argue that yes, there has been a change and that, yes, it does concern among other things how real action-space is formed and constructed. I further argue that, yes, some of the decision-making has moved from one political level (the city) to another (the municipalities) thereby placing it closer to the population. Even though this has happened, the new power-order is not without problems, and the study shows that the municipalities are far from realising their political potential. This might be explained by the fact that they are still in an institutional-building phase, and that it is thereby too early to make a definite assessment of the political results in relation to the political idea of the self-governing municipalities. Eventually, their potential may be fulfilled in the time to come.

In the first section of the chapter, I examine the new political level in Russia in relation to the Soviet system, and how the issue of local self-government evolved in the 1990s. This is followed by a section that focuses on the Ligovo municipality and its Council, and what it has accomplished during its first terms of office 1998–2000. In the third part of the chapter the analysis of the Ligovo municipality is paired with an account of the media situation in Sankt-Peterburg, and the political role of the local television station in Krasnosel'skii raion. Concerning the local TV-station, I firstly show that it is an active medium of political communication, which strives to affect people in a way that has a direct bearing in their everyday lives. Secondly, I show its political role as a check on the self-governing municipalities. It is the regional authorities that control the TV-station and it is thus outside the control of the municipalities.

The method employed here is to understand the case of the Ligovo municipality from its own point of view, on the basis of what it publishes, and on the basis of a discussion and interview with a local politician, and also to relate the case to the political communication carried out in local media. The case presented here is, I believe, also largely valid for other parts of Sankt-Peterburg. Although differences do exist between the many municipalities in the city, they by and large share the same political environment (laws, economy etc.) and thus to a certain extent share similar opportunities and restrictions as each other.

7.1 The new local democracy – introduction

The right to "local self-government" (*mestnoe samoupravlenie*) is guaranteed in the Russian constitution from 1993, when it was introduced in Russian society for the first time since the revolution.[74] It was implemented in federal law in 1995, and in 1997 Sankt-Peterburg instituted regional laws to start to implement the federal demands. The city was divided into 111 municipal administrative districts, of which seven lie in Krasnosel'skii raion. The Russian name of such a district is *munitsipal'nyi okrug*, which literally means municipal circuit. District or borough would be alternative translations of the word *okrug*, but circuit is the most literal and direct translation. Besides, the term "district" is often used for the raion-level (e.g. Krasnosel'skii raion), which is part of the next level of the political territorial hierarchy in Russia, i.e. the regional level. The term *munitsipal'noe obrazovanie*, meaning municipal formation is more or less interchangeably used with *okrug* in Sankt-Peterburg. The municipal level is referred to as the "third" level of power in Russia, the first two being the federal and regional levels. The raions are controlled by the regional level of political territorial entities, and they are not self-governing entities.

The Ligovo municipality is called "Munitsipal'nyi okrug No 40 'Uritsk'", and its borders coincide with the borders of historical Ligovo discussed in Chapters 4 and 5. The Municipality, moreover, contains the *zhiloi raion* of Ligovo and the delimitation of the municipal circuits followed the "local community" principle, supposedly concordant with the settlement structure

---

74 Also before the revolution, the *zemstvo* in rural areas and the municipal self-government in cities had very limited *self-governing* powers. They should rather be seen as local administrative branches of the state (Mitchneck 1997, Lapteva 1996). This view, however, has lateley been challenged and the independence of the *zemstvo* and the success of the poltical reforms of the late tsarist times is now considered important from a local democracy-viewpoint by many scholars and intellectuals (Porter & Seregny 2004, Evans Jr. 2004).

of Sankt-Peterburg.[75] The circuits do not have much (real) power, and are mostly involved with issues regarding social assistence, and aspects of local physical planning such as organising play grounds for children, or places were people can sell their own produce. Nevertheless, the politically important idea is that this level should be locally self-governing.

The circuits are run by a Municipal Council (*Munitsipal'nyi Sovet*) and the deputies in the council receive their mandate in popular elections, and from the constitutional right to local self-government. Hereby, they have another base of power than the district (raion) level that receives their mandate of executive powers from the Governor (*gubernator*) of the city. The Governor, who is the leader of the city as a federal subject *and* a representative of state power, cannot supervise the local municipalities. The constitution reads: "Agencies of local self-government do not form part of the system of state power" (Article 12, quoted in Lapteva 1996:319, see also Barabashev 1994, Gel'man 2003:48, Wollman 2004). The concept of local self-government in Russia means, following Liudmila Lapteva (1996:318), that a locally elected body of political administration has the right and the possibility to make and implement independent decisions within the area of its legal competence.[76] The area of legal competence that the municipalities (in Sankt-Peterburg) may engage themselves in is rather large, and covers an extensive range of issues concerning the social, economic and built environment as well as the ecological environment (see the specification in Appendix A).

So, the issues the municipalities may engage in, and the idea of local self-government seem clear enough. However, as I will show, financial as well as other kinds of dependencies, among them the media situation, circumvents the potential for the municipalities to fulfil their functions and to live up to the constitutional right to local self-government. This problem is

---

75 The basic territorial unit of local self-government did hereby not follow the existing borders of the raions or political districts of other kinds. See Wollman (2004:113) for a discussion of how the municipal circuits were delimited in Russia.

76 The concept is also used with regards to non-territorial subjects, such as universities (Lapteva 1996). Here I am only interested in the territorial aspects of the concept, which according to Lapteva is similar to the concept of self-government as it is practised in Western Europe. The municipalities may also be made to carry out state functions, if they are given the means for these particular functions (Wollman 2004).

also in line with the general findings of Vladimir Gel'man (2003, see also Lankina 2002, cf. Kirkow 1997). Gel'man writes:

> Both the legal and the political dimensions of autonomy in Russian local government are so limited that their reason for existence is unclear. In fact, the political impact of local autonomy in Russia is largely limited to municipal elections, which are hard to regard as free and fair and which have much lower voter turnouts than national and regional elections. Contrary to legal declarations, the state does not delegate its powers (or resources) to local governments. At the same time, federal and regional authorities pursue policies of handing over the social obligations of the state (health care, education, public transportation, infrastructure etc.) to local governments, further contributing to the burden on local budgets. (Gel'man 2003:48)[77]

And though the state is handing over many of the obligations of what were formerly state responsibilities, the local governments are to a large extent bounded as to how these should be carried out. Jerome Gallagher et al. writes:

> Local governments in Russia now have primary responsibility for the administration of social assistance programmes thanks to a combination of decentralization of some responsibilities from higher levels of government and the transfer of certain administrative functions from state enterprises to municipalities. /.../ Municipalities have some role in determining programme parameters, but programme design is nonetheless substantially determined at the national level. (Gallagher et al. 2003:177)[78]

Moreover, amendments made in 2000 to the federal law on local governments made it possible for the President of Russia, and for regional Governors, to dismiss local assemblies if they violated federal and/or regional

---

77 The municipal budgets in Russia in 2001 had responsibilities for 32% of all expenditures of the consolidated budget of Russia, but controlled only 17% of its total revenues (Gel'man 2003:48).
78 See Gallagher et al. (2003) for a study of the administration of social assistance in Arzamas in Nizhnii Novgorod.

laws. This, as Gel'man (2003:49) points out, made the "power of immunity" for local politicians weak and he concludes that in total

> the early 2000s can be regarded, if not as a "municipal counter-revolution", then as a partial restoration of the subordinate status of local government typical of the Soviet period. (Gel'man 2003:49)

An account of the local political system in the Soviet Union and Russia will provide the necessary backdrop to understand the new system of self-governing municipalities in Russia. The backdrop is also motivated by the fact that the municipal level in Russia has not been examined to any significant extent in geographical research, or for that matter in political science, which normally focuses on the regional and/or federal levels of the political structure (Lankina 2001:398–399, Belokurova 2000:21, see also Gel'man 2004:1).

7.2 Soviet and post-Soviet political structures

During the Soviet era, the local soviets, which were elected within the one-party system, had some of the functions normally related to self-governing districts, e.g. to represent local interests and resolve local problems. However, the local soviets were an integrated part of the hierarchy of state government, and primarily represented the interests of the state, and not that of the electorate. To put it simply, the role of the local soviets was to carry out the policies decided upon at higher political instances, and the local districts were not self-governing (Lapteva 1996).

The same logic also applied to the regional level of decision-making. In Leningrad, as elsewhere, the role of the regional soviet was to approve the policies worked out by the executive branches (*ispolkom*) of the regional authorities. These policies had been guided by and formulated in close co-operation with the regional branch of the communist party, which in its turn followed the priorities set up by the central organs of the party. Vladimir Gel'man and Mary McAuley summarise:

> The main policy guidelines, and the major part of the budget, were determined in Moscow. Key institutions such as the police, the

KGB, and the prosecutor's office came under central government jurisdiction, and much of Leningrad's industry was controlled by All-Union ministries. Whole areas of decision making therefore lay outside the [city] soviet's reach. (Gel'man & McAuley 1994:19)

Concerning urban policy and development in individual cities and districts, this meant that the determining factor was national, and not local or even regional, priorities. This should, however, be modified by the lobbying and informal networking of the districts (and individual cities) to influence policy and decisions concerning capital allocation at the higher levels of decision-making (Mitchneck 1997:96). Moreover, city planners in various cities in the Baltic countries experienced themselves as having power locally and sharing the responsibility with the central Soviet authorities in Moscow. According to the local city planners' experience, they had real influence on local matters (Berglund 2002:35). Further modification of the overarching policies at the national level comes from the actual role and practices of the local and regional governments. The national priorities did not, as Theodore Friedgut put it,

mean that the soviets had no independent functions at the local level. In addition to being the transmission belts for central instructions and agendas, the oblast, city, and district (raion) soviets (both rural and urban) were charged with operating a great part of the consumer services in their territories. These included far more than the sanitation, education, public hygiene, and housing functions that almost everywhere are the province of local government and that were known in the Soviet administrative parlance as "the communal economy" (*kommunal'noe khoziaistvo*). The Soviet Union defined itself as a socialist state, and its particular definition of socialism (by no means the only possible definition) prescribed not only state ownership or control, but also state *operation* of the overwhelming majority of economic and social facilities. There was thus a broad potential field for local authorities' activities. Theatres, tea-rooms, dry cleaners, bakeries, grocery stores, appliance repairs, production of foodstuffs and construction materials for the local market—the entire local consumer economy (*bytovoe khoziaistvo*)—all these were the property and the operational responsibility of local government. (Friedgut 1994:5–6, *original emphasis*)

Although the local soviets were officially responsible for the bulk of both the "communal economy" and the "consumer economy", i.e. the non-productive sectors of the economy, the power of the soviets was limited by the Executive Committees (*ispolkomy*), who were meant to perform the local services. The salaried officials in these committees tended to take over from the soviets and in practice, the power over these kinds of local decisions lay with the officials of the local executive power, which as noted earlier worked in close co-operation with the communist party. Besides the political role of the executive committees, the local government (soviets and *ispolkomy*) had very limited control over the incomes. In the local budgets, only about ten percent came from locally controlled sources (Friedgut 1994, Mitchneck 1994 in Friedgut 1994, see also Urban 1990).

An additional problem for local government was that large state companies connected to the republic and the all-union ministries of production, who had the resources the soviets lacked, acted more or less independently of the soviets and encroached on their responsibilities by supplying large portions of the communal and consumer economies (*kommunal'noe khoziaistvo, bytovoe khoziaistvo*) in order to provide the services included in these for their workforce (Bater 1980, 1996, Ruble 1995, Gaddy 1996, Healey, Leksin & Svetsov 1999).

Moreover, the local soviet was not a self-governing unit since it was dependent both on the local branch of the Communist party, and on the overarching territorial soviet (e.g. the city or oblast' levels). If conflicts between these institutions occurred, they were likely to be submitted and resolved at a higher political institutional level, rather than in constitutional courts. The soviets of the higher territorial level were in turn dependent on the republic-level of soviets, and the chain of subordinate territorial levels continued straight up to the Supreme Soviet (Lapteva 1996, Ruble 1990). To put it simply, the local soviet's right of authority, although side-stepped by the *ispolkom*, was given to them from above, and was constituted in political practice rather than legal practice. According to Tomila Lankina (2001:400), the political role of the local soviets together with the local executive branches (*ispolkomy*), i.e. the local government, was to consolidate control over local societies.

> In fact, before 1985 the very term "self-government" was rarely, if ever, used in the political vocabulary of the Russian people. Since democratic centralism was the over-riding principle both in theory and in practice, nobody dared speak of local self-government.
> (Lapteva 1996:318)

With the advent of perestroika in the mid-1980s, the political discussions opened up and issues relating to self-government came onto the political agenda. Gorbachev's reforms did not, however, include local self-government as defined above but were rather a decentralisation of state administration, and with the elections in 1990 also a democratisation. With the elections, Gorbachev tried to reform the Soviet system and to gain support for his political programme, as well as to shield off a potential backlash from the conservatives. Lankina writes that the local

> councils, which had lost or indeed never had any substantial power in the Soviet system, were now to be invigorated and the weight of decision-making was to shift to the representative bodies and their elected presidiums. They were also made more independent from the higher-level soviets in what represented Gorbachev's effort to break the principle of "democratic centralism".
> (Lankina 2001:400)

Power was thus decentralised, and a result of this was that local, subregional entities emerged as important and more or less independent political actors at the regional level. In Leningrad this development meant that the city was divided into 21 districts (*raiony v gorade*). All of them had a soviet with more than a hundred popularly elected deputies in each, as well as their own executive branch (*raiispolkom*). The idea of this arrangement was that the soviets should decide the policy and the *raiispolkom* should carry them out. To shift power from the executive branches to the newly elected soviets was, however, more easily said than done and the new system did not work smoothly; it was, for example, often unclear who had decided the policies. In addition to such problems, the national legislation was not clear-cut on who owned what, which led the district soviets into conflict with the city soviet on issues concerning control of property. Sankt-Peterburg's

Mayor Anatolii Sobchak also opposed the district soviets (Gel'man & McAuley 1994:22–23, Mitchneck 1997:98–99)[79]

At the federal level, the evolution of local soviets invested with power did not suit Boris Yeltsin and, in a row of decrees following the October crisis in 1993, he limited their power and shifted control back to the local executive branches. The local authorities thereby again became part of a general executive power vertical that was controlled by the regional authorities. This also strengthened the position of the regions, not only vis-à-vis the local subregional entities, but also vis-à-vis the central federal authorities. This development may be said to have started already in 1991, when the leaders of the executive branches at the local level were again appointed from above rather than through popular elections (Lankina 2001:400–401, Gel'man 2003:50). Thus in 1993, thanks to the developments at the federal level, the old order with strong executive branches at the local level was restored. In Sankt-Peterburg:

> The district soviet deputies were locked out of their offices and the district soviet bank accounts were frozen. These actions ended the Soviet legacy of elected, representative local government at the district level in St Petersburg. (Mitchneck 1997:97–98)

This was done a couple of months before the new Russian constitution, which contained the right to local self-government, came into effect. However, for the time being it had suited Yeltsin to strengthen the regions, which made up a large part of his federal power-base, at the expense of the local authorities.

A couple of years later, the increasing sovereignty of the regions came to be viewed as a threat to the federal interests and measures were taken do reduce their influence. The political role of local self-government in national affairs was thus again focused as

> [t]he Yeltsin administration had come to regard local government as a political check against regional regimes, as a political machine to mobilise opposition to them, and as an agency that has in

---

79 For a detailed analyses of Sankt-Peterburg city politics during the first two to three years of the 1990s, see Vladimir Gel'man and Mary McAuley (1994), and Robert Orttung (1995). For a case study of Petrodvorets, a satellite city (*sputnik gorod*) of Sankt-Peterburg for the same period, see Beth Mitchneck (1997).

the past and could in the future deliver the pro-Yeltsin vote where the republican and regional regimes had failed to do so. (Lankina 2001:401)

Subsequently, the local level was strengthened – this time at the expense of the regions – by formulating the federal law of 1995 that made it possible to implement local self-government as granted by the constitution.

Not surprisingly, this development was not appreciated by the regional governments and in Sankt-Peterburg the Mayor Anatolii Sobchak seem to have done what he could to delay the implementation of the law (Kirkow 1997:46–49, Lankina 2001)[80] Indeed, it was only after his resignation in 1996 that the implementation of self-governing municipalities could take off, and the first elections, which might have taken place although he had still been the Mayor, to the municipal councils were held in September 1997, as decided by Yeltsin in 1995 (Wollman 2004:116). However, because voter turnout was too low, the elections were only approved in 32 of the 111 municipalities (Hedenskog 1999:46). New elections in the remaining municipalities were held in February 1998. In these elections no minimum level of voter turnout was demanded.

In June of the same year Ligovo was able to form a functional political municipality of local self-government. The following account of the Ligovo municipality is based on field-notes taken during talks with one of the local deputies in the Municipal Circuit, and also from my own observations and from the written material that the circuit has published.[81]

---

[80] See Peter Kirkow (1997) for a study of the development of local self-government in Russia concerning the years 1994–1996.

[81] *Munitsipal'naia zhizn'*, *vypusk* no 1 (2), 23 July 1999, and *Munitsipal'naia zhizn'*, *vypusk* no 2 (5), 17 Mars 2000. These are the only two papers Munitsipal'noe obrazovanie no. 40 "Uritsk" published during my stay in Ligovo, and they are directed to the inhabitants of the municipality. See also the municipality's homepage *Munitsipal'nyi okrug No. 40 "Uritsk"* (22 July 2003), and the homepage for Sankt-Peterburg's self-governing municipalities in general *Local Self-Governement in St. Petersburg* (22 July 2003). Both are informative and publish quite a large amount of documents related to their activities.

7.3 Munitsipal'nyi okrug No 40 "Uritsk"

My first close contact with the local administration took place just before the elections in March 2000. Elena had suddenly said that she was going to their office to yell. She was upset about the holes in the pavement in the yard and that the stairs in the house looked awful. I asked if I could go with her and at the same time asked if she would point out and discuss these problems with me. At the time she declined but I decided to make a visit by myself as she had made me understand that these were the people who were politically responsible for planning issues nearest to home. As it happened, my visit to the Municipality's office turned out to be during the opening hours for social questions (*sotsial'nanaia sluzhba*). I step into a room where people are seated along the walls and which is centred on a woman seated behind a desk. A man is standing beside her. Both of them are around 50 years old and they are very helpful and expedient. Along the walls in the room are chairs and here mainly elderly people, mostly women, sit and wait for their turn. I take a seat and wait for my turn, and learn that all the people are here to apply for economic support (*materialnaia pomoshch*). The woman behind the desk says out loud to everybody that they will try to give them support as soon as possible, hopefully before the elections (March 2000) but that she is not sure if they will manage to help all of them before then. I see and hear her help the applicants fill in the forms, tell them what documents they need to file with the application and make copies of the ones they have brought with them. The man is helping the people in the same way but spends more time talking about the political system. He says that the laws are crazy and that they do not have enough money in the Municipality. This man, Anatolii Nikolaevich Grachev, is the one who helps me when it is my turn.

I present myself and explain what I am doing there and Anatolii Nikolaevich, whose own field in the Municipality is concerned with social help, starts to talk freely about the local political system. He says that the leadership of the Municipality is organised in a Municipal Council (*Munitsipal'nyi Sovet*) with 20 deputies, and that the Municipality is divided into four parts, or constituencies, and that from each part five of the deputies of the Council are elected. This is a pity, he thinks, since every deputy of the Council works for the whole Municipality and not only for his or her constituency. As a result of this it happens that he helps people who cannot later vote for him. He says that there is also a risk that discord and enmity can arise between the deputies as individual members might try to get more of the resources for their part of the Municipality. He adds that the deputies of the Municipal Council do not have to live in the part, or even in the Municipality in which they are elected, and that private entrepreneurs that are elected mainly see to their own company's interest, and not to the good of the area.

He is getting all the more upset as we speak, and exemplifies how bad everything is with the pensions for the elderly, about 400 rubles a month (less than 15 US dollars), that do not cover anything but mere survival. He underlines that he is a *belaia vorona* (white crow) and with this he means that he is different, that he is honest and follows the laws, in contrast to all the others (the black crows). The law is what should apply, and he says that I am lucky to have met him since none of the others would be so frank on the state of affairs. He means that he can talk freely and that he does not care if someone tries to order him around, and this is due to the fact that in his professional life he was a military in the submarine navy and that it is in the nature of that profession to be independent also during difficult conditions.

He continues complaining that the municipalities in Sankt-Peterburg only get half of a percent of the city budget, and says that the only thing that the people in the city government do is to put money in their own pockets. He is upset and seems to mean that all people in the city government and the 50 deputies in the city parliament – or at least most of them – take bribes and are only there to make sure that their own pockets are lined. Maybe the fact that in 1999 he had been an assistant (*pomoshnik*) to one of the deputies in the legislative assembly in Sankt-Peterburg (Zakonodatel'nogo Sobraniia SPb) renders this talk more value than mere slander would.

The political climate in Sankt-Peterburg during the 1990s was infected and extremely raw and hard, which is illustrated by the discussion during the years around 2000 in Sankt-Peterburg that persons in the top management of the city was involved in organised crime and even in political murders. Whether this is true or not, according to Jakob Hedenskog (1999:46), some persons were apparently bothered by this information, and they had, according to Hedenskog, difficulties accounting for their activities during the time shortly after the murder of the popular politician Galina Starovoitova. The latter is said to have possibly been in possession of taped telephone conversations that may have connected the top management to organised crime.

Hedenskog (1999:44–52) writes about six additional political murders in Sankt-Peterburg that occurred at the end of the decade and most of these were in some way connected to the business interests of the victims. Political murders are the uttermost form of the criminalisation of politics and, besides these, there existed a range of lower forms of criminalisation, one example being the accusations of corruption in the city leadership during the tenure of the former Mayor Anatolii Sobchak. The trials that were initiated in connection to these charges have been regarded as politically motivated. Less serious, but still part of the criminalisation of politics, were the vandalisation of political posters and fake candidates ("doubles" with the same names as real politicians), which were interfering with the campaigns of the real candidates and confusing the voters on the election day. The tone of voice used in political life was highly raised with dirty attacks and severe accusations, and there were candidates in the elections that supposedly represented organised crime. The raw political climate, the politically related crimes and the many political murders contributed to the city being given the epithet "Criminal Capital of Russia".

Anatolii Nikolaevich, who nowadays is part of the political game in the city, shows me his deputy-card and says that it gives him the right to meet people in the city government, and to get any documents sent to him within ten days. I ask if there are more printed materials about the Municipality than the paper *Munitsipal'naia zhizn'* of which I already had the first two issues. But there is no more material, and he says that the Municipality does not have the money for that, but then gives me a special edition of *Smena* (3 June 1998), which contains the charter that regulates the work of the Municipality. He also shows me two issues of *Kodeks* (No. 4-2 October 1997, and No. 4, January 1998), a journal that deals with laws, and he looks up certain paragraphs to show me that the city had passed a law that did not provide the municipalities with the same scope of action that the federal law stipulates that they should have. Repeatedly he states how wrong this is since federal legislation should count before the regional laws of the city. Anatolii Nikolaevich says that the municipalities were established so that Russia would be able to join the Council of Europe, and that the laws on self-government had been rushed through solely to fulfil the demands of this international body. I have not been able to verify this statement in full, but Hellmut Wollman writes that in 1995 President Yeltsin "surprisingly signed the bill [regulating local self-government] without further ado, perhaps in view of the pending decision by the Council of Europe on admitting Russia as a new member" (2004:114). The Council of Europe demands that power within a country should be decentralised for it to be regarded as democratic.

Anatolii Nikolaevich is also irritated by the fact that the city has used the word *elektorat* (electorate) in connection with the municipal elections. It is a foreign word, he says, that not many people understand, especially not the elderly. People are used to the word *izberateli* (voters) but would not understand the meaning of *elektorat*. Difficult words, he insinuates, are used on purpose, and he continues his critique by saying that no information has been issued on the municipal elections that were to take place in just a few days time. The only information available, he says, is on the presidential election, and continues by saying in a rather agitated tone that when people come to vote in the presidential election and then discover that an additional election is taking place, they will just be surprised and throw away the papers concerning the election to the Municipal Council. Anatolii Nikolaevich means that the preparations for the election are clearly insufficient and that only those who have masterminded the political game can understand how it should work, and he, who has lived here all his life, cannot.

It should also be mentioned that at the same time as the presidential and municipal elections, there would also be regional elections in Sankt-Peterburg. Elena Alekseevna knew very well that the municipal election would take place, so Anatolii Nikolaevich's concern was at least in this case unfounded. There was the risk, however, that the rather limited information that the Municipality was able to disseminate would disappear in the otherwise extensive flows of information and news on the regional and national elections. Aside from what the mass media was writing about the elections and the different candidates running for the posts of Governor, President etc., flyers, brochures and other material on the issues are delivered by people all around the city. In Ligovo these people are lined up at the booths outside Dom Tkanei at the central crossing. I collect a few flyers and try to speak with some of the people. A few argue for their political cause, but many were not at all interested in discussing politics. A tall man in his 30s who really wanted me to take his brochures says – here, take more of them, I'm getting paid to do this, I don't care what they stand for, take the flyers, I'm just doing a job.

The candidates running for posts in the Municipal Council do, however, possess a proximity to the voters that the candidates in the other elections do not have. In Ligovo there are 13 to 14,000 inhabitants in each of the four parts of the Municipality, and they live in high-rise buildings that, in each of these parts, are concentrated on less than three quarters of a square kilometre of land. In addition, the fact that the post-boxes for each apartment are grouped at the entrances of the buildings does make possible a rather effective and relatively speedy distribution of information. A further direct channel to the voters is the notice-boards that the Municipality has set up at the entrance to each staircase in every apartment block. On these boards, the candidates – who are elected through direct representation – put up election posters of themselves (see Figure 7.1). The posters are A4-sheets of paper, and all of them follow the same pattern; they contain the name and year of birth of the candidate, a portrait photograph and a short text on his or her background and family. The posters also briefly describe the candidate's political ideas, and usually also include a slogan. Anatolii Nikolaevich's slogan is: As long as there is strength, I want to be useful to people (*Poka est' sily, khochy byt' polezen liudiam*).

The slogans of the policemen on the photograph are "Law and order!" and "Order in the streets and yards!" respectively. Both were subsequently elected to the Municipal Council, and of the women, Ul'ianova was elected. Anatolii Nikolaevich carries out his election campaign also by walking around the Municipality talking to people.

MEETING PLACES 215

Figure 7.1 Election posters in Munitsipal'nyi okrug No 40 "Uritsk" (2000). (Photo: Thomas Borén)

We take a walk together and he points out to me in an annoyed manner how the posters have been torn down from the notice boards. He says that someone is paying young hooligans to destroy the posters, not for specific candidates, but rather to ruin the election. I had no means of verifying whether this was correct or not. Apart from the many torn-down posters that I saw, I also noted that candidates were rather quick to re-poster the notice-boards.

The talks with Anatolii Nikolaevich started in the office of the Municipality, and he speaks freely even though there are many people around us. While talking he continues to serve people and to answer his phone which rings intermittently, he also occasionally leaves the room for shorter periods. We leave the office together to take a walk in the Municipality, and at the end of our meeting he asks if I would like to be an election observer (*nabliudateliam*), and says that he will find out if it is possible. I agree of course, but he subsequently tells me that the answer had been "preferably not", and I decide not to push the issue. We decide, however, that he will try to arrange things so that I can be present for an hour so that I will be able to see how the election is conducted. This does not happen, but on the election day Elena Alekseevna's daughter Tania and I go together to some of the polling-stations to have a quick look. She does not vote herself, neither in the local ward election nor in any other election for that matter since "it is anyway not we who decide". Elena Alekseevna on the other hand follows both the elections and the news carefully, and always has an opinion on whom to support and why. The polling stations, which have information and material on the different candidates available, are organized in public buildings like schools and hospitals where people sit at long tables and handle the proceedings and the voters. I do not meet Anatolii Nikolaevich at any of them and I was to subsequently lose contact with him. He managed well in the elections, however, and a couple of years later (2003) he is the Vice-Chairman in the Municipal Council. Apart from our talks in the office of the Municipality and during the walk, we spoke a few times on the phone.

7.4 The Municipal Council and its influence

The first 20 deputies were elected to the Municipal Council in Ligovo in February 1998. Of these it is only the Chairman (*glava soveta*) and the Vice-Chairman (*zamestitel' glavy soveta*) that are paid on a full-time basis for their work in the Council, whereas the other deputies work on a voluntary basis (*na obshchestvennykh nachalakh*). In March of 1998 the charter for the Municipality was passed, in May the charter was officially registered by the city, and at the beginning of June it was published in *Smena* (3 June 1998). Ligovo was hereby one of the first municipalities in Sankt-Peterburg to begin operating on a legal basis.

The first group of deputies served for two years up until the election in 2000, when seven of them were re-elected. Starting in 2000, the term of office is four years and thus adjusted to the length of the terms of office in the other elections (Duma, President etc.). The characteristics of the deputies regarding their age, gender, work, personal ties to the area, etc. are presented in Appendix B. The appendix treats the groups that were elected in the elections of both 1998 and 2000.

The Municipal Council that was elected in 2000 has organised themselves into seven Commissions (*komissiia*) and a Supervisory Unit (*rukovodstvo*). The latter consists of the Chairman and the Vice-Chairman, and the former of three to five deputies, including a President (*predsedatel' komissii*). The seven Commissions have different areas of responsibility. A deputy may be a member of several Commissions at the same time. The Commissions are:

- Commission of budget and finance, 5 deputies.
- Commission of equipping with facilities and services (*blagoustroistvu*) and greening (*ozeleneniiu*), 5 deputies.
- Commission of local markets (*potrebitel'skomu rynku*), 5 deputies.
- Commission of education, culture and youth (*delam molodezhi*), 5 deputies.
- Commission of law and order (*zakonnisti i pravoporiadku*), 4 deputies.

- Commission of public health (*zdravookhraneniio*), ecology and medical-sanitary well-being (*sanitarnamu blagopoluchiiu*), 4 deputies.
- Commission for social questions, 3 deputies.

But what then has the Municipality accomplished apart from organising themselves into a political working body? In the second paper produced by the Municipal Council, dated 17 March 2000, they summarise what has been achieved for the Municipality during the first two years of its existence. Below I list the accomplishments and have categorised them into three groups. The categorisation is followed by an account of the finances and future plans of the Municipality. The paragraphs are based on a text written by Valerii Neunyvakin, the Chairman of the Municipal Council, and published in the same paper.

7.5 Direct impact on the place

The first category is about configuring the outdoor environment according to certain ideals. Measures in this category have a direct impact on how the place is constructed. It contains two sub-categories; 1) adding physical constructions to form and shape the place, and 2) removal of material from the area. Both of these are important to the outdoor qualities of the place.

- Repaired 2440 square metres of yard surfacing in the Circuit, [and] carried out partial repairs of the potholes in the yards' thoroughfares.
- Restored street lighting in the yards.
- Equipped ten playgrounds and five sports grounds.
- Set up 40 public benches.
- With the participation of the deputies in the Municipal Council, Schools No. 217 and No. 399 have been equipped with basketball facilities.
- Closed pedestrian paths for motor transport in some places.
- Removed more than 30 abandoned cars.
- Abandoned market booths have, with the assistance of the Municipal Council, been taken away from area at the "Ligovo" railway station.

- Conducted a volunteer (*provedeny sobbotniki*) cleaning of the pavements of Ulitsa Partizana Germana, [and] also of the vacant plots [*pustyrei*] located within the borders of the Circuit.

7.6   Financial and organisational help

The social assistance that the Municipality engages in is directed to children and youth-related activities, and to older people. In terms of the latter, this mainly concerns those who, in some way or another, took part in the Great Patriotic War. These measures address people and the internal space of buildings, and do not other than marginally affect the outdoor qualities of the place.

- Assisted in organising public works to equip Schools No. 208, 217, 237, 383 and 399, and the children's clinic with services and utilities.
- Provided financial help to support the implementation of a summer sanitary campaign in all the schools in the Circuit, the "Rubezh" youth club, the "Spartak" sports club, and the child clinic.
- Provided assistance for the New Year's Eve festivities for children – provided Christmas trees to all schools and day-care centres in the Municipal Circuit, and to child clinics, and the "Ligovo" and "Rubezh" youth clubs.
- Provided humanitarian assistance for a 30-day long hike (*pokhoda*) for youths from the war-patriotic club "Rubezh".
- To honour the 55 anniversary of the liberation of Leningrad from the blockade, [the Municipal Council] gave help in the form of a selection of food-stuffs to 400 blockade-veterans (*veteranam-blokadnikam*).
- Organised a festive evening for 150 war veterans to honour the Day of Victory [9 May].

7.7 Control and safety measures

The third group is concerned with control and safety measures although the first of the issues mentioned below had not yet been realized (spring 2000), and had therefore had no direct influence on the place or people's behaviour. The second issue, however, has significantly changed the place and, among other things, implies greater restrictions to movement in formerly accessible spaces. The locks were put up directly after the house bombings in Moscow in 1999. Earlier, nearly no basements, garbage rooms or similar spaces had locks that worked.

- According to an agreement with RUVD, introduced the post of municipal policeman, whose duties include controlling the observance of rules regarding equipping with facilities and services (*blagoustroistva*), and commerce.
- Acquired and installed more than 200 locks to secure the basement premises (*podval'nikh pomeshchenii*).

7.8 Finances, plans and problems

The income of the Municipality mainly derives from the city, and from company taxation. Concerning the transfers from the city, in 1999 the 111 municipalities shared 0.5 percent of the city budget, and 1.5 percent for the year 2000. An additional source of income derives from the taxation of companies. These, however, are not evenly spread throughout the city and Neunyvakin writes that Ligovo unfortunately does not have any larger companies within its borders, and that the Municipality must survive on "subsidies" (*dotatsii*). A third major source of income derives from fines of different kinds. In total, the incomes of the budget for 2000 were 4,437,000 rubles (scarcely 150,000 US dollars). In the budget for 2001, the total income amounts to 5,047,000 rubles.

Regarding the expenditures in the budget for 2000, the major portion is directed towards improvement of the yards, relief payments of different kinds, and to the running of the Municipality itself. Neunyvakin writes that the Municipality especially strives to do the following in year 2000:

- To conduct a partial repair of the asphalt surface in the yards.
- To provide more than 100 public benches.
- To provide more than 50 refuse bins.
- To equip more than ten play- and sports grounds.
- To restore the street lighting in the yards.

In addition to this, writes Neunyvakin, the city plans to allocate a portion of their resources to repair the road surfaces in the yards, to put up metal doors in the apartment blocks, to repair and replace the post-boxes, and to equip four sport complexes for children.

These intentions aside, if one compares the lists of accomplishments with the list of responsibilities (see Appendix A), one can conclude that the Municipality is far from achieving its potential influence over the place and in people's everyday lives. One reason for this relates to the limited amount of funds that the Municipality controls, while another concerns the uncertain legal situation. Neunyvakin writes that the Municipality lacks the legal and financial means to carry out its responsibilities. He states that all of the municipalities in the city have the same problem, and that nothing has been done to alter the legislation although the municipalities have submitted over 100 law proposals (*zakonoproektov*) to Sankt-Peterburg's legislative assembly. He writes that the legal and financial shortcomings are

> clear signs of the slowing down of the municipal movement, [and] of the wish to reduce it to the role of a public organisation without rights. In such a situation, of all the attempts of the organs of local self-government to concretely realize their authority, only the declaration of intentions is left. (p.1, *my translation*)

An additional reason for the limited power of municipalities is that, although the municipalities have the primary responsibility for the various programmes, e.g. concerning social assistance, the main design of the programmes is not locally or even regionally determined, but, as has been mentioned earlier, is to a large extent determined at the national level (Gallagher et al. 2003:177). As if the problems concerning finance, laws and program designs were not enough, the existing local media works in favour of the city.

7.9 Local media

Concerning newspapers, Leningrad had one of the largest, most varied and most lively free presses in the former Soviet Union at the end of the 1980s. In 1990, the city had more than 600 periodical publications, a sharp contrast to the pre-perestroika years when the total amounted to only a handful (Krekola 2000:74, 79). However, at the beginning of the 1990s the editions of these publications started to decrease, and in tandem with the large increases in the costs of printing and distribution, many papers found it necessary to seek financial support from the city administration. By the end of the 1990s there were only three newspapers that operated independently from the influence of the city administration. One of these is in English (*St. Petersburg Times,* issued twice a week), the second is a business newspaper (*Delovoi Peterburg,* issued three times a week), and the third is the weekly *Peterburgskii chas pik*. Jointly, these have a total edition of about 60,000 copies, which amounts to about 60 percent of the biggest paper – *St-Peterburgskie vedomosti*, which is partly owned by the city authorities (Hedenskog 1999:9–10). It should be emphasised that three "free" papers is a small number in a city the size of Sankt-Peterburg.

The development of the media situation in Sankt-Peterburg follows the general pattern in Russia during the 1990s. In other cities, and at the national level, the press freedom that existed at the time of perestroika and at beginning of the 1990s has come to end. The main reason is that Russian media is to a very large degree dependent on "sponsors" since they do not have sufficient incomes from circulation and from selling commercial space. These sponsors are all to some extent politicised and often affect the daily work of editors and journalists (Hagström 2000, Belin 2001). Some commentators even mean that the control that the authorities now have over the media has given rise to a new wave of *samizdat* publications (Pugachev 1998 in Hagström 2000:232). According to Laura Belin

(2001:340–341), not one of the 89 regions in Russia (Sankt-Peterburg included) have conditions conducive to the existence of a genuinely free press, and often the regional leaders are able to totally monopolise the political content in the regional media.

The great majority of Russian media is thus not a free press in the Western sense of the term. However, this does not mean that only one view dominates to the extent that was the case during the Soviet times. Rather, conflicting political interests try to use the segments of the media that they influence to promote their points of view. The result of this is that the sum total of views dispersed via media is diverse. It should be pointed out, however, that for a consumer to gain a good insight into the news, it is necessary to read half a dozen papers and watch several TV-channels, and this is not what the people in general do (Belin 2001, Hagström 2000). When there are no media alternatives, as would be the case in most local (and regional) settings in Russia, the role of the "local newspaper", as pointed out by Tomila Lankina, "becomes particularly salient" (2002:1045) in shaping public opinion.

7.10 The media situation in Ligovo

Ligovo, which has about 54,000 inhabitants, does not have a local newspaper, and other printed mass media seem to neglect this part of the city. The local press that does exist in Ligovo consists of two to three commercial letters that are delivered freely in the mailboxes on a regular basis. The letters have no editorial material but consist solely of short commercial announcements. In the other newspapers in the city, Ligovo and Krasnosel'skii raion are only sporadically covered.

In a survey of all published books and articles in newspapers and journals in Leningrad/Sankt-Peterburg from January 1989 to December 1991, only one concerned Ligovo/Uritsk.[82] Krasnosel'skii raion at large was covered by 14 articles. Ulitsa Partizana Germana, the street where I lived, was not covered at all, and Prospekt Veteranov, the main thoroughfare in the

---

82   This is D.A. Aminov's article in *Dialog* (1990).

district, was covered twice. To put this in some wider context, during the same period a total of sixty-six articles covered Nevskii Prospekt. High-rise suburbs in general are covered slightly better, but the articles are still few and mainly concern the built environment and housing questions.[83]

But what then of the local libraries? Wouldn't they have collected what the newspapers were writing about their raion and *mikro-raion* in 1990s? In the local library called "Ligovo", there was a folder of newspaper articles and papers written by pupils from the local schools, and in the central library of the raion there were a few more items. I went through the material, but it only confirmed the picture that Ligovo and Krasnosel'skii raion are represented in the media to only a very limited extent.

Thus, there is very little press that concern Ligovo and for local news the people have to make do with the local TV-channel. This is an organ of the regional level of power, i.e. the city and the raions, and it is used to reach out to the people in the area. Furthermore, it is explicitly used for political purposes.

7.11 The local TV-channel

The most influential of the local media in Ligovo is the cable TV-channel which, in 1999, opened a local studio in Krasnosel'skii raion. The studio belongs to the state company "Telekompaniia Sankt-Peterburskoe kabel'noe televidenie" and the company also has studios in ten other raions in Sankt-Peterburg and in Vyborg. According to an article in the paper *Nevskoe vremia* (No. 44, 12 March 1999) more studios are planned. The local studio in Krasnosel'skii broadcasts two hours of locally produced material con-

---

[83] The figures stem from a perusal of the subject index of six editions of the bibliography *Novaia literatura o Leningrade* with followings (editions 4–9) issued by the Rossiiskaia natsional'naia biblioteka (National Library of Russia) in Sankt-Peterburg. The English title is *New Literature on Leningrad*. The followings are named *Novaia literatura o Leningrade – Sankt Peterburge* and *Novaia literatura o Sankt Peterburge*. This bibliography lists all articles concerning Leningrad and Sankt-Peterburg in newspapers and journals. In the 4th edition the surveyed newspapers and journals amounted to 115, and in the 9th edition to 311. In each of the editions there are a couple of thousand references to articles on varying subjects which all concern the city.

cerning the raion each week as two one-hour programmes. These two one-hour programmes are then repeated so the total broadcasting time amounts to four hours a week spread over four days. In addition to these, they send a ten-minute show called "Question of the week" every Sunday. The channel's cable network covers the whole of Ligovo and some, but not all, of the other parts of Krasnosel'skii raion.

In connection with an interview this studio did with Anatolii Mikhailovich and myself, I ask for an interview with Liudmila, the interviewer. I meet her at the small studio situated on the top floor of a high-rise housing building in the district, and she, a young journalist, starts telling me about the local television station where she has worked for about six months. We sit in the part of the room that is used for tea and coffee breaks. No doors seclude the place, which has room for about five people, and the whole of the short side is open to the corridor.

Liudmila means that local television is good, and when I ask what the viewers think, she says that people like to watch themselves, their acquaintances and neighbours, and that through local television they gain a sense of pride and importance about both themselves and their raion. She can not, however, answer any of my questions concerning the channels public viewing ratings. But although she is unaware of the exact numbers, she says that despite the cable net not being fully developed in the whole of the raion the studio does get many calls from the viewers, except for programmes that deal with basic information from the authorities. And, she adds, since the channel has advertisers, they most likely have viewers as well. An additional albeit small indication that people actually watch the channel is that when they broadcasted the interview with Anatolii Mikhailovich and myself, a couple of neighbours immediately called Elena Alekseevna and to tell her that I was on TV.

Since the interview with Liudmila was the only one I carried out on the role of the local media, I will use long excerpts from it in an attempt to "show" that she talks about the role of the station in a self-evident way, just pointing out the basics to an ignorant foreigner in a helpful way. It could perhaps be said that she tells me those things regarding the local media that are non-contested. That we sat openly somewhat supports this view. I would also argue that her view of me as an ignorant foreigner worked to my advantage, as she talks to me as though everything she says needs to be explained. The interview turned out to be very revealing in terms of the power relations in the district, and at the end of the interview, when we talk explicitly on these issues, she lowers her voice a bit.

Liudmila tells me that the television is *gosudarstvennyi* (State, public) and that it was organised by the state in 1989 so that the inhabitants of the districts (raions) would receive "reliable" information about "what is going on in their raion, concretely".

> That is, we tell (*rasskazyvaem*) about what is happening in our territorial administration, that is the information we give. That is, the heads of office of their [respective] branch of activity – that is culture, construction, equipping with facilities and services (*blagoustroistvo*), you know, roads, organs – you know – of internal affairs (you know that is the police), inspectorate of minors, you know GAI – they tell, you know on television, they tell the inhabitants what is going on in the raion at present. This is very useful information about concrete events, and about how one should behave (*kak sleduet sebia vesti*). That is, this is a kind of legal, you know, a kind of legal advice (*iuridicheskaia pomoshch'*), advice, you know, for families.[84]

Apart from providing information about what the local authorities do and how the citizens can make use of them, the channel also broadcasts on issues concerning "the life of the raion", e.g. activities taking place at the libraries such as exhibitions of local material and Peterburgian artists. The employment centre provides information concerning job vacancies, and the GAI provides information on matters pertaining to traffic including new rules and news regarding roads and such things.[85] In these cases there are no doubt that the TV channel is the voice of the city administration and that it is used to reach and talk to the inhabitants.

---

84   Liudmila's answers are interspersed with the words *vot* (lit. that is) and *kak by* (lit. as if). I have translated both these expressions to "you know" and kept some of them in the transcripts presented here, but also, for the sake of reading, excluded many when editing the text.
85   GAI is the police, or militia, that is responsible for roads and traffic. Their official name changed at the end of the 1990s, but colloquially they are still known as GAI.

The broadcasts also have another side to them; they are not only informational. Some of the broadcasts contain information on how to behave regarding social problems. This is done with a lawful purpose, but it is nonetheless illustrative about issues regarding social regulation and spatial obedience. As always, these issues seem to be most apparent concerning those groups that do not conform to social norms, and maybe especially so if youths are involved. Apart from information about social problems, the viewers receive information about which institutions they can turn to if they want to translate the information into practical measures. Liudmila continues:

> Not long ago we made a series of broadcasts connected to the problems of drug addicts in the raion. According to the statistics, the amount of drug addicts among teenagers, among children, you know, rose very fast. At first it was not very much, but then it rose very fast, you know, [enough] to cause alarm and we told about this. We have [in the raion] an inspector of minors (*inspektor po delam nesovershennoletnikh*), [and he] gave an interview, [and] told: how the statistics are like, how one fights it, [and] how one looks after (*otslezhivaiut*) the criminals. [And] a part of the police department told what crime teenagers commit. Imagine! Teenagers – it is topsoil for drug addicts, how can they! We filmed operative raids among their nests (*pritonam*). This is the kind of information, that is useful, you know, and we [also] told what kind of medical centres we have that can help, you know, not for the sake to get out [of the habit, but] there they have prophylactics of narcotics. [We also told] where one can turn [concerning] difficult teenagers, [and that t]hey have an informational phone (*telefon doveriia*). If the mother sees, you know, some kind of problems with the child, she can call them, take her child there, and they direct him to a job (*napraviat na rabotu*). But now, you know, it is really very difficult exactly for these difficult children, who do not want to study, but one has to fix them up. Well, that is the kind of information we tell.

On matters concerning bringing up children, the TV channel also provides positive examples:

We also have a very strong connection with a child-teenager's centre. The teenager's centre "Ligovo" includes child clubs of all kinds. We have special institutions, where specialised teachers work with various study groups, and where children can go after school to not hang-out (*boltaiutsia*) in the street. You know, to not try narcotics or something else. Well, in general this is very important. They go there and engage in what they like. There they draw, sculpture, dance, sing, do things, sew, there yes, there are girls and yes there are boys, who build rockets, yes? There they engage in sports, [they have] all kinds of different sports sections. And we show when they have some kind of event or concert, or a fashion show, or some kind of sports competition. All this we also show. Also to show the parents where they can send their children, we really tell of all the clubs, which one is closest to their house, it is just that not everybody knows this. Very many difficult children, when they start school, stop being difficult. Well, you know what difficult children are, there is all this kinds of children ... well, you have probably been walking in the raion, you see a ten year old boy, and there he stands and smokes, yes? You have met those, well, you can imagine yourself what that is. But there [in the clubs] they engage in something and that is good, you know.

Liudmila uses the verb *rasskazyvat'/rasskazat'*, which means to tell and to relate something to someone, and not the verb *pokazyvat'/pokazat'*, which means to show, which she uses later in the interview concerning productions that do not only confine their content to operational information from the authorities. This choice of words further underlines the channel's role of providing information from a certain perspective, and with certain objectives. That is, the channel is in some respects simply a medium for projecting someone's interest; it works in the interest of (regional) authorities. Regarding young drug-addicts, the TV-channel provides a view that is in line with many people's norms (and also mine), but drugs are nonetheless a contested field, especially among young people. The information hereby becomes part of the authorities' disciplinary practices, although these interests coincide with norms commonly shared by the public.

For comparison, this example is similar to Soviet media praxis. In the Soviet Union, social problems were presented in the news as something that concerned society as a whole, and journalism was to play a part in solving these problems rather than merely reporting them. The following quote from the media researcher Jukka Pietiläinen is illustrative:

> Journalism was part of the ideological apparatus and neither could nor should define the situation on its own or use quoted statements solely to prove its own conclusions. Journalism need not disguise its role. Soviet journalism did not try to set itself over the events it reported on. The events were not "up there", they were at the same level as journalism and the general public. The aim of the news report was not to remain on the sidelines, but to influence the shaping of reality. (Pietiläinen 2000:121)

7.12 Local TV as a political tool at the local level

In addition to trying to help with issues that have become social problems, and spreading positive examples on how one should act, the local TV-channel also fulfils another function. Liudmila describes how they can raise questions from below, so that the leaders at the municipal level, that is the lowest level of territorial administration, attend to their duties:

> And we had a subject, dedicated to the municipal formations. In every raion we have municipal circuits. They enclose a small number of houses, and in every circuit their own elected deputies works. They engage in problems, you know, of the immediate surroundings (*neposredstvennogo ustroistva*), [and] equipping with facilities and services (*blagoustroistvo*). That is, you know, these roads, you know, these play grounds, these market places. You have been around, yes? Somewhere you probably saw that in some market places it is very dirty, and in other places it is the other way around, its good and clean. All this is what these municipal formations are engaged in.
>
> And we did a subject dedicated to [this, and] a deputy of a municipal formation she told us of what they had done in their area

[circuit]. She showed the playgrounds, that appeared not long ago, in the summer, and she showed a very well equipped quarter (*kvartal*). Very nice. In the results of this, we had a call from a viewer and she told us that in the neighbouring quarter, literally on the other side of the road, terrible things were going on. That is, they had no playgrounds, and the children had nowhere to play. Everything was broke, there were no lawns, the cars were driving [into the yards], and were simply standing under the windows. That is, no one looked after this, and no one was in charge of it. [But] we had this subject, and asked the municipal formation to comment. They put the blame on the lack of money, but the question had been raised.

Thus, the viewers have already understood, that when some kind of problem appears, it is not worth to sit and wait for something to happen, [or to sit and wait for] someone to come and enrich them. It follows that oneself has to turn to these organs of power and, you know, to us. We can tell of this and the very same organs of power may think twice on what they do.

The local television thus helps the inhabitants to keep track of the municipal authorities. By doing so, they also help the raion and other city authorities to keep the municipalities in check. This is thus not only done with financial and political means, but also by the way they are treated in the media. Significant here is the fact that the TV-channel is controlled by the city's structures of power, of which the municipalities are not part. To some extent this is also true at the level of the raion. Liudmila says that on a number of occasions the channel has managed to raise questions that the local authorities at the raion level must attend to, and in general, she says, the problems they illuminate are attended to.

To be sure, this is an old Soviet power technique as well. It was not permissible for the Soviet system to be criticised, but within the system, people could use the media to complain about the way the policies were carried out locally. Thus, the media was a means for the top authorities to keep local and middle-range authorities in check by letting the media be the organ for people's complaints. In this case, the principle is the same

although it now takes the form of one democratic structure controlling another. Liudmila continues:
> That is, to me it seems that this kind of television is very important in order to solve these problems. You must understand that among people there are still Soviet relics left, and they can not demand what is theirs. They do not understand, that these organs of power must engage in what they are called for and do something, and not fill their own pockets or the like, but engage in what comes up and do something concrete. They have to start to do something.
>
> And we explain this to people, you know, that they are not alone, that they have to do all this, that they must turn to them, must call, and must make demands. They are taxpayers, and they pay taxes in order to have them [the authorities] do this for them. If these taxes disappear somewhere, you know, it is of course intolerable. In principle that is the kind of jerk towards democratic transformation in our country, yes. From this viewpoint, the local television, the television of the scale of the raions, is very important. This is exactly so.

The interview with the journalist takes another turn as I begin to ask her about social problems and what is good and what is bad about this particular raion. The best thing, she says, is that there are so many enthusiastic people who work hard for almost nothing in return aside from the satisfaction of doing a good job. They are engaged, she says, and not indifferent, and she has especially high regard for the special teachers and methodologists working at the above mentioned clubs and for the people who work in other types of "self sacrificing" jobs.

The worst thing in the raion, she continues, are people who are indifferent. When speaking of indifference, Liudmila make parallels to the people in power and says that the root of the problems is that they talk more than they do; that it seems as if talk has replaced action. Those in power, she says, "in the majority of cases get off with some kinds of general phrases". I ask if they at the studio criticise these authorities. Liudmila answers:
> Well, we try to criticise, but we are dependent on our territorial authorities. And in fact it is a state company and they support us. Yes.

That is, we have guaranteed a supply to them, yes, and assume [we need] some kind of equipment, they help. Because of this, our broadcast of course, you know, of course support and strengthen their image in the raion. But if something appalling shows up, an error in accounting, something actual, and something real, like shortcomings, which you can't hide, we of course show this, you know, as we can. But to say that we are a free television and that we can practise open, well, all the same, this censorship, it works on us.

Liudmila then rounds off the interview by saying that in practically every raion old "party leaders" are still in power and "very few new people, that is, are democrats". Apart from the few "new people", she considers the rest as "relics" of the Soviet system, and these people "are morally very dependent on the management. They need their support morally, not only materially, they can not work freely".

7.13 Conclusions

Local self-government was implemented in Russia during the 1990s. Whether this was due to a desire for democracy among the top leaders and the public at large seems unlikely, except maybe concerning the initial reforms during the perestroika. Giving autonomy to elected local bodies was instead initially used to *break* Soviet power structures (both in 1990 and in 1993), and then to break regional power structures (in 1995), rather than to *build* a democratic political structure. Brought to a head, it seems as if democratic local self-government was used as a tool to reform a system that the top leadership wanted to do away with, rather than an instrument to form the future.

Nevertheless, whatever the purposes of democratic reform have been, the evolution of local self-government has implied a change in the political system of the country, although it is far from fulfilling the role it could have. Concerning the empirical question put forward in this chapter – i.e. whether local self-government works – the main conclusion is that the Municipality in Ligovo has thus far had less influence than would have been the case had it been given the legal and financial means to work in the political fields that the municipalities in Sankt-Peterburg have responsibility for. The Municipality lacks the financial and the juridical wherewithal to be a self-governing body in any practical sense, except for smaller measures in the fields of physical planning and social assistance. Nor do they control any efficient form of mass media through which to channel political communication other than the use of posters and fliers, and even control of these is limited as they are repeatedly torn down. The political communication that does exist in Ligovo can hardly be said to belong to the "free press". Nevertheless the local TV-channel does help to control the municipalities and may hereby work as the mouthpiece of the public, at least if the opinions expressed do not work against the city, the controller of the channel. Although this type of management of political communication may, in certain circumstances, give the public a voice, it still acts to subordinate the municipalities, and hereby also makes their self-governing capabilities less powerful.

But what then of the changes that have actually taken place? Well, although the subordinate status of the municipalities might be regarded as a failure when it comes to questions of autonomy and self-government in "heavy" political issues involving large sums of money, some of the decisions that are important to people concerning their everyday environment have been moved closer to the users of that very environment. The concrete issues concerning the outdoor environment in which the Municipality has been active include things like: sports and playgrounds for youth and children; street lightning in the yards (important for the feeling of safety); benches (important for social life); cleaning and removal of heavy garbage and repairing potholes (important for the general impression of a district) and; issues relating to safety (the locks and the agreement with the police).

Regarding issues like these, it is now easier for people's complaints to be effective as the contacts with the local decision-makers are closer and more direct than before. The office of the Municipality is situated within walking distance of all the inhabitants, and may easily be visited. Many, but far from all, of the deputies work or live in the Municipality, and the Municipality's homepage features their pictures and provides short presentations. The deputies are not anonymous[86] and they are directly connected to the electorate, an electorate that has the real power to replace them at the ballot box. In Ligovo only seven of the deputies were re-elected in 2000. The public may also use the local TV-channel to raise their complaints. The public's control over the lived environment must therefore be said to have increased as a result of the municipal reform.

Hereby it can also be concluded that the Municipality, or rather the course-relations that stem from it, has changed the balance of the place-forming forces. The balance in forming real action-space has changed in favour of the lifeworld as the spatial competence of the system is, in terms of scale, now closer to the actual users of the place. This is at least the case concerning the issues that the Municipality has engaged itself in and which are important aspects of the lived environment and the lifeworld. The place as a meeting-place has become better integrated, and although this is not carried out to its full potential, a platform has been laid that might help in forming and creating the values connected to a functioning democratic governance and to a self-governing society in which control over space is to larger extent based on local prerequisites.

This would, with the introductory quote to this chapter in mind, eventually turn the localities from being top-down "out-reach" instruments of state politics to bottom-up public participatory tools in discussions on how issues of local importance could and should be solved for the wellbeing of the district.

---

86 The majority of the Municipal Councils in Sankt-Peterburg do not, however, publish this kind of information on the web.

8 Ligovo essays of Sankt-Peterburg – Conclusions

> Without specific works presenting the local characteristics of countries and regions, there is no geography. (Anuchin 1977:258)

Vsevolod Anuchin's quote above introduces the beginning of the end of the Ligovo essays of Sankt-Peterburg. Geography is about the local characteristics, the differences, on the surface of the earth. But, as Anuchin very well knows from the uproar he brought about in Soviet geography in the 1960s, the characteristics that should be focused on, and how they should be interpreted, are not self-evident. Geography as a science changes and as the discipline (in the West) moved from an absolute conception of space via a relative to a relational, the focus of the studies shifted to how space comes into being as a social product. Generally speaking, the construction of space in relation to society has constituted the focus of interest among geographers from the 1980s and onwards.

In this thesis the construction of space is understood on the basis of a model that secures the geographical understanding of this construction in relation to scale-dependent factors of space and time. The overarching aim with the model is to make the idea of the landscape of courses methodologically researchable, so as to "bring closer" concrete research and the ideas on which it is theoretically grounded. Theory-wise, the thinking inherent in the model contains the funnelling of focus from the worldview, or ontology, of time-geography via its epistemological landscape equivalent (landscape of courses) to a methodologically applicable model of that landscape. The model is meant to provide a way to theoretically ground research questions in (or rather to excerpt them from) geographic ideas of the complexity and totality of reality, without compromising the importance of the idea of the co-existence of various phenomena in that totality. A research question in this context is conceived of in a broad sense, and includes both heuristic and explorative searches for insights as well as specific questions.

This chapter begins with an assessment of the model. The assessment is conducted both with regards to theory, and with regards to the empirical results of the studies; on the basis of what might be called a double hermeneutic circle. Following my assessment of the model, I discuss spatial change more freely and try, by way of abstraction, to generalise time-space into a number of types of change.

8.1 The double hermeneutic circle

To construct the model was the first purpose of the study, and to conclude the thesis not only should the model be assessed in relation to its theoretical background, but also to the results of the empirically oriented chapters in which the model has directed the interpretations. This will be done in relation to what might be called a double hermeneutic circle, as, in regards to the ontology of time-geography and the epistemology of a landscape of courses, the model must firstly be seen in its parts, that taken together ultimately strengthen the idea of that ontology and epistemology. This, of course, is nothing but a variant of the good old hermeneutic circle. But secondly, in regards to the empirical material, it is the model that should be seen as the whole, and the empirical results as the parts that taken together ideally should strengthen the idea of the model. This constitutes the second of the two circles in the double hermeneutic circle.

Put somewhat differently, in the second circle the model is the whole on which reality can be read, and the chapters are readings with the model comprising the analytical glasses. In this way, the empirically oriented chapters are parts created to support the model, which stands for the whole. In the first circle the perspective is turned around and the components of the model become the parts that should be assessed in relation to a whole, and that whole is time-geographic theory in general and the idea of a landscape of courses in particular. Figure 8.1 sums up the idea of putting the model through what I call a double hermeneutic circle.

MEETING PLACES 237

The figure also illustrates the intended role of the model as a research tool situated in-between geographic theory (the ontology and epistemology of time-geography and the landscape of courses), and the concrete research setting (in this case an urban district, or place).

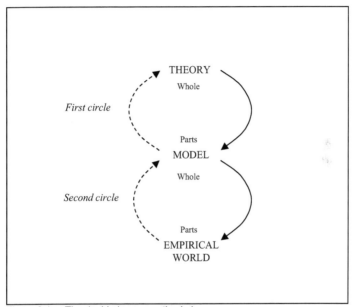

Figure 8.1 The double hermeneutic circle

8.2 Theoretical assessment – the first hermeneutic circle

With regards to the first circle (and Chapters 1–3), the question is how well founded the components of the model are in theoretical reason that relate to time-geography and the landscape of courses. Well, if the main idea of time-geography and the landscape of courses is the co-existence of various phenomena and how they spatially relate to each other over time, then the idea of meeting-places, i.e. a time-space constituted by the courses (and their relations) that stems from different action-spaces, and which form the very space in which they meet, can be regarded as theoretically well-grounded. The reason for this is that all three (ontology, epistemology and the parts of the model) are firmly connected to the principle of nearness, which I take as the founding principle that can not be questioned without also questioning geography as a subject (and here is not the place for such a discussion).

In the model, courses and course-relations are given a prominent position. Behind the force of the courses to form space there are, in many cases, decisions being made by social actors, and some parts of the model look to social theory for concepts to help understand the nature of the social world. The parts of the model that concern social theory should ideally also be made to fit into the ontology of time-geography and the epistemology of the landscape of courses. In doing this, it should not matter that time-geographic ontology has been more concerned with corporeal aspects of the world. This is because time-geography, according to the principle of nearness, recognises that all that is present (and thus not only the corporeal) is of interest in understanding the totality of reality. The concepts borrowed from social theory are then put to use in the model according to their "geographic potential", i.e. their potential to enhance the understanding of the construction of space. Social theory and its concepts are hereby spatialised from the point of view of their relevance to understand the world in accordance with the principle of nearness. Subsequently they become part of the conceptual dismantling of the world into the geographical categories that relate to how space is constructed over time.

One consequence of incorporating social theory to conceptually dismantle the world is that the ontology of time-geography and the epistemology of the landscape of courses meet the epistemology of cultural geography (in which I place social theory in general). This should not present any insurmountable problems because they are not mutually exclusive. This is firstly because the landscapes of courses are dependent on social evolution (processes of the world as lived and experienced – lifeworlds, and the governed world – the system) and hence the epistemology of the landscape of courses should not be insensitive to social issues, and secondly, because the epistemology of cultural geography does not reject the materiality of the world. Rather, the different objects of study (courses in the first case and representations, cultural semiotics and practices in the second) that the two epistemologies relate to, are always intertwined with each other and together form space in what I have called meeting-places. The social construction of epistemologies should thus not be able to prevent an understanding of the world as a totality of various phenomena that co-exist. After all, to understand the world (in a geographically legitimate way) is just a matter of how the hermeneutic animal is tamed, and what logical inferences that are possible to make. The history of geography in particular, and of science in general, is important in doing this, as much of our preconceptions of the world lies within it.

To sum up the first hermeneutic circle, the main parts of the model relate well to geographic theory and the ontology and epistemology from which the model has sprung. The model can hereby, although the assessment is short and only focused on the most pertinent issues, be said to be theoretically grounded.

8.3 Empirical assessment – the second hermeneutic circle

To know whether the model also works in regards to concrete empirical studies, it will have to be assessed in relation to the results of the material presented in Chapters 5–7. This assessment will here be conducted in relation to two main questions. The first question is whether the answers (or empirical results) that come out of the research questions that are theoretically grounded in the model fulfil relevant demands for validity, i.e. do the answers really concern the construction of space as a meeting-place of forces stemming from various scale levels? The second question is whether the model is useful for constructing new theoretical propositions that enhance the understanding of the construction of space? To assess the empirical chapters with regards to how well the model has helped to generate new theoretical propositions might at first seem awkward. However, to my mind one of the main roles of science is to produce new generalised knowledge, and if the model were a functional research tool, it would facilitate that goal. If it works, this would also mean that the model is "future oriented", for lack of a better word, and not only a way to describe the current situation. To develop new theory is also a way to avoid circular definitions and arguments in assessing the model. These two questions will only concern Chapters 5–7, as Chapter 4 is chiefly meant to provide a background to the type of space and empirical setting that are analysed in the subsequent three chapters.

Nevertheless, a short comment on Chapter 4 is of value because it contains a number of concrete, although more implicit than explicit, examples of how the model works. Especially pertinent in this respect is the greenery in the area, and the façades, in which the force of the course-relations that stem from the lifeworlds of people and the system together have formed space over time. But the thinking inherent in the model would also be important to explain other spatial details in the district. The parking of cars, the benches on which people sit, and, by no means least, in the attempts of the system to form the identity of Soviet people by shaping the cultural landscape and load it with ideological representations in the form of monuments. To what extent the system really succeeded in achieving this goal might be a question for further research, but from the described examples of how certain details in the district are formed, it seems that the thinking inherent in the model and the questions that can be grounded in this thinking, generate answers that live up to the demands of validity that necessarily pertain for models of this kind.

In Chapter 5, the total action space is focused upon with regards to the new codes that are used to understand Ligovo and Sankt-Peterburg at large. In the case of Ligovo, we have seen how one author working in the medium of serious enthusiasm draws upon certain codes to construct the history of the place. This provides language as a medium in the actual action-spaces of people with a larger repertoire of codes to use to understand and to practice the new possible spatialities of post-Soviet Sankt-Peterburg. According to the model, the new meta-project to which these codes belong constitutes parts of the new total action-space. The old codes are marginalised, or fully replaced, when people act upon the new codes and put them into spatial practice. Moreover, hereby they are also realising the implicit or explicit intentions of the new meta-project of the city. The cultural space of Ligovo is constructed in the meeting of course-relations that flow through the serious enthusiasm of a writer (Rozhkov) and through the history and physical remnants of the place, which he uses to achieve his objective. Additionally, in Ligovo's cultural space, the course-relations that stem from his work also meet the codes that are developed in total action-space of post-Soviet Sankt-Peterburg at large, and which he draws upon in writing the history of Ligovo.

In this chapter, the model thus functioned to enhance the understanding of scale-related cultural issues, such as identity and the meaning of place. And in case the significances (webs of meaning) that people assign to a place is a part of the construction of that space as a meeting-place, the results of the research questions developed in relation to the model seem to fulfil the demands for validity required of the model. It could be noted, however, that had the new codes of how Sankt-Peterburg is understood had any significant impact in how space is also concretely constructed in Ligovo, e.g. renaming streets, putting up new monuments and the like, the validity claims would be even stronger. This has, with a few minor exceptions, not happened (yet). It could be noted, however, that after I finished my fieldwork, a very large hammer and sickle, located in Park Lenina, was removed and this might be taken to mean that the specific Soviet cultural landscape is starting to be dismantled. Concerning the assessment of the results in relation to the second question, i.e. if the results generate new theoretical propositions that enhance the understanding of that space, then the answer may be affirmative if the formulations of the codes and juxtapositions count as theoretical propositions. Based on these conclusions, I argue that Chapter 5, as a part of the thesis of logic pursued in this work, strengthens the general ideas of the model, and hereby this part also contributes to closing the second hermeneutic circle.

In the following chapter (Chapter 6), the strength of the model to understand space at different scale levels with regards to the different action-spaces is shown. Ligovo as a meeting-place of course-relations stemming from different scale levels is explored in relation to maps and mental maps. It is argued that the Soviet authorities of the real action-space tried to prevent the formation of accurate perceptions of space among the public, and that this was part of an informational strategy to protect the meta-project of the state, i.e. what was rhetorically expressed as the building of communism. However, this policy was counter-productive in that it forced people to construct mental representations of space that were more accurate than the maps, so that they could orient themselves in the stiff landscape of Soviet shops.

To assess the chapter in relation to the question concerning new theoretical propositions is not a problem as the idea of a stiff landscape, and that of better mental representations of space, had to be developed to answer the research questions posed in the chapter. The question concerning validity could also, I believe, be answered affirmatively. The Soviet map policy was part of the system, and people had to develop their own local mental maps. From both of these aspects there stemmed forces that shaped peoples spatialities and the courses related to this are part of the construction of space as a meeting-place. With regards to the second hermeneutic circle, this chapter may also be seen to have supported the claims of the model.

In Chapter 7, the analyses concern the Russian political system at the most local level, which during the 1980s and 1990s went through major changes. Self-governing municipalities were introduced, and although the idea of self-government clearly breaks with the political tradition of Russia and the Soviet Union, the concrete results of this reform have not fulfilled the potential for autonomous and place-based governance that they could have. Nevertheless, although far from having fulfilled its potential, the reform has to some extent changed the balance of course-relations, and the formation of space has subsequently also changed. Some of the forces that shape space are now located closer to the place itself and it can be concluded that, to some extent, the municipalities in Sankt-Peterburg as meeting-places are better socially integrated with regards to lifeworlds and the system.

Assessing this chapter with regards to the first question concerning validity is not problematic, as it seems clear that the research question based in the model does generate results that explain the change in the shaping of space as a meeting-place. The chapter, however, has not resulted in any new theoretical propositions on the local political system in Russia. Hereby, some part of the model, or the way it has been applied, has failed. The results are, no doubt, in line with what other researchers have found, but the chapter does not enhance the theoretical understanding of the local political system in any other way than is already evident in the model. Accordingly, to avoid circular definitions and arguments in assessing the model with regards to the second hermeneutic circle, it is clear that Chapter 7 does not support the general ideas in the model in any other way than what can be based in the issue of validity.

In summing up the second hermeneutic circle and the assessment of the model in relation to the empirically oriented chapters, it seems as if the model by and large works as intended. Concerning the first question regarding the validity of the model, it may be concluded from the assessment of Chapters 5–7 that the idea of the model is strengthened. Hereby, it may also be concluded that the model is one way to make the landscape of courses researchable, i.e. the model is a way to make that landscape methodologically applicable to research questions that are theoretically grounded (as assessed in the first hermeneutic circle).

In relation to the second question concerning whether the model facilitates new theoretical propositions, the answer is not as clear-cut, although the potential is clearly evident in Chapters 5 and 6. In Chapter 7, however, this was not the case. To speculate why the chapter failed to generate new theory, I believe that one reason might be that my point of entry into the local politics of Sankt-Peterburg was too theoretically and empirically limited. I did not, for example, make explicit use of cultural semiotics to understand the course-relations, and I also believe that more aspects of the model should have been empirically explicated. As this was not done, the chapter only reaches the current general level of knowledge of the local political system. It seems to confirm other researchers' results rather than to produce new ideas, and the chapter was thus unable to proceed in developing new knowledge in the form of theoretical propositions.

More reasons may also exist, and one of them, which I find interesting, is that the idea of self-government is new to Russian governance and might thus not fit in with my general understanding of Russia, which would make it harder to draw conclusions based on logical inference. If this proposition is correct it may be indicative of an on-going larger change in Russia as the new political system may, for the time being at least, not be in line with how we as researchers understand the socio-cultural base on which that system is built. If that is so, the failure of the model to facilitate new theoretical propositions in this specific and concrete research setting has actually led to the argument that the understanding of the socio-cultural base in Russia in some way will have to be complemented.

This, of course, is for now pure speculation, but could as such be a suggestion for further research. The questioning of what we know often starts, I believe, with a measure of speculation, and it is only later that the hermeneutic animal is tamed, forcing the speculations, if they are to survive critical attention, into controlled interpretations. And the control of the interpretations is made with regards to what else is known about a certain research setting (the specific and concrete), and/or with regards to theory (the general and abstract).

To sum up the assessment according to the double hermeneutic circle, it may be concluded on the basis of that assessment that the model is theoretically grounded, and that it works when applied in a specific research setting. Hereby the thesis that this study has pursued seems to hold true: the model is a functional research tool that makes the worldview of time-geography and the epistemology of the landscape of courses applicable to concrete research.

8.4 Generalising spatial change – looking forward

Lets try to proceed to a more general view of spatial change – a view that, although based in the model with its relativistic features, would nevertheless treat spatial change in such an abstract manner that it gets closer to universalistic presumptions on geography as a theoretical, and abstract, science. If spatial change is regarded as the result of course-relations that direct a force towards spatial change, the spatial outcome of the forces of the course-relations could be generalised into the following abstraction (Figure 8.2). The figure shows four fields relating to two axes. The vertical axis represents the *speed of change* and the horizontal represents the *degree of change*. When the surface between the axes is divided into four fields, each one of the fields represents a different type of time-spatial change.

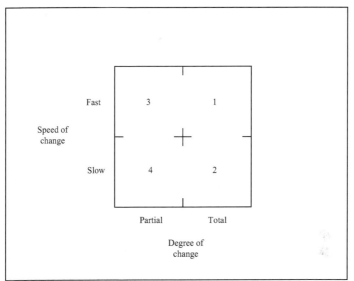

Figure 8.2   Fields of different types of spatial change

The first field represents change that is both quick and total. The second field also represents total change although this has occurred more slowly than in the first. The third field represents a quick, but partial change of space. And the fourth a slow and partial change.

To each of the fields of the abstraction certain research questions could be posed. The specificity of these questions are that they are extracted from the geographical totality without compromising how that totality has come together in the first place. A couple of examples: In the first and second fields, why is the force of the course-relations insufficient to bring about a quick change? And correspondingly, if the third or fourth field applies, how comes that the force-relations of the place manage to sustain continuity in some parts, but not in others? To sum up, questions like these would all concern power in some way, the power to change space or the power to resist it.

To this "total" model of spatial change could be added a fifth square outside the model. This could be placed at the bottom left hand corner where the two axes form the first coordinate of the diagram. This could be called the zero-alternative and it represents space that is not changed at all (i.e.

not quickly, slowly, partially or totally). This state of affairs can hardly be said to exist in any concrete time-spatial setting and, in terms of the thinking inherent in the idea of the landscape of courses, implies an impossible situation. However, lets imagine a space that does not change over time, and lets think of it as a prolonged "now" in time. Let's call such an abstract spatial situation the "geographical now".

The geographical now would exist in between periods of change. In this text, I have discussed how course-relations form space, as a certain space is a meeting-place for course-relations. However, when the forces of the course-relations *balance* each other, then meeting-places and hence space would logically not change, but just continue being more or less as before. Thus we would get periods of time, in which the concept of the geographical now would apply to describe this kind of hypothetical situation in time-space. But what is this construct good for? Well, as an abstract construct it might, I imagine, be of help as a zero-reference in assessing change when studying spatial change.

This zero-reference might also be given to time-spatial situations that are changing in a constant or regular way, and the studies would then focus on the changes of the regularity. This might be better illustrated with lines than fields.

8.5 Lines, instead of fields

Another way, as compared to Figure 8.2, to show the different types of spatial change is illustrated in Figure 8.3. In the diagram of Figure 8.3 the fields of Figure 8.2 are represented by correspondingly numbered lines.

These lines are just another way of presenting the same idea as above, but lines might, when one is added to another, be a better way to illustrate the changes of spatial change itself. For example, in empirical studies it would be expected that when a certain meeting-place for the course-relations is singled out for study, the types of change explicated above would not be as pure as they are when abstracted and generalised in the figures. Depending on the time-spatial-scale one chooses, it would most likely be possible in such an empirical study to see how the different types of spatial change (field or line 1, 2 etc) subsequently follow one another. Rather than only stating that after one type of change another follows, the process could be shown in the following type of diagram (Figure 8.4).

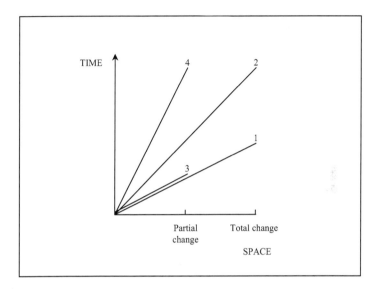

Figure 8.3   Lines of different types of spatial change

From the curved lines in this diagram, similar questions as from Figure 8.2 and 8.3 could be excerpted. Why is the change initially slow but then rapid? Is it because some of the course-relations only have limited durability? Or because others gain momentum and force only after some time? And why would that be? How come that change is first rapid and then slow? Could it be that some course-relations mobilise force to fight off change only after change had started? Or was the force of the initial course-relation too weak to totally transform space? Or had there been any unanticipated chain reactions? How is this dynamic structured?

As is shown in the figure, the interface between different types of change in time-space has been smoothed and marked. It may be ventured that these interfaces would be the most interesting to study, at least if one wants to understand the forces behind the different course-relations.

Maybe of special interest would be the hypothetical interface in time-space when change ceases and turns into the imaginable zero-alternative, i.e. when the course-relations perfectly balance each other. Would such a question provide answers that relate to the limits of spatial change? Would it explain stiff landscapes?

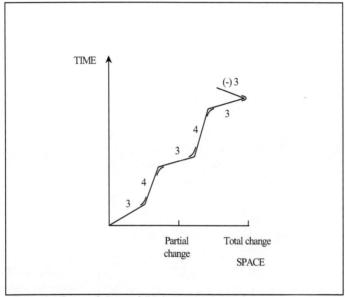

Figure 8.4 Types of change following each other

Hypothetical questions like these could be formulated almost ad infinitum, as the number of combinations in the generalised model of spatial change be-comes rather large. However, to put questions in relation to the abstractions presented here would not only be interesting in itself, but would, I hope, facilitate the analyses of time-space in what might be called a regional sense. This, however, would be a kind of regional geography adapted to include internal as well as external (f)actors, and how they evolve and affect space over time.

Now, would it be possible, on the basis on these suggestions, to be more specific and concrete with regards to interesting questions to study?

As was shown in Chapter 2, there is very little research on Russia that could be said to qualify as cultural geography. This means that there is scope for much future research to be carried out concerning how places and landscapes are con-structed, both historically and today. This would be especially interesting with regards not only to the special era of the Soviet Union, about which little is known concerning everyday life, but also to the latest tendencies of Russian politics towards re-centralising the power and political administration of the country. The de-Sovietisation of the country in the 1990s opened up for free speech and relatively free and open political elections in which the political leadership could be replaced. For some years now, this is a statement that needs modification. Few mass media are independent of the political power structures and this affects both free speech and the possibility to hold fair elections. Within the light of this it would be interesting to continue to study the role of spatial representations and how different actors relate to them. What, for example, will come after the current meta-project of Sankt-Peterburg? How will different actors use it? What languages (codes) will evolve? Will there be a new set of maps, both ordinary and performative? Or will they degenerate into pure falsifications and propaganda? Moreover, what about the speculation concerning a larger cultural transformation of Russia that has yet to be included in the preconceptions of research on Russia?

Related and more specific suggestions for future research concern the system of local self-government in Russia and Sankt-Peterburg. As has been discussed above, local self-government and a factual civic influence are new to Russia. In terms of democratisation, it is important that such local civic influence has a central position in the political life of the country, and research into the processes relating to the local political administration would be of the utmost interest. This is not only for the sake of the maturation of democracy, but also for the reason that local politics and citizens' active interest in local politics and in their district is central to the construction of places and space.

The above questions on local self-government are the ones I perceive as the most important in future research. This is for two main reasons. Firstly, that further research into this aspect may lead to changes in the research community's preconceptions on Russia. Secondly, and partly for more personal reasons, I conceive of a democratic evolution of society as very important, and research discussions should be useful in illuminating the question concerning Russia's democratisation.

To raise the covetous eye a bit, it is in the political system at the local level and in concrete places where the democratic changes would make themselves most noticeable for society at large. With a political system that fosters local civic influence, it is not difficult to imagine that the democratisation of Russia at large would be facilitated. Local self-government is about much more than local influence over where cars should be parked, or which benches should be repaired. At the base of these issues one finds the prerequisites for the social discussion, or dialogue, necessary to solve common problems. This is, in short, about reaching agreement on fair and sustainable principles for how time-space and its resources should best be put to use. In future research it would be interesting to follow this evolution, on media, politics and identity mirrored by places and the local, which is the level of scale at which true change is factual and manifests itself for the citizens with direct and concrete implications for how life is actually lived, and for how the earth is formed to the home of humanity.

Appendix A: Issues of local self-government

The following issues are the responsibility of local self-government in Sankt-Peterburg's municipal circuits:

1) Acceptance and change of the charter of municipal formation, [and] the control of its observance.
2) Possession, using, disposal of the asset which is in the property of municipal formations according to the current legislation.
3) Formation, ratification and execution of the local budget.
4) Introduction and cancellation of local taxes and tax collections, definition of concrete rates and granting of privileges on payment of taxes and tax collections according to the current legislation.
5) Acceptance of plans and programs of development of municipal formation.
6) Maintenance and use of a municipal available housing [(*zhilishchnogo fonda*)] and the uninhabited premises transferred to the municipal property by laws of St. Petersburg.
7) Organization, maintenance and development of municipal establishments of preschool and basic general education.
8) Organization, the maintenance (contents) and development of municipal establishments of social protection of the population, culture, physical training and sports, [and] public health services.
9) Distribution of sanctions to marriage to the persons who have reached age of sixteen years in the order established by the family legislation.
10) Organization and realization of trusteeship and guardianship, including children who have stayed without care of parents, according to federal laws and laws of St. Petersburg.
11) Maintenance of sanitary well-being of the population of [the] municipal formation, realization of actions for preservation of the environment in [the] territory of [the] municipal formation.

12) Establishment of the municipal organizations, including the unitary enterprises based on the right of economic conducting.
13) Repairing and gardening of house and courtyard territories.
14) Organization and maintenance of municipal archives.
15) Maintenance of municipal information service.
16) Maintenance of activity of mass media of [the] municipal formation.
17) Creation of conditions for maintenance of the population of [the] municipal formation with services of trade, public catering and consumer services.
18) Organization of fuel supply for the population of [the] municipal formation and [the] municipal establishments.
19) Organization and maintenance of protection of [the] social order at the expense of [the] local budgets of [the] municipal bodies.
20) Maintenance of granting of social services to the population of [the] municipal formation due to means of local budgets.
21) Assistance of employment of the population of [the] municipal formation due to means of local budgets.
22) Organization of work on military-patriotic education of [the] citizens of the Russian Federation in [the] territory of municipal formation.
23) Maintenance and development of public transport.
24) Organization and realization of actions for protection of the population and [the] territories from extreme situations of natural and technogenic character.

The list is published in Russian in *Munitsipal'naia zhizn'*, *vypusk* no 2 (5), 17 March 2000, and in English on the common homepage of Sankt-Peterburg's self-governing municipalities (Local Self-Government in St. Petersburg, July 2003).

Appendix B: The Municipal Council

In this appendix, I describe the characteristics of the deputies in the Municipal Council (*Munitsipal'nyi Sovet*) in Munitsipal'nyi okrug No 40 "Uritsk", which is the formal name of the Municipal Circuit in Ligovo.

The account is based on the deputies' self-descriptions, which are published on the Municipality's homepage (Munitsipal'nyi okrug No 40 "Uritsk", 2003). The deputies in the first Council (1998–2000) are only presented with name, year of birth and occupation, wheras the deputies of the second Council (2000–2004) present themselves with a portrait photograph and a short text. The text regards their personal history and in most cases this includes information concerning where they currently live and work, their education and earlier careers. Directly or indirectly, many also explain their connection to the neighbourhood and most of them state their family background and present family situation, e.g. if they are married and have children.

Age, sex, profession and education among the deputies

During the first term of office 1998–2000, the Council comprised seven female deputies and thirteen male deputies. Both the Chairman and the Vice-Chairman were men. The average age among the deputies was relatively low, ten being born in the 1960s and one in the 1970s. In this group the men dominated; nine were men and two were women. The other deputies were older, five being born in the 1950s, three in the 1940s and one in the 1930s. Of these, five were women and four were men.

The Municipality employed two of the twenty deputies. Four were teachers (one at a technical college, *tekhnikum*) and one was the headmaster of a local school. Three persons ran their own businesses, two were policemen and one was a guard. Two were pensioners and among the rest, there was one senior physician (*glavnyi vrach*), one engineer, one technician, one deputy superior (*zam. nachal'nika*) and one shop manager (*administrator v khoz. magazine*).

Concerning the deputies elected in 2000, of the nineteen persons about which there is information, the picture regarding the age distribution is about the same as in the first group of deputies; ten are born in the 1960s and one in the 1970s. Of these, nine are men and two are women. In the older group five are men (three were born in the 1950s and two in the 1940s) and three are women (two were born in the 1950s and one in the 1940s). Both the Chairman, who was re-elected to the post, and the Vice-Chairman, who is new to the post, are men. The picture of the male gender biased leadership of the Municipality is somewhat balanced by the fact that four of the seven Commissions are headed by women.

The average age of deputies in the Council is relatively low in both the first and the second terms of office. The gender distribution has changed however between the two terms to an increased male dominance. It is striking, however, that in both terms, the gender distribution is in balance in the group of older deputies (born in the 1950s or earlier), whereas men heavily dominate the younger group in both terms.

In the group of deputies from 2000, an additional factor that many of them point out in their self-presentations is a link to the military. This is so also for the women. Two of the five women have a connection to the military via their families, and one woman states that her parents were blockade survivors (*blokadniki*). Among the men, ten emphasise their background in the military. Eight of these have, aside from compulsory military service, been employed in military service at some point in life. Of the other two, one person relates where he did his compulsory service, and one states that his family has a military background. In total, a majority of the deputies (twelve persons) refer directly to the military in their self-presentations.

None of these, however, are now active military personnel although several of them state that they are now policemen (*militsioner*). On the portrait photographs these six are dressed in their police uniform. A military pensioner wears his military uniform, and one of the former servicemen wears his military marks of distinction (*ordenskaia planka*) on his civilian clothes.

The occupational group that is most heavily over-represented among the 19 deputies is the police. As has been mentioned above, six of the deputies work as policemen, three of them as police officers (three persons are *ychastkovym inspektorom*, and three persons are *starshym ychastkovym inspektorom*). All six of them are stationed at the same department (No. 54 Krasnosel'skii raion) but work in different parts of the district (the raion).

Among the other thirteen persons there is one teacher, one headmaster (both at School 383 situated within the borders of the Municipal Circuit), one senior physician (*glavnyi vrach*), one journalist, one technician, one youth worker, four civil servants and one is a higher salaried employee in private business. The Chairman has a background as engineer and the Vice-Chairman (Anatolii Nikolaevich, see Chapter 7) is a retired military from the navy. These two now work full-time for the Municipality.

All but four of the nineteen are highly educated and of the highly educated, two also have post-graduate education (*kandidat nauk*). Several of the deputies declare that their children study at the university. Only one states a working-class family background. Two of the deputies are married to each other.

The ethnic, or national (*national'nost'*), composition is not evident from the self-presentations except in two cases in which the persons state that they are Russians. Concerning the others, all but two have traditionally Russian first names and patronymics. The surnames are more varied but the vast majority (15 persons) have surnames that are typically Russian. As far as physical looks are indicative of ethnic background, of the portrait photographs only two do not have typical Russian features, and the names of these are not typically Russian either. It thus seems as if the Municipal Council is clearly dominated by ethnic Russians.[87]

---

87   The analyses of names and physical appearance have been double-checked with a native Russian.

Local connection and earlier political experience of the deputies

An important question in relation to how *local* the local democracy actually is, concerns the degree of affiliation the deputies have to the Municipality in which they are elected as representatives. In the group of deputies elected at the 2000 election, only three do not refer to any type of local connection in their self-presentations (one of them being the Chairman).

The degree of local connection among the others may be divided in two groups. The first is made up by those who have strong ties to the Municipality, either by living in Ligovo, or by working in Ligovo. The second group are those who have weak ties to the Municipality, and these are the deputies that either live or work in other parts of Krasnosel'skii raion. According to the self-presentations of the sixteen deputies in these two groups, their grade of local connectedness is as follows:

Strong ties
– Four persons state that they live in Ligovo. Of these, two persons (the married couple) also relate that they have children in one of the schools in the Municipality;

– Seven persons state that they work in Ligovo.

Weak ties
– Three persons state that they live in Krasnosel'skii raion (of which two also work in the raion);

– Two persons state that they work in Krasnosel'skii raion (apart from the two mentioned above)

Of the nineteen deputies, seven state that they had been proposed by the voters in the Circuit ("*vydvinyt izbirateliami okruga*"), and only one person states that she had been proposed by a political party (Iablako). The latter person is one of seven who have previous experience of political work. Of the remaining six, some have been politicians themselves and others have worked close to political decision-makers, and could thus be said to know what political life is about.

According to the self-presentations of the rest of the deputies, their political work in the Municipality seems to be their first personal involvement in political life. Concerning the Commissions, four of the seven Presidents belong to the group that has had some earlier political experience, as defined above.

According to the self-presentations, the number of deputies with a local connection in terms of living and working in (strong ties) or near (weak ties) Ligovo seems to be rather high. Sixteen persons, a clear majority of the total of deputies belong to this group. However, only four persons (among them a married couple) explicitly state that they live within the borders of the Municipality, which is a rather low number of the total.

Among the leaders of the Municipal Council, the Vice-Chairman (Anatolii Nikolaevich, see Chapter 7) has strong connections to Ligovo. He is born in Leningrad and has lived in the Circuit for more than 20 years (as of 2000). The Chairman does not state where he lives, and from his self-presentation it is not possible to know where he worked before he became involved in the Municipal Council.

Among the Presidents of the Commissions, only the President of the Commission for Social Questions lives in Ligovo. Judging from the amount of deputies it engages (three persons), and its position at the bottom of the list, this Commission is considered the least important of them all. The important Commission of Budget and Finance, which is listed first among the Commissions and which engages five deputies, is, on the other hand, headed by a President who does not even live in Krasnosel'skii raion but in another part of the city. He does not seem to have any other connection to the Municipality other than being an elected member of the Municipal Council. Of the remaining Commissions, a deputy who works in Ligovo heads the important Commission for Education, Culture and Youth. The other Commissions are presided over by persons with weak ties to Ligovo (they either work or live in the adjoining raion).

To sum up, most of the deputies have some connection to Ligovo in that they live or work there, or nearby. However, only a minority lives in Ligovo. The Chairman is not strongly connected to Ligovo and neither is the President of the most important Commission. However, the Vice-Chairman and two of the Presidents have close connections (strong ties) with the place. The other four are connected to Ligovo only indirectly (they work or live in the Krasnosel'skii raion). If it is regarded as positive that the deputies have a close connection to Ligovo, then the current situation could be better. The total picture of the grade of connectedness among the deputies to the place that they are mandated to administer is maybe best described as mixed.

Bibliography

Agar, John (1978) Maps and Propaganda, *Bulletin – Society of University Cartographers* 11, 1–15.

Agar, Michael H. (1996) *The Professional Stranger: An Informal Introduction to Ethnography* (2nd edition), San Diego & London: Academic Press.

Alvesson, Mats & Kaj Sköldberg (1994) *Tolkning och reflektion: vetenskapsfilosofi och kvalitativ metod* [Interpretation and Reflection: Philosophy of Science and Qualitative Method], Lund: Studentlitteratur.

Aminov, Daud A. (1996) Po Petergofskoi i Krasnosel'skoi...[Along Petergof and Krasnosel'skoi...], *Neva* No. 2: 233–238.

Aminov, Daud A. (1990) Iz istorii nashevo goroda: Ligovo – Uritsk [From the History of our City: Ligovo – Uritsk], *Dialog* 33 (November): 25–32.

Aminov, Daud A. (1988) Byla takaia rechka Liga... [Once was the Small River Liga...], *Leningradskaia Panorama* No 4: 33–34.

AN (1993) CIA Guide to St. Petersburg, *Geographical Magazine* 65, 7: 6.

Anderberg, Stefan (1996) *Flödesanalys i den hållbara utvecklingens tjänst. Reflektioner kring en "metabolism"-studie av Rehnområdets utveckling* [Flow-analysis in the Service of Sustainable Development: Reflections on a "Metabolism"-study of the Development of the Rhine Valley], Meddelanden från Lunds universitets geografiska institutioner, avhandlingar 128, Lund: Lund University Press.

Anderson Kay, Mona Domosh, Steve Pile & Nigel Thrift (eds) (2003) *Handbook of Cultural Geography*, London: Sage.

Anuchin, Vsevolod A (1977) *Theoretical problems of geography*, edited by R.J. Fuchs & G.J. Demko, Columbus: Ohio State University Press.

Arnstberg, Karl-Olov (1997) *Fältetnologi* [Field Ethnology], Stockholm: Carlssons.

Arnstberg, Karl-Olov (1996) Humanvetenskapliga aspekter [Aspects of the Human Sciences], in *Människa och miljö* [Man and Environment], Stockholm: Byggnadsforskningsrådet G3.

Asplund, Johan (1983) *Tid, rum, individ och kollektiv* [Time, Space, Individual and Collective], Stockholm: Liber.

Åquist, Ann-Cathrine (1992) *Tidsgeografi i samspel med samhällsteori* [Time-geography in Association with Social Theory], Meddelanden från Lunds geografiska institutioner, avhandlingar nr 115, Lund: Lund Unversity Press.

Bandlamudi, Lakshmi (1994) Dialogics of Understanding Self/Culture, *Ethos* 22, 4: 460–493.

Barabashev, Georgii V. (1994) Main Currents in the Development of Russian Local Self-Government, in T.H. Friedgut & J.W. Hahn (eds) *Local Power and Post-Soviet Politics*, London: M.E Sharpe.

Barnes, Trevor J. & James S. Duncan (1992) Introduction: Writing Worlds, in T.J. Barnes & J.S. Duncan (eds) *Writing Worlds: Discourse, Text and Metaphor in the Representation of the Landscape*, London & New York: Routledge.

Bassin, Mark (2000) Landscape and Identity in Russian and Soviet Art: An Introduction, *Ecumene* 7, 3: 249–251.

Bassin, Mark (1999) *Imperial Visions: Nationalist Imagination and Geographical Expansion in the Russian Far East, 1840–1865*, Cambridge: Cambridge University Press.

Bassin, Mark (1992) Geographical Determinism in Fin-de-Siècle Marxism: Georgii Plekhanov and the Environmental Basis of Russian history, *Annals of the Association of American Geographers* 82, 1: 3–22.

Bassin, Mark (1991) Russia between Europe and Asia: The Ideological Construction of Geographical Space, *Slavic Review* 50, 1: 1–17.

Bassin, Mark (1988) Expansion and Colonialism on the Eastern Frontier: Views of Siberia and the Far East in Pre-Petrine Russia, *Journal of Historical Geography* 14, 1: 3–21.

Bassin, Mark (1983) The Russian Geographical Society, the "Amur Epoch," and the Great Siberian Expedition 1855–1863, *Annals of the Association of American Geographers* 73, 2: 240–256.

Bater, James H. (1996) *Russia and the Post-Soviet Scene: A Geographical Perspective*, London: Arnold.

Bater, James H. (1980) *The Soviet City: Ideal and Reality*, London: Arnold.

Bater, James H. (1976) *St Petersburg: Industrialization and Change*, London: Edward Arnold.

Baxter, Jamie & John Eyles (1997) Evaluating Qualitive Research in Social Geography: Establishing 'Rigour' in Interview Analysis, *Transactions of the Institute of British Geographers* 22, 4: 505–525.

Bäckman, Jennie (2001) Nätverk i olika sociala rum. IT:s påverkan på mänskligt handlingsutrymme, räckhåll och rörelsemönster [Networks in Different Social Spaces: Information Technology and its Impact on Human Action-Space, Reach, and Patterns of Mobility]. Unpublished Master thesis (D-uppsats), Södertörn University College, Human Geography.

Belin, Laura (2001) Political Bias and Self-Censorship in the Russian Media, in A. Brown (ed.) *Contemporary Russian Politics: A Reader*, Oxford: Oxford University Press.

Belokurova, Elena (2000) Russian Political Science on Regional Politics: An Overview, Södertörns University College: *Working paper* 3/2000.

Bengtsson, Jan (1999) Introduktion. Livets spontanitet och tolkning. Alfred Schütz' fenomenologiska samhällsteori [Introduction: The Spontanity and Interpretation of Life – Alfred Schütz' Phenomenological Social Theory], in J. Bengtsson (ed.) *Den sociala världens fenomenologi* [The Phenomenology of the Social World], Göteborg: Daidalos.

Berglund, Ulla (2002) Privatisation, segregation and local engagement: a Latvian case study, in I. Marana & S. Tsenkova (eds) *Challenges and opportunities in housing: new concepts, policies and initiatives*, Riga: CIB Working Commission 69 Housing Sociology.

Berman, Marshall (1990) *Allt som är fast förflyktigas: modernism och modernitet* [All that is Solid Melts into Air: The Experience of Modernity], 2nd edition, Lund: Arkiv.

BES: Bol'shoi entsiklopedicheskii slovar' [BES: The Large Encyclopedia] (2nd edition), Moskva: Nauchnoe izdatel'stvo "Bol'shaia Rossiiskaia entsiklopediia" & Sankt-Peterburg: Norint, 1998.

Bethea, David M. (1997) Bakhtinian Prosaics versus Lotmanian "Poetic Thinking": The Code and its Relation to Literary Biography, *The Slavic and East European Journal* 41, 1: 1–15.

Bodin, Per-Arne (2003) S:t Petersburg som ett litterärt storverk [Sankt-Peterburg as a Literary Masterpeace], *Svenska Dagbladet* 27 May, page 7.

Bodin, Per-Arne (1995) Ryssland och arvet från Bysans [Russia and the Legacy of Byzantium], in B. Furuhagen (ed.) *Ryssland – ett annat Europa. Historia och samhälle under 1000 år* [Russia – An other Europe: History and Society during 1000 years], Stockholm: SNS Förlag.

Bodin, Per-Arne (1993) *Ryssland och Europa. En kulturhistorisk studie* [Russia and Europe: A Cultural-Historical Study], Stockholm: Natur och Kultur.

Bodin, Per-Arne (1987) *Världen som ikon* [The World as Icon], Skellefteå: Artos.

Bodström, Kerstin (2000) *Balansgång – på sin plats: reflektioner och rannsakan kring en fältstudie i Stockholmsförorten Alby* [Balancing in Alby: The Research Situation in a Fragile Suburban Environment], Kulturgeografiskt Seminarium 3/00. Stockholm: Kulturgeografiska institutionen, Stockholms universitet.

Bond, Andrew R. (1989) Soviet Official admits Past Policy of Deliberate Map Distortion: Calls for Increased Access to Large-Scale Maps and Images Mount, *Mapping Sciences and Remote Sensing* 26, 2: 160–163.

Book, Tommy (2000) *Symbolskriften i det politiska landskapet. Namn – heraldik – monument* [Landscapes of Political Symbolism: Names – Heraldry – Monuments], Acta Wexionensia nr 3 Geografi, Växjö: Växjö University Press.

Book, Tommy (1996a) Stadskartor i Östeuropa – information eller desinformation? [City Maps in Eastern Europe – Information or Disinformation?], Sydsvenska Geografiska Sällskapet: *Svensk Geografisk Årsbok* 72: 35–39.

Book, Tommy (1996b) *Balkanstaden – i ständig förvandling stadsbyggnadsmässigt och etniskt* [The Balkan City – Planning and Ethnicity undergoing Continual Change], Acta Wexionensia. Social Sciences, No. 1/96. Växjö: Högskolan i Växjö.

Book, Tommy (1991) *Berlin – sönderbrutet och hopfogat, en politiskgeografisk studie* [Berlin – Broken Apart and Joined Together, a Politico-

Geographical Study], Acta Wexionensia Series 1, History and Geography No. 7. Växjö: Högskolan i Växjö.

Borén, Thomas (2003a) What are Friends for? Rationales of Informal Exchange in Russian Everyday Life, in K-O. Arnstberg & T. Borén (eds) *Everyday Economy in Russia, Poland and Latvia*, Södertörn Academic Studies 16, Huddinge: Södertörn University College. Stockholm: Almqvist & Wiksell International.

Borén, Thomas (2003b) Den sovjetiska förorten som livsmiljö: fallet Ligovo i St Petersburg [The Soviet High-rise Suburb as a Milieu for Living: The Case of Ligovo in St. Petersburg], in B. Henningsen; A. Wischmann & H. Graf (eds) *Städtischer Wandel in der Ostseeregion heute – Städers omvandling i dagens östersjöregion*. Berlin: Berliner Wissenschafts-Verlag.

Borén, Thomas (2002) *Ryssland, Baltikum och östra Europa i svenska geografiska tidskrifter 1980–2001. Bibliografi med kommentar* [Russia, the Baltic States and Eastern Europe in Swedish Geographical Periodicals 1980–2001: A Bibliography with an Introduction], Kulturgeografiskt Seminarium 2/02, Stockholm: Kulturgeografiska institutionen, Stockholms universitet.

Borén, Thomas (1999) *Källsortering för hållbar utveckling? Kretsloppssamhälle och förloppslandskap* [Sorting Waste at the Source for Sustainable Development? A Society of Circulation and the Landscape of Courses], Stockholm Geographical Reports No. 3. Stockholm: Kulturgeografiska institutionen, Stockholms universitet.

Bourdieu, Pierre (1990) *The Logic of Practice*, Cambridge: Polity Press.

Bourdieu, Pierre (1977) *Outline of a Theory of Practice*, Cambridge: Cambridge University Press.

Boym, Svetlana (1994) *Common Places: Mythologies of Everyday Life in Russia*, Cambridge: Harvard University Press.

Bradshaw, Michael J. (1990) New Regional Geography, Foreign-Area Studies and Perestroika, *Area* 22, 4: 315–322.

Brodsky, Joseph (1987) Guide till en omdöpt stad [Guide to a Renamed City], in *Att behaga en skugga. Valda essäer* [Less than One: Selected Essays], Stockholm: Wahlström & Widstrand.

Burnett, Alan (1985) Propaganda Cartography, in D. Pepper & A. Jenkins (eds) *The Geography of Peace and War*, Oxford: Basil Blackwell.

Bylinkina, N.P. & A.V. Riabushina (eds) (1985) *Sovremennaia Sovetskaia Arkhitektura 1955–1980 gg.* [Contemporary Soviet Architecture 1955–1980], Moskva: Stroiizdat.

Carlestam, Gösta & Barbro Sollbe (eds) (1991) *Om tidens vidd och tingens ordning. Texter av Torsten Hägerstrand* [On the Width of Time and the Order of Things: Texts by Torsten Hägerstrand], Stockholm: Byggnadsforskningsrådet.

Casey, Edward S. (2002) *Representing Place: Landscape Painting and Maps*, Minneapolis: University of Minnesota Press.

Cele, Sofia (2004) *Children in interaction with urban space*, Seminar Manuscript at the Department of Human Geography, Stockholm University.

Certeau, Michel de (1984) *The Practice of Everyday Life*, Berkeley: University of California Press.

Clifford, James (1986) On Ethnographic Allegory, in J. Clifford & G.E. Marcus (eds) *Writing Culture: The Poetics and Politics of Ethnography*, Berkeley: University of California Press.

Cloke, Paul et al. (2004) *Practising Human Geography*, London: Sage.

Cosgrove, Denis & Luciana L. Martins (2001) Millenial Geographics, in C. Minca (ed.) *Postmodern Geography: Theory and Praxis*, Oxford: Blackwell.

Crang, Mike (2002) Qualitative Methods: The New Orthodoxy? *Progress in Human Geography* 26, 5: 647–655.

Czaplicka, John J. & Blair A. Ruble (eds) (2003) *Composing Urban History and the Constitution of Civic Rights*, Washington D.C.: Woodrow Wilson Center Press.

Dawson, Andrew (1999) From Glittering Icon..., *The Geographical Journal* 165, 2: 154–160.

De Souza, Peter (1989) *Territorial Production Complexes in the Soviet Union – with Special Focus on Siberia*, Department of Human and Economic Geography: School of Economics and Legal Science, University of Gothenburg: Series B nr 80.

Dear, Michael (2000) *The Postmodern Urban Condition*, Oxford: Blackwell.

DeLyser, Dydia & Paul F. Starrs (2001) Doing Fieldwork: Editiors' Introduction, *Geographical Review* 91, 1 & 2: iv–viii.

Demeritt, David & Sarah Dyer (2002) Dialogue, Metaphors of Dialogue and Understandings of Geography, *Area* 34, 3: 229–241.

Dewsbury, J.D. & S. Naylor (2002) Practicing Geographical Knowledge: Fields, Bodies and Dissemination, *Area* 34, 3: 253–260.

Dingsdale, Alan (1999) New Geographies of Post-Socialist Europe, *The Geographical Journal* 165, 2: 145–153.

Doniger, Wendy (1979) Foreword, in C. Lévi-Strauss *Myth and Meaning: Cracking the Code of Culture*, New York: Schocken Books.

Driver, Felix (2000) Editorial: Field-work in Geography, *Transactions of the Institute of British Geographers* 25, 3: 267–268.

Duncan, James S. (1990) *The City as Text: The Politics of Landscape Interpretation in the Kandyan Kingdom*, Cambridge: Cambridge University Press.

Duncan, James S. & Nancy G Duncan (2001) Theory in the Field, *Geographical Review* 91, 1 & 2: 399–406.

Duncan, James S. & David Ley (1993) Introduction: Representing the Place of Culture, in J.S. Duncan & D. Ley (eds) *Place/Culture/Representation*, London & New York: Routledge.

Eco, Umberto (1992a) Overinterpreting Texts, in S. Collini (ed.) *Interpretation and Overinterpretation*, Cambridge: Cambridge University Press.

Eco, Umberto (1992b) Between Author and Text, in S. Collini (ed.) *Interpretation and Overinterpretation*, Cambridge: Cambridge University Press.

Eco, Umberto (1990) Introduction, in Y. Lotman, *Universe of the Mind: A Semiotic Theory of Culture*, London & New York: I.B. Tauris & Co.

Eco, Umberto (1977/1987) De nya filosoferna [The New Philosophers], in *Vad kostar ett mästerverk?* [How Much for a Master-peace?], Stockholm: Brombergs.

Eco, Umberto (1967/1987) Cogito Interruptus, in *Vad kostar ett mästerverk?* [How Much for a Master-peace?], Stockholm: Brombergs.

Ehrensvärd, Ulla (2000) Svensk kartläggning i Baltikum [Swedish Mapping in the Baltic States], Svenska Sällskapet för Antropologi och Geografi: *Ymer* 120: 225–239.

Ellegård, Kajsa & Bo Lenntorp (1980) Teknisk förändring och produktionsstruktur. En ansats till analys med exempel från mejerihanteringen [Technical Change and the Structure of Production: An Attempt at an Analysis, with Examples from Dairying], Sydsvenska Geografiska Sällskapet: *Svensk Geografisk Årsbok* 56: 75–88.

England, Kim V.L. (1994) Gettting Personal: Reflexivity, Positionality, and Feminist Research, *The Professional Geographer* 46, 1: 80–89.

Evans, Mel (1988) Participant Observation: The Researcher as Research Tool, in J. Eyles & D.M. Smith (eds) *Qualitative Methods in Human Geography*, Cambridge: Polity Press.

Evans Jr., Alfred B. (2004) Contemporary Russian Scholars' Changing Views on Local Government in Late Tsarist Russia, in A.B. Evans Jr. & V. Gel'man (eds) *The Politics of Local Government in Russia*, Oxford: Rowman & Littlefield Publishers.

Forest, Benjamin & Juliet Johnson (2002) Unraveling the Threads of History: Soviet Era Monuments and Post-Soviet National Identity in Moscow, *Annals of the Association of American Geographers* 92, 3: 524–547.

French, R. Antony (1979) The Individuality of the Soviet city, in R.A. French & F.E. Ian Hamilton (eds) *The Socialist City: Spatial Structure and Urban Policy*, Chichester: John Wiley & Sons.

French, R. Antony & F.E. Ian Hamilton (eds) (1979) *The Socialist City: Spatial Structure and Urban Policy*, Chichester: John Wiley & Sons.

Friedgut, Theodore H. (1994) Introduction: Local Government under the Old Regime, in T.H. Friedgut & J.W. Hahn (eds) *Local Power and Post-Soviet Politics*, Armonk & London: M.E. Sharpe.

Gaddy, Clifford G. (1996) *The Price of the Past: Russia's Struggle with the Legacy of a Militarized Economy*, Washington D.C.: Brookings Institution Press.

Gallagher, L. Jerome; Raymond J. Struyk & Ludmila Nikonova (2003) Savings from Integrating Administrative Systems for Social Assistance

Programmes in Russia, *Public Administration and Development* 23, 177–195.

Geertz, Clifford (1973) *The Interpretation of Cultures*, New York: Basic Books.

Gel'man, Vladimir (2004) Introduction: The Politics of Local Government in Russia: A Framework for Analysis, in A.B. Evans Jr. & V. Gel'man (eds) *The Politics of Local Government in Russia*, Oxford: Rowman & Littlefield Publishers.

Gel'man, Vladimir (2003) In Search of Local Autonomy: The Politics of Big Cities in Russia's Transition, *International Journal of Urban and Regional Research* 27, 1: 48–61.

Gel'man, Vladimir & Mary McAuley (1994) The Politics of City Government: Leningrad/St. Petersburg, 1990–1992, in T.H. Friedgut & J.W. Hahn (eds) *Local Power and Post-Soviet Politics*, Armonk & London: M.E. Sharpe.

Gentile, Michael (2004a) Segregation by Socio-Economic Status and Housing Quality in a Post-Soviet City: Evidence from Ust'-Kamenogorsk, Kazakhstan, in M. Gentile *Studies in the Transformation of Post-Soviet Cities: Case Studies from Kazakhstan*, Geografiska Regionstudier nr 59, Uppsala: Uppsala University, Department of Social and Economic Geography.

Gentile, Michael (2004b) Former Closed Cities and Urbanisation in the ex-USSR: An Exploration in Kazakhstan, *Europe-Asia Studies* 56, 2: 263–278.

Gentile, Michael (2003) Residential Segregation in a Medium-Sized Post-Soviet City: Ust'-Kamenogorsk, Kazakhstan, *Tijdschrift voor Economische en Sociale Geografie* 94, 5: 589–605.

Gerasimov, Innokenty (1981) The Historical Background to Russian and Soviet Geography, in L.N Kudriashcheva (ed.) *Soviet Geography Today: Aspects of Theory*, Moscow: Progress.

Giddens, Anthony (1985) Jürgen Habermas, in Q. Skinner (ed.) *The Return of Grand Theory in the Human Sciences*, Cambridge: Cambridge University Press.

Gohstand, Robert (1993) Book Review (of Lappo & Petrov 1992, see below), *Slavic Review* 52, 3: 653–656.

Gorbachevich, K. & E. Khablo (1998) *Pochemu tak nazvany?* [Why That Name?] (5th edition), Sankt-Peterburg: Norint.

Gosporov, Boris (1985) Introduction, in A.D. Nakhimovsky & A. Stone Nakhimovsky (eds) *The Semiotics of Russian Cultural History: Essays by Iurii M. Lotman, Lidiia Ia. Ginsburg, Boris A. Uspenskii*, Itacha & London: Cornell University Press.

Gregory, Derek & John Urry (1985) Introduction, in D. Gregory & J. Urry (eds) *Social Relations and Spatial Structures*, London: MacMillan Publishers.

Gregson, Nicky (2003) Reclaiming "the Social" in Social and Cultural Geography, in K. Anderson, M. Domosh, S. Pile & N. Thrift (eds) *Handbook of Cultural Geography*, London: Sage.

Gren, Martin (1994) *Earth Writing: Exploring Representation and Social Geography in-between Meaning/Matter*, Departments of Geography, University of Gothenburg, Series B, No. 85, Gothenburg: Department of Human and Economic Geography, University of Gothenburg.

Gren, Martin & Per-Olof Hallin (2003) *Kulturgeografi. En ämnesteoretisk introduktion* [Human Geography: A Theoretical Introduction to the Subject], Malmö: Liber.

Habermas, Jürgen (1987a) *The Theory of Communicative Action: The Critique of Functionalist Reason, vol. 2*, Cambridge: Polity Press.

Habermas, Jürgen (1987b) *The Philosophical Discourse of Modernity: Twelve Lectures*, Cambridge: Polity Press.

Habermas, Jürgen (1984) *The Theory of Communicative Action: Reason and the Rationalization of Society, Vol. 1*, Boston: Beacon Press.

Hagström, Martin (2000) Control over the Media in Post-Soviet Russia, in J. Ekekrantz & K. Olofsson (eds) *Russian Reports: Studies in Post-Communist Transformation of Media and Journalism*, Södertörn Academic Studies 2, Stockholm: Almqvist & Wiksell International.

Hannerz, Ulf (1983) *Över gränser* [Crossing Borders], Lund: LiberFörlag.

Hapke, Holly M. & Devan Ayyankeril (2001) Of "Loose" Women and "Guides," or, Relationships in the Field, *Geographical Review* 91, 1 & 2: 342–352.

Harley, J. Brian (1989/1997) Deconstructing the Map, in T. Barnes & D. Gregory (eds) *Reading Human Geography: The Poetics and Politics of Inquiry*, London: Arnold.

Harley, J. Brian (1988) Maps, Knowledge, and Power, in D. Cosgrove & S. Daniels (eds) *The Iconography of Landscape: Essays on the Symbolic Representation, Design and Use of Past Environments*, Cambridge: Cambridge University Press.

Harrison, Dick (1998/2003) *Skapelsens geografi. Föreställningar om rymd och rum i medeltidens Europa* [The Geography of The Creation: Representations on Space in Medieval Europe], Svenska Humanistiska Förbundet 110, Stockholm: Ordfront.

Harvey, David (1985a) *The Urbanization of Capital*, Oxford: Basil Blackwell.

Harvey, David (1985b) The Geopolitics of Capitalism, in D. Gregory & J. Urry (eds) *Social Relations and Spatial Structures*, London: MacMillan Publishers.

Hägerstrand, Torsten (1993) Samhälle och natur [Society and Nature], *NordREFO* 1993, 1: 14–59.

Hägerstrand, Torsten (1991) Tidsgeografi [Time-Geography], in G. Carlestam & B. Sollbe (eds) *Om tidens vidd och tingens ordning. Texter av Torsten Hägerstrand* [On the Width of Time and the Order of Things: Texts by Torsten Hägerstrand], Stockholm: Byggnadsforskningsrådet.

Hägerstrand, Torsten (1985a) Den geografiska traditionens kärnområde [The Core of the Geographic Tradition], *Geografiska Notiser* 43, 3: 3–7.

Hägerstrand, Torsten (1985b) Time-Geography: Focus on the Corporeality of Man, Society, and Environment, in *The Science and Praxis of Complexity*, Tokyo: United Nations University.

Hägerstrand, Torsten (1970) Konturerna av en tidsgeografisk samhällsmodell [The Contours of a Time-Geographic Model of Society], in *Urbaniseringen av Sverige* [The Urbanisation of Sweden], Stockholm: Statens Offentliga Utredningar 1970:14, bilaga 1:4.

Healey, Nigel M; Vladimir Leksin & Aleksandr Svetsov (1999) The Municipalization of Enterprise-owned "Social Assets" in Russia, *Post-Soviet Affairs* 15, 3: 262–280.

Hedenskog, Jakob (1999) *Mellan självstyre och centralstyre. S:t Petersburg och dess förhållande till centralmakten under 1990-talet* [Between

Autonomy and Central Government: St. Petersburg and Its Relationship to the Federal Powers in the 1990s], Stockholm: Defence Research Establishment, Division for Defense Analysis.

Hedlund, Stefan (1992) *Öststatsekonomi* [Economy of the Eastern States] (2nd edition), Lund: Dialogos.

Hellberg-Hirn, Elena (2003) *Imperial Imprints: Post-Soviet St Petersburg*, Helsinki: SKS Finnish Literature Society.

Hellstedt, Jane (1988) *S:t Petersburg – Leningrad*, Vagnhärad: Seminarium.

Herbert, Steve (2001) From Spy to Okay Guy: Trust and Validity in Fieldwork with the Police, *Geographical Review* 91, 1 & 2: 304–310.

Herbert, Steve (2000) For Ethnography, *Progress in Human Geography* 24, 4: 550–568.

Herrold, Melinda (2001) Which Truth? Cultural Politics and Vodka in Rural Russia, *Geographical Review* 91, 1 & 2: 295–303.

Holloway, Julian & James Kneale (2000) Mikhail Bakhtin: Dialogics of Space, in M. Crang & N. Thrift (eds) *Thinking Space*, London & New York: Routledge.

Holt-Jensen, Arild (1999) *Geography: History and Concepts, a Students' Guide* (3rd edition), London: Sage Publications.

Hooson, David J.M (1984) The Soviet Union, in R.J. Johnston & P. Claval (eds) *Geography since the Second World War: An International Survey*, London: Croom Helm.

Hooson, David J.M. (1968) The Development of Geography in Pre-Soviet Russia, *Annals of the Association of American Geographers* 58, 2: 250–272.

Jackson, Peter (2000) Rematerializing Social and Cultural Geography, *Social & Cultural Geography* 1, 1: 9–14.

Jackson, Peter (1985) Urban Ethnography, *Progress in Human Geography* 9, 2: 157–176.

Jackson, Peter (1983) Principles and Problems of Participant Observation, *Geografiska Annaler* 65 B, 1: 39–47.

Jagomägi, J. & H. Mardiste (1994) Maps and Mapping in Estonia, *GeoJournal* 33, 1: 81–90.

Jangfeldt, Bengt (1998) *Svenska vägar till S:t Petersburg. Kapitel ur historien om svenskarna vid Nevans stränder* [Swedish Ways to Sankt-Peterburg: Chapters from the History of the Swedes at the River-banks of Neva], Stockholm: Wahlström & Widstrand.

Jangfeldt, Bengt (1987) Estetiken är etikens moder. Ett samtal med Joseph Brodsky [Aesthetics is the Mother of Ethics: A Conversation with Joseph Brodsky], in J. Brodsky *Att behaga en skugga. Valda essäer* [Less than One: Selected Essays], Stockholm: Wahlström & Widstrand.

Jansson, Ulf (2003) Inledning – med landskapet i centrum [Introduction – With the Landscape at the Centre], in U. Jansson (ed.) *Med landskapet i centrum. Kulturgeografiska perspektiv på nutida och historiska landskap* [With the Landscape at the Centre: Perspectives of Human Geography on Contemporary and Historical Landscapes], Meddelanden från Kulturgeografiska institutionen vid Stockholms universitet 119, Stockholm: Kulturgeografiska institutionen, Stockholms universitet.

Johnston, R.J. (1997) *Geography and Geographers: Anglo-American Human Geography since 1945* (5th edition), London: Arnold.

Kapuściński, Ryszard (1996) *Imperiet* [The Empire], Stockholm: Bonnier Alba.

Karimov, Alexei (1999) Russian Cadastrial Surveys before and after Peter the Great, *The Cartographic Journal* 36, 2: 125–132.

Kirkow, Peter (1997) Local Self-Government in Russia: Awakening from Slumber? *Europe-Asia Studies* 49, 1: 43–58.

Komarov, A. (1988) Krasnosel'skii raion [Krasnosel'skii raion], *Dialog* No. 29 (October): 2–6.

Komedchikov, N.N. (2000) Cartography in the USSR Academy of Sciences, 1917–1991, *Mapping Sciences and Remote Sensing* 37, 1: 17–39.

Kotkin, Stephen (2001) *Armageddon Averted: The Soviet Collapse 1970–2000*, Oxford: Oxford University Press.

Kotkin, Stephen (1991) *Steeltown, USSR: Soviet Society in the Gorbachev Era*, Berkeley: University of California Press.

Krekola, Tamara (2000) The Alternative Press in St. Petersburg, 1987–1991, in J. Ekekrantz & K. Olofsson (eds) *Russian Reports: Studies in*

Post-Communist Transformation of Media and Journalism, Södertörn Academic Studies 2, Stockholm: Almqvist & Wiksell International.

Kropotkin, Peter (1962) *En anarkists minnen* [Memoirs of a Revolutionist], Stockholm: Forum.

Kull, Anu (1990) Trends in the Development of Human Geography in Estonia after the Second World War, *Geografiska Annaler* 72 B, 1: 27–33.

Lankina, Tomila (2002) Local Administration and Ethno-Social Consensus in Russia, *Europe-Asia Studies* 54, 7: 1037–1053.

Lankina, Tomila (2001) Local Government and Ethnic and Social Activism in Russia, in A. Brown (ed.) *Contemporary Russian Politics: A Reader*, Oxford: Oxford University Press.

Lapteva, Liudmila (1996) Problems of Local Self-Government in Russia, *The Russian Review* 55: 317–324.

Lees, Loretta (2002) Rematerializing Geography: The "New" Urban Geography, *Progress in Human Geography* 26, 1: 101–112.

Ledeneva, Alena V. (1998) *Russia's Economy of Favours: Blat, Networking and Informal Exchange*, Cambridge: Cambridge University Press.

Lenina, Valentina (1993) Doroga na Dudergof [The Road to Dudergof], *Neva* No. 7: 263–272.

Leningrad and Its Environs: A Guide (1979) Moscow: Progress.

Leningrad: A Guide (1990) (2nd edition) Moscow: Planeta Publishers.

Lenntorp, Bo (1998) Orienteringsanvisningar i ett forskningslandskap [Directions of Orientation in a Landscape of Research], in M. Gren & P.O. Hallin (eds) *Svensk kulturgeografi. En exkursion inför 2000-talet* [Swedish Human Geography: An Excursion on the Eve of the 21st Century], Lund: Studentlitteratur.

Lenntorp, Bo (1995) Kulturgeografi, speglat i dess avhandlingar [Human Geography as Reflected in its Dissertations], *Geografiska Notiser* 53, 3: 160–165.

Lenntorp, Bo (1993) De fyra nordiska husen – en empirisk studie av materialflöden i samband med husbyggnation [The Four Nordic Houses – An Empirical Study of Material Flows in Connection with the Construction of Houses], *NordREFO* 1993, 1: 76–111.

Lévi-Strauss, Claude (1979) *Myth and Meaning: Cracking the Code of Culture*, New York: Schocken Books.
Ley, David & James Duncan (1993) Epilogue, in J. Duncan & D. Ley (eds) *Place/Culture/Representation*, London & New York: Routledge.
Limb, Melanie & Claire Dwyer (eds) (2002) *Qualitative Methodologies for Geographers: Issues and Debates*, London: Arnold.
Lindgren, Stefan (1990) *Leningrad – på andra stranden* [Leningrad – On the other Shore], Stockholm: Ordfront.
Lisovskii, V.G (1983) *Leningrad. Raiony novostroek* [Leningrad: Newbuilt Districts], Leningrad: Lenizdat.
Lorimer, Hayden & Nick Spedding (2002) Editorial: Putting Philosophies of Geography into Practice, *Area* 34, 3: 227–228.
Lotman, Yuri M. (1990) *Universe of the Mind: A Semiotic Theory of Culture*, London & New York: I.B. Tauris & Co.
Lotman, Jurij M. (1984) The Poetics of Everyday Behaviour in Russian Eighteenth Century Culture, in A. Shukman (ed.) *The Semiotics of Russian Culture*, Department of Slavic Languages and Literatures, University of Michigan: Ann Arbor. *Michigan Slavic Contributions* No. 11.
Lotman, Jurij M. & Boris A. Uspenskij (1984a) Authors' introduction, in A. Shukman (ed.) *The Semiotics of Russian Culture*, Department of Slavic Languages and Literatures, University of Michigan: Ann Arbor. *Michigan Slavic Contributions* No. 11.
Lotman, Jurij M. & Boris A. Uspenskij (1984b) Echoes of the Notion "Moscow as the Third Rome" in Peter the Great's Ideology, in A. Shukman (ed.) *The Semiotics of Russian Culture*, Department of Slavic Languages and Literatures, University of Michigan: Ann Arbor. *Michigan Slavic Contributions* No. 11.
Lotman, Iurii M. & Boris A. Uspenskii (1977/1985) Binary Models in the Dynamics of Russian Culture (to the End of the Eighteenth Century), in A.D. Nakhimovsky & A. Stone Nakhimovsky (eds) *The Semiotics of Russian Cultural History: Essays by Iurii M. Lotman, Lidiia Ia. Ginsburg, Boris A. Uspenskii*, Itacha & London: Cornell University Press.
Lotman Ju.M.; B.A. Uspenskij; V.V. Ivanov; V.N. Toporov & A.M. Pjatigorskij (1975) *Theses on the semiotic study of culture*, Lisse: The Peter de Ridder Press, *Semiotics of Culture* 2.

Loukaki, A. (1997) Whose Genius Loci? Contrasting Interpretations of the "Sacred Rock of Athenian Acropolis", *Annals of the Association of American Geographers* 87, 2: 306–329.

Lundén, Thomas (2002) *Över gränsen. Om människan vid territoriets slut* [On the Boundary: About Humans at the End of Territory], Lund: Studentlitteratur.

Lundén, Thomas & Tommy Book (eds) (2003) *Det bergiga Balkan – konflikternas halvö* [The Mountainious Balkans – The Peninsula of Conflicts], Svenska Sällskapet för Antropologi och Geografi: *Ymer* 123.

Lynn, Nicholas J. (1999) Geography and Transition: Reconceptualizing Systematic Change in the former Soviet Union, *Slavic Review* 58, 4: 824–840.

Marcus, George E. (1992) "More (Critically) Reflexive than Thou": The Current Identity Politics of Representation, *Society & Space: Environment and Planning D*, 10, 5: 489–493.

Marcus, George E. & Michael M.J. Fischer (1986) *Anthropology as Cultural Critique: An Experimental Moment in the Human Sciences*, Chicago & London: University of Chicago Press.

Matless, David (1997) The Geographical Self, the Nature of the Social and Geoaesthetics: Work in Social and Cultural Geography 1996, *Progress in Human Geography* 21, 3: 393–405.

Mazurkiewicz, Ludwik (1992) *Human Geography in Eastern Europe and the Former Soviet Union*, London: Belhaven Press.

Månson, Per (1998) Jürgen Habermas och moderniteten [Jürgen Habermas and Modernity], in P. Månson (ed.) *Moderna samhällsteorier. Traditioner, riktningar, teoretiker* [Modern Social Theory: Traditions, Directions, Theorists] (5th edition), Stockholm: Prisma.

Medvedev, Sergei (1999) A General Theory of Russian Space: A Gay Science and a Rigorous Science, in J. Smith (ed.) *Beyond the Limits: The Concept of Space in Russian History and Culture*, Helsinki: SHS, Studia Historica 62.

Mehnert, Klaus (1959) *Sovjetmänniskan. Försök till porträtt efter tretton resor till Sovjetunionen 1929—1959* [Soviet Man: An Attempt at a Portrait after Thirteen Journeys to the Soviet Union 1929—1959], Stockholm: Albert Bonniers förlag.

Milner-Gulland, Robin (1994) Symbolic Landscapes in Muscovite Russia, in R. Reid, J. Andrew & V. Polukhina (eds) *Structure and Tradition in Russian Society: Papers from an International Conference on the Occasion of the Seventieth Birthday of Yury Mikhailovich Lotman*, Helsinki: Department of Slavonic Languages, University of Helsinki, Slavica Helsingiensia 14.

Minca, Claudio (2001) Prelude, in C. Minca (ed.) *Postmodern Geography: Theory and Praxis*, Oxford: Blackwell.

Mitchneck, Beth (1997) The Emergence of Local Government in Russia, in M.J. Bradshaw (ed.) *Geography and Transition in the Post-Soviet republics*, Chichester: John Wiley & Sons.

Monmonier, Mark (1996) *How to Lie with Maps* (2nd edition), Chicago: University of Chicago Press.

Munitsipal'naia zhizn' [Municipal life], vypusk no 2 (5), 17 Mars 2000.

Munitsipal'naia zhizn' [Municipal life], vypusk no 1 (2), 23 July 1999.

Nast, Heidi J. (1994) Women in the Field, *The Professional Geographer* 46, 1: 54–66.

Neumann, Iver B. (1996) *Russia and the Idea of Europe: A Study in Identity and International relations*, London: Routledge.

Nevskoe Vremia no 44, 12 March 1999, "S kazhdogo kodeksa – po strochke?" ["Picking up a Line from each Code?"] See www.nvrem.dux.ru/arts/nevrem-1925-art-23.html (18 July 2003).

Nordell, Kersti (2002) *Kvinnors hälsa – en fråga om medvetenhet, möjligheter och makt: att öka förståelsen för människors livssammanhang genom tidsgeografisk analys* [Women's Health – About Awareness, Possibilities and Power], Meddelanden från Göteborgs universitets geografiska institutioner, serie B, nr 101. Göteborg: Kulturgeografiska institutionen, Handelshögskolan vid Göteborgs universitet.

Novaia literatura o Leningrade [New Literature on Leningrad] with followings (editions 4–9), Leningrad and Sankt-Peterburg: Rossiiskaia natsional'naia biblioteka.

Oinas, Päivi (1999) Voices and Silences: The Problem of Access to Embeddedness, *Geoforum* 30, 4: 351–361.

Olsson, Gunnar (1998a) Towards a Critique of Cartographical Reason, *Ethics, place and environment* 1, 2: 146–155.

Olsson, Gunnar (1998b) Stadier på livets väg [Phases in the Track of Life], in G. Olsson (ed.) *Att famna en ton* [To Encompass a Tone], Uppsala: Acta Universitatis Upsaliensis 63.

Olsson, Gunnar (1992) Lines of Power, in T.J. Barnes & J.S. Duncan (eds) *Writing Worlds: Discourse, Text and Metaphor in the Representation of the Landscape*, London & New York: Routledge.

Olsson, Jan Olof (1967) *Leningrad – S:t Petersburg*, Stockholm: Alders/Bonniers.

Ormeling Jr., F.J. (1974) Cartographic Consequences of a Planned Economy – 50 Years of Soviet Cartography, *The American Cartographer* 1, 1: 39–50.

Ortner, Sherry (1984) Theory in Anthropology since the Sixties, *Comparative Studies in Society and History* 26: 126–166.

Orttung, Robert W. (1995) *From Leningrad to St. Petersburg: Democratization in a Russian city*, New York: St. Martin's Press.

Paasi, Anssi (2003) Boundaries in a Globalizing World, in K. Anderson, M. Domosh, S. Pile & N. Thrift (eds) *Handbook of Cultural Geography*, London: Sage.

Painter, Joe (2000) Pierre Bourdieu, in M. Crang & N. Thrift (eds) *Thinking space*, London & New York: Routledge.

Peet, Richard (1998) *Modern Geographical Thought*, Oxford: Blackwell.

Peil, Tiina (1999) *Islescapes: Estonian Small Islands and Islanders through Three Centuries*, Acta Universitatis Stockholmiensis / Stockholm Studies in Human Geography 8. Stockholm: Almqvist & Wiksell International.

Philo, Chris (2000) More Words, More Worlds: Reflections on the "Cultural Turn" and Human Geography, in I. Cook, D. Crouch, S. Naylor & J.R. Ryan (eds) *Cultural Turns/Geographical Turns: Perspectives on Cultural Geography*, Harlow: Prentice Hall.

Pickles, John (1992) Texts, Hermeneutics and Propaganda Maps, in T.J. Barnes & J.S. Duncan (eds) *Writing Worlds: Discourse, Text and Metaphor in the Representation of the Landscape*, London & New York: Routledge.

Pickles, John & Adrian Smith (eds) (1998) *Theorising Transition: The Political Economy of Post-Communist Transformations*, London: Routledge.

Pietiläinen, Jukka (2000) Changing Journalism in a Changing Society: The Case of the Karelian Republic, in J. Ekekrantz & K. Olofsson (eds) *Russian Reports: Studies in Post-Communist Transformation of Media and Journalism*, Södertörn Academic Studies 2, Stockholm: Almqvist & Wiksell International.

Piirainen, Timo (1997) *Towards a New Social Order in Russia: Transforming Structures and Everyday Life*, Aldershot: Dartmouth.

Pred, Allan (1986) Power, Practice, and Consciousness: One's Place in the World, the World in One's Place, *Svensk geografisk årsbok 62*, Lund: Sydsvenska geografiska sällskapet.

Price, Marie & Martin Lewis (1993) The Reinvention of Cultural Geography, *Annals of the Association of American Geographers* 83, 1: 1–17.

Porter, Thomas Earl & Scott Seregny (2004) The Zemstvo Reconsidered, in A.B. Evans Jr. & V. Gel'man (eds) *The Politics of Local Government in Russia*, Oxford: Rowman & Littlefield Publishers.

Postnikov, Alexey V. (2002) Maps for Ordinary Consumers versus Maps for the Military: Double Standards of Map Accuracy in Soviet Cartography, 1917–1991, *Cartography and Geographic Information Service* 29, 3: 243–260.

Postnikov, Aleksei Vladimirovic (1996) Russia in Maps: A History of the Geographical Study and Cartography of the Country, Moscow: Nas Dom – L'Age d'Homme.

Raiony Sankt-Peterburga –99: Ofitsial'noe izdanie [Districts of Sankt-Peterburg – 99: Official Edition] (2000), Sankt-Peterburg: Sankt-Peterburgskii komitet gosudarstvennoi statistiki.

Raiony Sankt-Peterburga –98: Ofitsial'noe izdanie [Districts of Sankt-Peterburg – 98: Official Edition] (1999), Sankt-Peterburg: Sankt-Peterburgskii komitet gosudarstvennoi statistiki.

Relph, Edward (1976) *Place and Placelessness*, London: Pion.

Riazantsev, M. (1987) Stantsiia Ligovo [The Ligovo Station], *Vechernii Leningrad* No 65: 3.

Ries, Nancy (1997) *Russian Talk: Culture and Conversation during Perestroika*, Ithaca & London: Cornell University Press.

Rose, Courtice (1988) The Concept of Reach and the Anglophone Minority in Quebec, in J. Eyles & D.M. Smith (eds) *Qualitative Methods in Human Geography*, Cambridge: Polity Press.

Rose, Gillian (1997) Situating Knowledges: Positionality, Reflexivities and other Tactics, *Progress in Human Geography* 21, 3: 305–320.

Rozhkov, Anatolii M. (1997) *Na iugo-zapade Sankt-Peterburga (Iz istorii Krasnosel'skovo raiona)* [In Sankt-Peterburg's South-west (From the History of Krasnosel'skii raion], Sankt-Peterburg: Liki Rossii.

Ruble, Blair A. (1995) *Money Sings: The Changing Politics of Urban Space in Post-Soviet Yaroslavl*, Cambridge: Woodrow Wilson Center Press & Cambridge University Press.

Ruble, Blair A. (1990) *Leningrad: Shaping a Soviet City*, Berkeley & Los Angeles: University of California Press.

Rugumayo, Caroline Rusten (1997) Locality Studies: The Case for the Narrative, *Nordisk Samhällsgeografisk Tidskrift* 24: 36–47.

Rukavishnikov, V.O. (1978a) Ethnosocial Aspects of Population Distribution in Cities in Tataria (On the Examples of Kazan and Al'met'evsk), *Soviet Sociology: A Journal of Translations* 8, 2: 59–79.

Rukavishnikov, V.O. (1978b) Etnosotsial'ye aspekty rasseleniia v gorodakh Tatarii (na primere Kazani i Al'met'evska) [Ethnosocial Aspects of Population Distribution in Cities in Tataria (On the Examples of Kazan and Al'met'evsk)], *Sovetskaia Etnografiia* 53, 1: 77–89.

Salishchev, K.A. (1989) The Seventieth Anniversary of Soviet Cartography – Some Achievements and Tasks of Restructuring, *Mapping Sciences and Remote Sensing* 26, 1: 14–19.

Salishchev, K.A. (1988) Problems and Achievements of Soviet Thematic Cartography, *Mapping Sciences and Remote Sensing* 25, 3: 179–187.

Sandler, Stephanie (1994) Pushkin as a Sign in Contemporary Russian Culture: the Example of Film, in R. Reid, J. Andrew & V. Polukhina (eds) *Structure and Tradition in Russian Society: Papers from an International Conference on the Occasion of the Seventieth Birthday of Yury Mikhailovich Lotman*, Helsinki: Department of Slavonic Languages, University of Helsinki, *Slavica Helsingiensia* 14.

Sankt-Peterburg, Petrograd, Leningrad: Entsiklopedicheskii spravochnik [Sankt-Peterburg, Petrograd, Leningrad: Encyclopedic Reference Book] (1992) Moskva: Nauchnoe Izdatel'stvo "Bol'shaia Rossiiskaia Entsiklopediia".

Sayer, Andrew (1992) Radical Geography and Marxist Political Economy: Towards a Re-evaluation, *Progress in Human Geography* 16, 3: 343–360.

Scott, James C. (1998) *Seeing Like a State: How Certain Schemes to Improve the Human Condition have Failed*, New Haven & London: Yale University Press.

Schütz, Alfred (1953/1999) Den vardagliga och den vetenskapliga tolkningen av mänskliga handlingar [Common-sense and Scientific Interpretation of Human Action], in J. Bengtsson (ed.) *Den sociala världens fenomenologi* [The Phenomenology of the Social World], Göteborg: Daidalos.

Schutz, Alfred (1953/1962) Common-sense and Scientific Interpretation of Human Action, in M. Natanson (ed.) *Collected Papers 1: The Problem of Social Reality*, The Hague: Martinus Nijhoff.

Schütz, Alfred (1946/1999) Den välinformerade medborgaren. En essä om den sociala fördelningen av kunskap [The Well-informed Citizen: An Essay on the Social Distribution of Knowledge], in J. Bengtsson (ed.) *Den sociala världens fenomenologi* [The Phenomenology of the Social World], Göteborg: Daidalos.

Schütz, Alfred (1945/1999) Om mångfalden av verkligheter [On Multiple Realities], in J. Bengtsson (ed.) *Den sociala världens fenomenologi* [The Phenomenology of the Social World], Göteborg: Daidalos.

Schutz, Alfred (1945/1962) On Multiple Realities, in M. Natanson (ed.) *Collected Papers 1: The Problem of Social Reality*, The Hague: Martinus Nijhoff.

Shaw, Denis J.B. (1978) Planning Leningrad, *Geographical Review* 68, 2: 183–200.

Sidarov, Dmitri (2000) National Monumentalization and the Politics of Scale: The Resurrections of the Cathedral of Christ the Saviour in Moscow, *Annals of the Association of American Geographers* 90, 3: 548–572.

Sjöberg, Örjan (1999) Shortage, Priority and Urban Growth: Towards a Theory of Urbanisation under Central Planning, *Urban Studies* 36, 13: 2217–2236.

Smith, Hedrick (1977) *Ryssarna* [The Russians], Stockholm: Bonnier.

Smith, Jeremy (1999) Introduction, in J. Smith (ed.) *Beyond the Limits: The Concept of Space in Russian History and Culture*, Helsinki: SHS, Studia Historica 62.

Smith, Susan J. (1984) Practicing Humanistic Geography, *Annals of the Association of American Geographers* 74, 3: 353–374.

Soviet Cartographic Falsification (1970) *The Military Engineer* 62, 410: 389–391.

Tammaru, Tiit (2001) Suburban Growth and Suburbanisation under Central Planning: The Case of Soviet Estonia, *Urban Studies* 38, 8: 1341–1357.

Thrift, Nigel (1996) "Strange Country": Meaning, Use and Style in Non-representational Theories, in N. Thrift *Spatial Formations*, London: Sage.

Thrift, Nigel (1985) Flies and Germs: A Geography of Knowledge, in D. Gregory & J. Urry (eds) *Social Relations and Spatial Structures*, London: MacMillan Publishers.

Tuan, Yi-Fu (1991) Language and the Making of Place: A Narrative-descriptive Approach, *Annals of the Association of American Geographers* 81, 4: 684–696.

Tyner, Judith A. (1982) Persuasive Cartography, *Journal of Geography* 84: 4, 140–144.

Umiker-Sebeok, D. Jean (1977) Semiotics of Culture: Great Britain and North America, *Annual Review of Anthropology* 6: 121–135.

Urban, Michael E. (1990) *More Power to the Soviets: The Democratic Revolution in the USSR*, Aldershot: Edward Elgar.

van Hoven, Bettina (ed.) (2004) *Europe: Lives in Transition*, Edinburgh: Pearson Education.

Varis, Eira & Sisko Porter (eds) (1996) *Karelia and St. Petersburg: From Lakeland Interior to European Metropolis*, Joensuu: Joensuu University Press.

Volkov, Solomon (1996) *St. Petersburg: A Cultural History*, London: Sinclair-Stevenson.

Wacquant, Loïc (2002) Scrutinizing the Street: Poverty, Morality, and the Pitfalls of Urban Ethnography, *American Journal of Sociology* 107, 6: 1468–1532.

Wollman, Hellmut (2004) Institutional Building of Local Self-Government in Russia: Between Legal Design and Power Politics, in A.B. Evans Jr. & V. Gel'man (eds) *The Politics of Local Government in Russia*, Oxford: Rowman & Littlefield Publishers.

Young, Craig & Duncan Light (2001) Place, National Identity and Post-Socialist Transformations: An Introduction, *Political Geography* 20: 941–955.

Zeigler, D.J. (2002) Post-Communist Eastern Europe and the Cartography of Independence, *Political Geography* 21, 5: 671–686.

Zelinsky, Wilbur (2001) The Geographer as Voyeur, *Geographical Review* 91, 1 & 2: 1–8.

Maps and atlases

Leningrad: Istoriko-geograficheskii atlas [Leningrad: Historico-geographical Atlas] (1981) Moskva: Glavnoe upravlenie geodezii i kartografii pri sovete ministrov SSSR.

Osnovnye magistral'ye proezdy g. Sankt-Peterburga, Sankt-Peterburg i Leningradskaia oblast' [Main Roads of the City of Sankt-Peterburg, Sankt-Peterburg and Leningrad Oblast'] (1996) Sankt-Peterburg: 444 Voenno-Kartograficheskaia Fabrika. Scale 1: 39,900.

Sankt-Peterburg 98 [Sankt-Peterburg 98] (1998) Sankt-Peterburg: ZAO "Karta". Scale 1:30,000.

Sankt Peterburg atlas goroda [Sankt-Peterburg City Atlas] (2002) Sankt-Peterburg: ZAO "Karta". Scale 1: 14,000. Pages 64–65.

Sankt Peterburg atlas goroda dlia zhitelei i gostei [Sankt-Peterburg City Atlas for Inhabitants and Guests] (2003) Sankt-Peterburg: ZAO "Karta" ltd. 2003. Scale 1: 34,000. Pages 46–47.

Sankt-Peterburg universal'nyi plan [St. Petersburg City Map] (1998) (9 vypusk). Karty Novogo Vremeni No. 118. Sankt-Peterburg: V.V. Vindina – Novoe Vremia. Scale not specified.

Turistu o Sankt-Peterburge [To a Tourist about Sankt-Peterburg] (1995) Sankt-Peterburg: 444 Voenno-Kartograficheskaia Fabrika & OOO Reklamno-Izdatel'skoe Agenstvo Fainder. Scale not specified.

Uchebnyi geograficheskii atlas Leningradskoi oblasti i Sankt-Peterburga [Geographic School Atlas of Leningrad Oblast' and Sankt-Peterburg] (1997) Sankt-Peterburg: Sankt-Peterburgskaia kartograficheskaia fabrika VSEGEI. Scale of referred map: 1: 114,000. Pages 30–31.

Films

Riazanova, El'dara (dir.) (1975) *Ironiia sud'by, ili s legkim parom* [The Irony of Faith], Gosteleradio SSSR.

Sukarov, Alexander (dir.) (2002) *Russkii kovcheg* [Russian Ark], The Hermitage Bridge Studio (Sankt-Peterburg) et al.

Homepages

Local Self-Government in St. Petersburg: http://spb.municip.nw.ru/# (22 July 2003).

Munitsipal'nyi okrug No 40 "Uritsk": http://mo40.municip.nw.ru/index.htm (22 July 2003).

SOVIET AND POST-SOVIET POLITICS AND SOCIETY

Edited by Dr. Andreas Umland

ISSN 1614-3515

1 *Андреас Умланд (ред.)*
Воплощение Европейской
конвенции по правам человека в
России
Философские, юридические и
эмпирические исследования
ISBN 3-89821-387-0

2 *Christian Wipperfürth*
Russland – ein vertrauenswürdiger
Partner?
Grundlagen, Hintergründe und Praxis
gegenwärtiger russischer Außenpolitik
Mit einem Vorwort von Heinz Timmermann
ISBN 3-89821-401-X

3 *Manja Hussner*
Die Übernahme internationalen Rechts
in die russische und deutsche
Rechtsordnung
Eine vergleichende Analyse zur
Völkerrechtsfreundlichkeit der Verfassungen
der Russländischen Föderation und der
Bundesrepublik Deutschland
Mit einem Vorwort von Rainer Arnold
ISBN 3-89821-438-9

4 *Matthew Tejada*
Bulgaria's Democratic Consolidation
and the Kozloduy Nuclear Power Plant
(KNPP)
The Unattainability of Closure
With a foreword by Richard J. Crampton
ISBN 3-89821-439-7

5 *Марк Григорьевич Меерович*
Квадратные метры, определяющие
сознание
Государственная жилищная политика в
СССР. 1921 – 1941 гг
ISBN 3-89821-474-5

6 *Andrei P. Tsygankov, Pavel
A.Tsygankov (Eds.)*
New Directions in Russian
International Studies
ISBN 3-89821-422-2

7 *Марк Григорьевич Меерович*
Как власть народ к труду приучала
Жилище в СССР – средство управления
людьми. 1917 – 1941 гг.
С предисловием Елены Осокиной
ISBN 3-89821-495-8

8 *David J. Galbreath*
Nation-Building and Minority Politics
in Post-Socialist States
Interests, Influence and Identities in Estonia
and Latvia
With a foreword by David J. Smith
ISBN 3-89821-467-2

9 *Алексей Юрьевич Безугольный*
Народы Кавказа в Вооруженных
силах СССР в годы Великой
Отечественной войны 1941-1945 гг.
С предисловием Николая Бугая
ISBN 3-89821-475-3

10 *Вячеслав Лихачев и Владимир
Прибыловский (ред.)*
Русское Национальное Единство,
1990-2000. В 2-х томах
ISBN 3-89821-523-7

11 *Николай Бугай (ред.)*
Народы стран Балтии в условиях
сталинизма (1940-е – 1950-е годы)
Документированная история
ISBN 3-89821-525-3

12 *Ingmar Bredies (Hrsg.)*
Zur Anatomie der Orange Revolution
in der Ukraine
Wechsel des Elitenregimes oder Triumph des
Parlamentarismus?
ISBN 3-89821-524-5

13 *Anastasia V. Mitrofanova*
The Politicization of Russian
Orthodoxy
Actors and Ideas
With a foreword by William C. Gay
ISBN 3-89821-481-8

14　*Nathan D. Larson*
　　Alexander Solzhenitsyn and the
　　Russo-Jewish Question
　　ISBN 3-89821-483-4

15　*Guido Houben*
　　Kulturpolitik und Ethnizität
　　Staatliche Kunstförderung im Russland der
　　neunziger Jahre
　　Mit einem Vorwort von Gert Weisskirchen
　　ISBN 3-89821-542-3

16　*Leonid Luks*
　　Der russische „Sonderweg"?
　　Aufsätze zur neuesten Geschichte Russlands
　　im europäischen Kontext
　　ISBN 3-89821-496-6

17　*Евгений Мороз*
　　История «Мёртвой воды» – от
　　страшной сказки к большой
　　политике
　　Политическое неоязычество в
　　постсоветской России
　　ISBN 3-89821-551-2

18　*Александр Верховский и Галина
　　Кожевникова (ред.)*
　　Этническая и религиозная
　　интолерантность в российских СМИ
　　Результаты мониторинга 2001-2004 гг.
　　ISBN 3-89821-569-5

19　*Christian Ganzer*
　　Sowjetisches Erbe und ukrainische
　　Nation
　　Das Museum der Geschichte des Zaporoger
　　Kosakentums auf der Insel Chortycja
　　Mit einem Vorwort von Frank Golczewski
　　ISBN 3-89821-504-0

20　*Эльза-Баир Гучинова*
　　Помнить нельзя забыть
　　Антропология депортационной травмы
　　калмыков
　　С предисловием Кэролайн Хамфри
　　ISBN 3-89821-506-7

21　*Юлия Лидерман*
　　Мотивы «проверки» и «испытания»
　　в постсоветской культуре
　　Советское прошлое в российском
　　кинематографе 1990-х годов
　　С предисловием Евгения Марголита
　　ISBN 3-89821-511-3

22　*Tanya Lokshina, Ray Thomas, Mary
　　Mayer (Eds.)*
　　The Imposition of a Fake Political
　　Settlement in the Northern Caucasus
　　The 2003 Chechen Presidential Election
　　ISBN 3-89821-436-2

23　*Timothy McCajor Hall, Rosie Read
　　(Eds.)*
　　Changes in the Heart of Europe
　　Recent Ethnographies of Czechs, Slovaks,
　　Roma, and Sorbs
　　With an afterword by Zdeněk Salzmann
　　ISBN 3-89821-606-3

24　*Christian Autengruber*
　　Die politischen Parteien in Bulgarien
　　und Rumänien
　　Eine vergleichende Analyse seit Beginn der
　　90er Jahre
　　Mit einem Vorwort von Dorothée de Nève
　　ISBN 3-89821-476-1

25　*Annette Freyberg-Inan with Radu
　　Cristescu*
　　The Ghosts in Our Classrooms, or:
　　John Dewey Meets Ceauşescu
　　The Promise and the Failures of Civic
　　Education in Romania
　　ISBN 3-89821-416-8

26　*John B. Dunlop*
　　The 2002 Dubrovka and 2004 Beslan
　　Hostage Crises
　　A Critique of Russian Counter-Terrorism
　　With a foreword by Donald N. Jensen
　　ISBN 3-89821-608-X

27　*Peter Koller*
　　Das touristische Potenzial von
　　Kam''janec'–Podil's'kyj
　　Eine fremdenverkehrsgeographische
　　Untersuchung der Zukunftsperspektiven und
　　Maßnahmenplanung zur
　　Destinationsentwicklung des „ukrainischen
　　Rothenburg"
　　Mit einem Vorwort von Kristiane Klemm
　　ISBN 3-89821-640-3

28　*Françoise Daucé, Elisabeth Sieca-
　　Kozlowski (Eds.)*
　　Dedovshchina in the Post-Soviet
　　Military
　　Hazing of Russian Army Conscripts in a
　　Comparative Perspective
　　With a foreword by Dale Herspring
　　ISBN 3-89821-616-0

29   *Florian Strasser*
     Zivilgesellschaftliche Einflüsse auf die
     Orange Revolution
     Die gewaltlose Massenbewegung und die
     ukrainische Wahlkrise 2004
     Mit einem Vorwort von Egbert Jahn
     ISBN 3-89821-648-9

30   *Rebecca S. Katz*
     The Georgian Regime Crisis of 2003-
     2004
     A Case Study in Post-Soviet Media
     Representation of Politics, Crime and
     Corruption
     ISBN 3-89821-413-3

31   *Vladimir Kantor*
     Willkür oder Freiheit
     Beiträge zur russischen Geschichtsphilosophie
     Ediert von Dagmar Herrmann sowie mit
     einem Vorwort versehen von Leonid Luks
     ISBN 3-89821-589-X

32   *Laura A. Victoir*
     The Russian Land Estate Today
     A Case Study of Cultural Politics in Post-
     Soviet Russia
     With a foreword by Priscilla Roosevelt
     ISBN 3-89821-426-5

33   *Ivan Katchanovski*
     Cleft Countries
     Regional Political Divisions and Cultures in
     Post-Soviet Ukraine and Moldova
     With a foreword by Francis Fukuyama
     ISBN 3-89821-558-X

34   *Florian Mühlfried*
     Postsowjetische Feiern
     Das Georgische Bankett im Wandel
     Mit einem Vorwort von Kevin Tuite
     ISBN 3-89821-601-2

35   *Roger Griffin, Werner Loh, Andreas
     Umland (Eds.)*
     Fascism Past and Present, West and
     East
     An International Debate on Concepts and
     Cases in the Comparative Study of the
     Extreme Right
     With an afterword by Walter Laqueur
     ISBN 3-89821-674-8

36   *Sebastian Schlegel*
     Der „Weiße Archipel"
     Sowjetische Atomstädte 1945-1991
     Mit einem Geleitwort von Thomas Bohn
     ISBN 3-89821-679-9

37   *Vyacheslav Likhachev*
     Political Anti-Semitism in Post-Soviet
     Russia
     Actors and Ideas in 1991-2003
     Edited and translated from Russian by Eugene
     Veklerov
     ISBN 3-89821-529-6

38   *Josette Baer (Ed.)*
     Preparing Liberty in Central Europe
     Political Texts from the Spring of Nations
     1848 to the Spring of Prague 1968
     With a foreword by Zdeněk V. David
     ISBN 3-89821-546-6

39   *Михаил Лукьянов*
     Российский консерватизм и
     реформа, 1907-1914
     С предисловием Марка Д. Стейнберга
     ISBN 3-89821-503-2

40   *Nicola Melloni*
     Market Without Economy
     The 1998 Russian Financial Crisis
     With a foreword by Eiji Furukawa
     ISBN 3-89821-407-9

41   *Dmitrij Chmelnizki*
     Die Architektur Stalins
     Bd. 1: Studien zu Ideologie und Stil
     Bd. 2: Bilddokumentation
     Mit einem Vorwort von Bruno Flierl
     ISBN 3-89821-515-6

42   *Katja Yafimava*
     Post-Soviet Russian-Belarussian
     Relationships
     The Role of Gas Transit Pipelines
     With a foreword by Jonathan P. Stern
     ISBN 3-89821-655-1

43   *Boris Chavkin*
     Verflechtungen der deutschen und
     russischen Zeitgeschichte
     Aufsätze und Archivfunde zu den
     Beziehungen Deutschlands und der
     Sowjetunion von 1917 bis 1991
     Ediert von Markus Edlinger sowie mit einem
     Vorwort versehen von Leonid Luks
     ISBN 3-89821-756-6

44   *Anastasija Grynenko in Zusammenarbeit mit Claudia Dathe*
Die Terminologie des Gerichtswesens der Ukraine und Deutschlands im Vergleich
Eine übersetzungswissenschaftliche Analyse juristischer Fachbegriffe im Deutschen, Ukrainischen und Russischen
Mit einem Vorwort von Ulrich Hartmann
ISBN 3-89821-691-8

45   *Anton Burkov*
The Impact of the European Convention on Human Rights on Russian Law
Legislation and Application in 1996-2006
With a foreword by Françoise Hampson
ISBN 978-3-89821-639-5

46   *Stina Torjesen, Indra Overland (Eds.)*
International Election Observers in Post-Soviet Azerbaijan
Geopolitical Pawns or Agents of Change?
ISBN 978-3-89821-743-9

47   *Taras Kuzio*
Ukraine – Crimea – Russia
Triangle of Conflict
ISBN 978-3-89821-761-3

48   *Claudia Šabić*
"Ich erinnere mich nicht, aber L'viv!"
Zur Funktion kultureller Faktoren für die Institutionalisierung und Entwicklung einer ukrainischen Region
Mit einem Vorwort von Melanie Tatur
ISBN 978-3-89821-752-1

49   *Marlies Bilz*
Tatarstan in der Transformation
Nationaler Diskurs und Politische Praxis 1988-1994
Mit einem Vorwort von Frank Golczewski
ISBN 978-3-89821-722-4

50   *Марлен Ларюэль (ред.)*
Современные интерпретации русского национализма
ISBN 978-3-89821-795-8

51   *Sonja Schüler*
Die ethnische Dimension der Armut
Roma im postsozialistischen Rumänien
Mit einem Vorwort von Anton Sterbling
ISBN 978-3-89821-776-7

52   *Галина Кожевникова*
Радикальный национализм в России и противодействие ему
Сборник докладов Центра «Сова» за 2004-2007 гг.
С предисловием Александра Верховского
ISBN 978-3-89821-721-7

53   *Галина Кожевникова и Владимир Прибыловский*
Российская власть в биографиях I
Высшие должностные лица РФ в 2004 г.
ISBN 978-3-89821-796-5

54   *Галина Кожевникова и Владимир Прибыловский*
Российская власть в биографиях II
Члены Правительства РФ в 2004 г.
ISBN 978-3-89821-797-2

55   *Галина Кожевникова и Владимир Прибыловский*
Российская власть в биографиях III
Руководители федеральных служб и агентств РФ в 2004 г.
ISBN 978-3-89821-798-9

56   *Ileana Petroniu*
Privatisierung in Transformationsökonomien
Determinanten der Restrukturierungs-Bereitschaft am Beispiel Polens, Rumäniens und der Ukraine
Mit einem Vorwort von Rainer W. Schäfer
ISBN 978-3-89821-790-3

57   *Christian Wipperfürth*
Russland und seine GUS-Nachbarn
Hintergründe, aktuelle Entwicklungen und Konflikte in einer ressourcenreichen Region
ISBN 978-3-89821-801-6

58   *Togzhan Kassenova*
From Antagonism to Partnership
The Uneasy Path of the U.S.-Russian Cooperative Threat Reduction
With a foreword by Christoph Bluth
ISBN 978-3-89821-707-1

59   *Alexander Höllwerth*
Das sakrale eurasische Imperium des Aleksandr Dugin
Eine Diskursanalyse zum postsowjetischen russischen Rechtsextremismus
Mit einem Vorwort von Dirk Uffelmann
ISBN 978-3-89821-813-9

60 Олег Рябов
    «Россия-Матушка»
    Национализм, гендер и война в России XX века
    С предисловием Елены Гощило
    ISBN 978-3-89821-487-2

61 Ivan Maistrenko
    Borot'bism
    A Chapter in the History of the Ukrainian Revolution
    With a new introduction by Chris Ford
    Translated by George S. N. Luckyj with the assistance of Ivan L. Rudnytsky
    ISBN 978-3-89821-697-5

62 Maryna Romanets
    Anamorphosic Texts and Reconfigured Visions
    Improvised Traditions in Contemporary Ukrainian and Irish Literature
    ISBN 978-3-89821-576-3

63 Paul D'Anieri and Taras Kuzio (Eds.)
    Aspects of the Orange Revolution I
    Democratization and Elections in Post-Communist Ukraine
    ISBN 978-3-89821-698-2

64 Bohdan Harasymiw in collaboration with Oleh S. Ilnytzkyj (Eds.)
    Aspects of the Orange Revolution II
    Information and Manipulation Strategies in the 2004 Ukrainian Presidential Elections
    ISBN 978-3-89821-699-9

65 Ingmar Bredies, Andreas Umland and Valentin Yakushik (Eds.)
    Aspects of the Orange Revolution III
    The Context and Dynamics of the 2004 Ukrainian Presidential Elections
    ISBN 978-3-89821-803-0

66 Ingmar Bredies, Andreas Umland and Valentin Yakushik (Eds.)
    Aspects of the Orange Revolution IV
    Foreign Assistance and Civic Action in the 2004 Ukrainian Presidential Elections
    ISBN 978-3-89821-808-5

67 Ingmar Bredies, Andreas Umland and Valentin Yakushik (Eds.)
    Aspects of the Orange Revolution V
    Institutional Observation Reports on the 2004 Ukrainian Presidential Elections
    ISBN 978-3-89821-809-2

68 Taras Kuzio (Ed.)
    Aspects of the Orange Revolution VI
    Post-Communist Democratic Revolutions in Comparative Perspective
    ISBN 978-3-89821-820-7

69 Tim Bohse
    Autoritarismus statt Selbstverwaltung
    Die Transformation der kommunalen Politik in der Stadt Kaliningrad 1990-2005
    Mit einem Geleitwort von Stefan Troebst
    ISBN 978-3-89821-782-8

70 David Rupp
    Die Rußländische Föderation und die russischsprachige Minderheit in Lettland
    Eine Fallstudie zur Anwaltspolitik Moskaus gegenüber den russophonen Minderheiten im „Nahen Ausland" von 1991 bis 2002
    Mit einem Vorwort von Helmut Wagner
    ISBN 978-3-89821-778-1

71 Taras Kuzio
    Theoretical and Comparative Perspectives on Nationalism
    New Directions in Cross-Cultural and Post-Communist Studies
    With a foreword by Paul Robert Magocsi
    ISBN 978-3-89821-815-3

72 Christine Teichmann
    Die Hochschultransformation im heutigen Osteuropa
    Kontinuität und Wandel bei der Entwicklung des postkommunistischen Universitätswesens
    Mit einem Vorwort von Oskar Anweiler
    ISBN 978-3-89821-842-9

73 Julia Kusznir
    Der politische Einfluss von Wirtschaftseliten in russischen Regionen
    Eine Analyse am Beispiel der Erdöl- und Erdgasindustrie, 1992-2005
    Mit einem Vorwort von Wolfgang Eichwede
    ISBN 978-3-89821-821-4

74 Alena Vysotskaya
    Russland, Belarus und die EU-Osterweiterung
    Zur Minderheitenfrage und zum Problem der Freizügigkeit des Personenverkehrs
    Mit einem Vorwort von Katlijn Malfliet
    ISBN 978-3-89821-822-1

75 Heiko Pleines (Hrsg.)
Corporate Governance in postsozialistischen Volkswirtschaften
ISBN 978-3-89821-766-8

76 Stefan Ihrig
Wer sind die Moldawier?
Rumänismus versus Moldowanismus in Historiographie und Schulbüchern der Republik Moldova, 1991-2006
Mit einem Vorwort von Holm Sundhaussen
ISBN 978-3-89821-466-7

77 Galina Kozhevnikova in collaboration with Alexander Verkhovsky and Eugene Veklerov
Ultra-Nationalism and Hate Crimes in Contemporary Russia
The 2004-2006 Annual Reports of Moscow's SOVA Center
With a foreword by Stephen D. Shenfield
ISBN 978-3-89821-868-9

78 Florian Küchler
The Role of the European Union in Moldova's Transnistria Conflict
With a foreword by Christopher Hill
ISBN 978-3-89821-850-4

79 Bernd Rechel
The Long Way Back to Europe
Minority Protection in Bulgaria
With a foreword by Richard Crampton
ISBN 978-3-89821-863-4

80 Peter W. Rodgers
Nation, Region and History in Post-Communist Transitions
Identity Politics in Ukraine, 1991-2006
With a foreword by Vera Tolz
ISBN 978-3-89821-903-7

81 Stephanie Solywoda
The Life and Work of Semen L. Frank
A Study of Russian Religious Philosophy
With a foreword by Philip Walters
ISBN 978-3-89821-457-5

82 Vera Sokolova
Cultural Politics of Ethnicity
Discourses on Roma in Communist Czechoslovakia
ISBN 978-3-89821-864-1

83 Natalya Shevchik Ketenci
Kazakhstani Enterprises in Transition
The Role of Historical Regional Development in Kazakhstan's Post-Soviet Economic Transformation
ISBN 978-3-89821-831-3

84 Martin Malek, Anna Schor-Tschudnowskaja (Hrsg.)
Europa im Tschetschenienkrieg
Zwischen politischer Ohnmacht und Gleichgültigkeit
Mit einem Vorwort von Lipchan Basajewa
ISBN 978-3-89821-676-0

85 Stefan Meister
Das postsowjetische Universitätswesen zwischen nationalem und internationalem Wandel
Die Entwicklung der regionalen Hochschule in Russland als Gradmesser der Systemtransformation
Mit einem Vorwort von Joan DeBardeleben
ISBN 978-3-89821-891-7

86 Konstantin Sheiko in collaboration with Stephen Brown
Nationalist Imaginings of the Russian Past
Anatolii Fomenko and the Rise of Alternative History in Post-Communist Russia
With a foreword by Donald Ostrowski
ISBN 978-3-89821-915-0

87 Sabine Jenni
Wie stark ist das „Einige Russland"?
Zur Parteibindung der Eliten und zum Wahlerfolg der Machtpartei im Dezember 2007
Mit einem Vorwort von Klaus Armingeon
ISBN 978-3-89821-961-7

88 Thomas Borén
Meeting-Places of Transformation
Urban Identity, Spatial Representations and Local Politics in Post-Soviet St Petersburg
ISBN 978-3-89821-739-2

FORTHCOMING (MANUSCRIPT WORKING TITLES)

Margaret Dikovitskaya
Arguing with the Photographs
Russian Imperial Colonial Attitudes in Visual Culture
ISBN 3-89821-462-1

Sergei M. Plekhanov
Russian Nationalism in the Age of Globalization
ISBN 3-89821-484-2

Robert Pyrah
Cultural Memory and Identity
Literature, Criticism and the Theatre in Lviv - Lwow - Lemberg, 1918-1939 and in post-Soviet Ukraine
ISBN 3-89821-505-9

Andrei Rogatchevski
The National-Bolshevik Party
ISBN 3-89821-532-6

Zenon Victor Wasyliw
Soviet Culture in the Ukrainian Village
The Transformation of Everyday Life and Values, 1921-1928
ISBN 3-89821-536-9

Nele Sass
Das gegenkulturelle Milieu im postsowjetischen Russland
ISBN 3-89821-543-1

Julie Elkner
Maternalism versus Militarism
The Russian Soldiers' Mothers Committee
ISBN 3-89821-575-X

Alexandra Kamarowsky
Russia's Post-crisis Growth
ISBN 3-89821-580-6

Martin Friessnegg
Das Problem der Medienfreiheit in Russland seit dem Ende der Sowjetunion
ISBN 3-89821-588-1

Nikolaj Nikiforowitsch Borobow
Führende Persönlichkeiten in Russland vom 12. bis 20. Jhd.: Ein Lexikon
Aus dem Russischen übersetzt und herausgegeben von Eberhard Schneider
ISBN 3-89821-638-1

Andreas Langenohl
Political Culture and Criticism of Society
Intellectual Articulations in Post-Soviet Russia
ISBN 3-89821-709-4

Lars Löckner
Sowjetrussland in der Beurteilung der Emigrantenzeitung 'Rul', 1920-1924
ISBN 3-89821-741-8

Ekaterina Taratuta
The Red Line of Construction
Semantics and Mythology of a Siberian Heliopolis
ISBN 3-89821-742-6

Bernd Kappenberg
Zeichen setzen für Europa
Der Gebrauch europäischer lateinischer Sonderzeichen in der deutschen Öffentlichkeit
ISBN 3-89821-749-3

Siegbert Klee, Martin Sandhop, Oxana Schwajka, Andreas Umland
Elitenbildung in der Postsowjetischen Ukraine
ISBN 978-389821-829-0

Elise Luckfiel
Zwischen Staat und externer Förderung - zivilgesellschaftliche Akteure in der Ukraine
Eine empirische Untersuchung von Kiewer NGOs
ISBN 978-3-89821-852-8

Eva Fuchslocher
Georgiens Nationenbildung
ISBN 978-3-89821-884-9

Oleh Kotsyuba
Ukrainian versus Russian Literature in the Post-Soviet Period
Overtaking and Surpassing America?
ISBN 978-3-89821-914-3

Mieste Hotopp-Riecke
Die Tataren der Krim zwischen Assimilation und Selbstbehauptung
Der Aufbau des krimtatarischen Bildungswesens nach Deportation und Heimkehr (1990-2005)
ISBN 978-3-89821-940-2

Alexander Schrepfer-Proskurjakov
Terror in Russland
Geschichte und Gegenwart
ISBN 978-3-89821-945-7

Quotes from reviews of SPPS volumes:

On vol. 1 – *The Implementation of the ECHR in Russia:* "Full of examples, experiences and valuable observations which could provide the basis for new strategies."

Diana Schmidt, *Неприкосновенный запас*

On vol. 2 – *Putins Russland:* "Wipperfürth draws attention to little known facts. For instance, the Russians have still more positive feelings towards Germany than to any other non-Slavic country."

Oldag Kaspar, *Süddeutsche Zeitung*

On vol. 3 – *Die Übernahme internationalen Rechts in die russische Rechtsordnung:* "Hussner's is an interesting, detailed and, at the same time, focused study which deals with all relevant aspects and contains insights into contemporary Russian legal thought."

Herbert Küpper, *Jahrbuch für Ostrecht*

On vol. 5 – *Квадратные метры, определяющие сознание:* "Meerovich provides a study that will be of considerable value to housing specialists and policy analysts."

Christina Varga-Harris, *Slavic Review*

On vol. 6 – *New Directions in Russian International Studies:* "A helpful step in the direction of an overdue dialogue between Western and Russian IR scholarly communities."

Diana Schmidt, *Europe-Asia Studies*

On vol. 8 – *Nation-Building and Minority Politics in Post-Socialist States:* "Galbreath's book is an admirable and craftsmanlike piece of work, and should be read by all specialists interested in the Baltic area."

Andrejs Plakans, *Slavic Review*

On vol. 9 – *Народы Кавказа в Вооружённых силах СССР:* "In this superb new book, Bezugolnyi skillfully fashions an accurate and candid record of how and why the Soviet Union mobilized and employed the various ethnic groups in the Caucasus region in the Red Army's World War II effort."

David J. Glantz, *Journal of Slavic Military Studies*

On vol. 10 – *Русское Национальное Единство:* "Pribylovskii's and Likhachev's work is likely to remain the definitive study of the Russian National Unity for a very long time."

Mischa Gabowitsch, *e-Extreme*

On vol. 13 – *The Politicization of Russian Orthodoxy:* "Mitrofanova's book is a fascinating study which raises important questions about the type of national ideology that will come to predominate in the new Russia."

Zoe Knox, *Europe-Asia Studies*

On vol. 13 – *The Politicization of Russian Orthodoxy*: "Mitrofanova's venerable study makes an important contribution to understanding the present ideological chaos in Russia."

Dmitry V. Pospielovsky, *Slavic Review*

On vol. 14 – *Aleksandr Solzhenitsyn and the Modern Russo-Jewish Question:* "Larson has written a well-balanced survey of Solzhenitsyn's writings on Russian-Jewish relations."

Nikolai Butkevich, *e-Extreme*

On vol. 16 – *Der russische Sonderweg?:* "Luks's remarkable knowledge of the history of this wide territory from the Elbe to the Pacific Ocean and his life experience give his observations a particular sharpness and his judgements an exceptional weight."

Peter Krupnikow, *Mitteilungen aus dem baltischen Leben*

On vol. 17 – *История «Мёртвой воды»:* "Moroz provides one of the best available surveys of Russian neo-paganism."

Mischa Gabowitsch, *e-Extreme*

On vol. 18 – *Этническая и религиозная интолерантность в российских СМИ:* "A constructive contribution to a crucial debate about media-endorsed intolerance which has once again flared up in Russia."

Mischa Gabowitsch, *e-Extreme*

On vol. 20 – *Помнить нельзя забыть:* "Guchinova's important book succeeds splendidly in recognizing the polymorphous quality of both history and memory."

Petra Rethmann, *Slavic Review*

On vol. 23 – *Changes in the Heart of Europe:* "An engaging book providing a useful overview of anthropological research in the Czech Republic and Slovakia at the present time."

Laura Cashman, *Europe-Asia Studies*

On vol. 25 – *The Ghosts in Our Classroom:* "Freyberg-Inan's well-researched and incisive monograph, balanced and informed about Romanian education in general, should be required reading for those Eurocrats who have shaped Romanian spending priorities since 2000."

Tom Gallagher, *Slavic Review*

On vol. 26 – *The 2002 Dubrovka and 2004 Beslan Hostage Crises:* "Dunlop's analysis will help to draw Western attention to the plight of those who have suffered by these terrorist acts, and the importance, for all Russians, of uncovering the truth of about what happened."

Amy Knight, *Times Literary Supplement*

On vol. 28 – *Dedovshchina in the Post-Soviet Military:* "This interdisciplinary panoply of analyses is an invaluable resource for any serious student of hazing in the Russian army, and a good first step toward understanding the complexity of this social ill."

Marybeth Ulrich, *The Russian Review*

On vol. 29 – *Zivilgesellschaftliche Einflüsse auf die Orange Revolution:* "Strasser's study constitutes an outstanding empirical analysis and well-grounded location of the subject within theory."

Heiko Pleines, *Osteuropa*

On vol. 31 – *Willkür oder Freiheit?:* "The German reader of Kantor's book is provided with first-hand experiences of current Russian thought – a gift for Western Slavic studies."

A.V. Mikhailovskii, *Вопросы философии*

On vol. 34 – *Postsowjetische Feiern:* "Mühlfried's book contains not only a solid ethnographic study, but also points at some problems emerging from Georgia's prevalent understanding of culture."

Godula Kosack, *Anthropos*

On vol. 35 – *Fascism Past and Present, West and East*: "Committed students will find much of interest in these sometimes barbed exchanges."

Robert Paxton, *Journal of Global History*

On vol. 37 – *Political Anti-Semitism in Post-Soviet Russia:* "Likhachev's book serves as a reliable compendium and a good starting point for future research on post-Soviet xenophobia and ultra-nationalist politics, with their accompanying anti-Semitism."

Kathleen Mikkelson, *Demokratizatsiya*

On vol. 39 – *Российский консерватизм и реформа 1907-1914:* "Luk'ianov's work is a well-researched, informative and valuable addition, and enhances our understanding of politics in late imperial Russia."

Matthew Rendle, *Revolutionary Russia*

On vol. 43 – *Verflechtungen der deutschen und russischen Zeitgeschichte:* "Khavkin's book should be of interest to everybody studying German-Soviet relations and highlights new aspects in that field."

Wiebke Bachmann, *Osteuropa*

On vol. 50 – *Современные интерпретации русского национализма:* "This thought-provoking and enlightening set of works offers valuable insights for anyone interested in understanding existing expressions and interpretations of Russian nationalism."

Andrew Konitzer, *The Russian Review*

On vol. 57 – *Russland und seine GUS-Nachbarn:* "Wipperfürth's enlightening and objective analysis documents detailed background knowledge and understanding of complex relationships. "

Julia Schatte, *Eurasisches Magazin*

On vol. 59 – *Das sakrale eurasische Imperium des Aleksandr Dugin:* "Höllwerth's outstanding 700-page dissertation is certainly the, so far, most ambitious attempt to decipher Dugin's body of thought."

Tanja Fichtner, *Osteuropa*

Series Subscription

Please enter my subscription to the series *Soviet and Post-Soviet Politics and Society*, ISSN 1614-3515, as follows:

❐ complete series   OR   ❐ English-language titles
                                                   ❐ German-language titles
                                                   ❐ Russian-language titles

starting with
❐ volume # 1
❐ volume # ___
     ❐ please also include the following volumes: #___, ___, ___, ___, ___, ___, ___
❐ the next volume being published
     ❐ please also include the following volumes: #___, ___, ___, ___, ___, ___, ___

❐ 1 copy per volume   OR   ❐ ___ copies per volume

Subscription within Germany:
You will receive every volume at 1st publication at the regular bookseller's price – incl. s & h and VAT.
Payment:
❐ Please bill me for every volume.
❐ Lastschriftverfahren: Ich/wir ermächtige(n) Sie hiermit widerruflich, den Rechnungsbetrag je Band von meinem/unserem folgendem Konto einzuziehen.

Kontoinhaber: _____ Kreditinstitut: _____
Kontonummer: _____ Bankleitzahl: _____

International Subscription:
Payment (incl. s & h and VAT) in advance for
❐ 10 volumes/copies (€ 319.80)   ❐ 20 volumes/copies (€ 599.80)
❐ 40 volumes/copies (€ 1,099.80)
Please send my books to:

NAME_____ DEPARTMENT_____
ADDRESS _____
POST/ZIP CODE_____ COUNTRY _____
TELEPHONE _____ EMAIL_____

date/signature_____

A hint for librarians in the former Soviet Union: Your academic library might be eligible to receive free-of-cost scholarly literature from Germany via the German Research Foundation. For Russian-language information on this program, see
        http://www.dfg.de/forschungsfoerderung/formulare/download/12_54.pdf.

Please fax to: **0511 / 262 2201 (+49 511 262 2201)**
or mail to: *ibidem*-Verlag, Julius-Leber-Weg 11, D-30457 Hannover, Germany
or send an e-mail: ibidem@ibidem-verlag.de

***ibidem*-Verlag**

Melchiorstr. 15

D-70439 Stuttgart

info@ibidem-verlag.de

www.ibidem-verlag.de
www.ibidem.eu
www.edition-noema.de
www.autorenbetreuung.de